Building Online Learning Communities

JB JOSSEY-BASS

Building Online Learning Communities

EFFECTIVE STRATEGIES FOR THE VIRTUAL CLASSROOM

SECOND EDITION OF *BUILDING LEARNING COMMUNITIES IN CYBERSPACE*

Rena M. Palloff
Keith Pratt

BICENTENNIAL
1807
WILEY
2007
BICENTENNIAL

Published by Jossey-Bass
A Wiley Imprint
989 Market Street, San Francisco, CA 94103-1741   www.josseybass.com

Readers should be aware that Internet Web sites offered as citations and/or sources for further information may have changed or disappeared between the time this was written and when it is read.

Jossey-Bass books and products are available through most bookstores. To contact Jossey-Bass directly call our Customer Care Department within the U.S. at 800-956-7739, outside the U.S. at 317-572-3986, or fax 317-572-4002.

Jossey-Bass also publishes its books in a variety of electronic formats. Some content that appears in print may not be available in electronic books.

Library of Congress Cataloging-in-Publication Data

Palloff, Rena M., 1950-
  Building online learning communities : effective strategies for the virtual classroom / Rena M. Palloff and Keith Pratt — 2nd ed.
      p. cm.
  Prev. ed.: Building Learning Communities in Cyberspace. c1999.
  Includes bibliographical references and index.
  ISBN 978-0-7879-8825-8 (pbk.)
  1. Distance education—United States. 2. College teaching—United States—Data processing. 3. Computer-assisted instruction—United States. I. Pratt, Keith, 1947- II. Palloff, Rena M., 1950- Building learning communities in cyberspace. III. Title.
  LC5805.P35 2007
    378.1'75—dc22   2007013435

Printed in the United States of America
SECOND EDITION
PB Printing   10 9 8 7 6 5 4 3 2 1

CONTENTS

LIST OF EXHIBITS

NINE

TEN

APPENDIX A

The Jossey-Bass Higher and Adult Education Series

To Gary and Dianne for your infinite patience and support;

the Fielding Graduate University for giving us our start;

and all of our students—past, present, and future.

PREFACE TO THE SECOND EDITION

When this book first appeared in 1999, online courses were a new and novel way of teaching and learning. The World Wide Web, as we know it now, had only been in existence for a few years. Few course management systems existed, and the only books available on the topic of online learning focused mainly on how to set up a Web page by using HTML, devoting little or no attention to how to teach online. As frustrated as our colleagues with the lack of literature on this topic, we set out to explore the territory of online teaching and not focus on the technology involved with course delivery. Our book was one of the first to address the issue of online teaching. Even so, given that so few instructors were actually teaching online at the time, it took a while before the book was "discovered." Once it was, however, it quickly became a popular text, and we were truly humbled by its success. We were two online instructors who were relatively new to the field ourselves and who were interested in sharing what we had learned thus far with our colleagues. We never imagined that the book would lead us to working with faculty all over the world, training them to develop good courses and to teach effectively online. Nor did we expect to continue to write about this area, as we have.

The world of online teaching has changed significantly since 1999, but the original version of this book continues to be read and used as a text in courses on instructional design and in online teaching. Consequently, there was a demand from our readers for an updated edition that would take us from where we were in our thinking about online learning communities in 1999 to where we are today, but with a request that many of the basic concepts be left untouched. The second edition, then, contains updated information about our approach and what we have continued to learn over the years in terms of best practices in online learning.

Many of the original resources cited in the 1999 edition have been used again in this one because they represent the work of the "pioneers" in this field, such as Linda Harasim and David Jonassen.

We predicted in 1999 that online learning communities would become an area of study, and it has. This book includes up-to-date research findings in the area of community-building online. In addition, we have updated the terminology used, provided current examples of the material discussed, and expanded those examples into disciplines beyond the social sciences. It is our hope that with this new, expanded, and updated information the book will continue to meet a need for both new and seasoned online instructors by addressing the important topic of how to maximize the human-to-human contact that is so important to the learning process online.

THE CURRENT LANDSCAPE OF ONLINE LEARNING

Since we wrote the first edition, online distance learning has become commonplace. The explosive growth of the Internet has contributed to the increasing popularity of this type of learning, along with a desire to reach students at a distance to increase enrollments and to provide a type of education that is in demand by students. The National Center for Educational Statistics (2003) reports that in 2000–2001, 52 percent of institutions that had undergraduate programs offered credit-granting distance education courses at the undergraduate level, and college-level, credit-granting distance education courses were offered at the graduate/first-professional level by 52 percent of institutions that had graduate/first-professional programs. Public two-year institutions had the largest number of enrollments in distance education offerings in 2000–2001, a trend that has continued since then. These statistics show that the original belief that online distance education was only for nontraditional, adult students has not held up over time. Granted, many nontraditional students are enrolled in two-year community college programs, but so are students right out of high school, who are also taking classes online.

Course offerings for online courses now span all disciplines. In the first edition of this book, we presented a sample of courses then being offered to illustrate that online learning was indeed growing. We smile now to think about how impressed we were then with an assortment of courses that included disciplines such as English, business, and computer science. Today, we see almost everything being offered online, from math and science classes to art and even dance. The emergence of new technologies has made almost anything possible—a trend that will continue into the future.

ONLINE LEARNING COMMUNITIES REVISITED

In this book we will be revisiting the concept of community building in online distance education, along with its inherent benefits, problems, and concerns. Online learning now takes more than one form, including the use of technology to enhance a face-to-face class, a hybrid class that combines both face-to-face meetings and online work, and fully online courses. Many of our colleagues have postulated that the technology enhancement of face-to-face courses has effectively begun to blur the distinctions between online and face-to-face classes. The use of synchronous media and virtual classrooms has grown and is affecting how we view community. Although most of our discussion relates to the use of asynchronous technologies for online discussion, we also discuss the use of synchronous media and its role in community building. Community building as the means by which online education is delivered pervades all forms of online learning and all forms of technology and needs to be considered regardless of how the course is delivered.

The shift to online distance learning continues to pose enormous challenges to instructors and their institutions. Some faculty members still believe that the online classroom is no different from the traditional one—that the approaches that work face-to-face will work when learners are separated from them and from each other by time and distance. Others feel that the online classroom is simply not as robust or rigorous and not worthy of their consideration, a belief that has caused those of us who teach online to overcompensate and create classes so full of content and activities that sometimes our students simply cannot keep up. When learning moves out of the classroom and into the online arena, we must pay attention to many issues that we take for granted in the face-to-face classroom. We need not apologize for online classes; when done well, they are every bit as rigorous as face-to-face education. But we do need to pay attention to the differences inherent in this form of teaching in order to develop high-quality courses that are every bit as rigorous as their face-to-face counterparts and perhaps even more so.

Some examples of difference that are brought to our attention every day by the faculty we train to do online work derive from questions such as, How do we know when a student is engaged with the subject matter? How do we account for attendance and participation? How do we deal with students who are not participating?

How can we recognize and deal with disagreement and conflict? How do we effectively use the discussion board? What has happened to the lecture? Is it really necessary to focus on community building at the start of a course? Educators and trainers who are already familiar with online education will find these issues still relevant because they relate to the ways in which the instructor establishes his or her own presence online and assists students in developing theirs, as well as how content is delivered.

Our early work in online learning helped create, for us, the beginnings of a model for effective online distance education. This model includes deliberate attempts to build community as a means of promoting collaborative learning. Embedded within community building are the active creation of knowledge and meaning, collaborative activities, opportunities for reflection, and the purposeful empowerment of participants to become experts at their own learning. We have concluded through our work that the construction of a learning community, with the instructor participating as an equal member, is the key to a successful outcome and is the vehicle through which online education is best delivered. What is most effective about our approach is its simplicity and the fact that it does not depend on any one form of technology. It is about using our best practices as educators and applying them in a completely different environment. Tried and true techniques used face-to-face in the classroom often do not work when the classroom is virtual.

Community building online and many other aspects of online learning have been and are currently under study in many venues. In fact, a large body of literature on these topics has appeared since the first edition of this book was released in 1999. We incorporate some of the recent thinking of our colleagues as well as our own to bring what we know about the online learning community into the present day.

This book also emerges out of our own experience as online faculty. We often tell our audiences when we speak and train that we have made every mistake possible in our online teaching, and those mistakes have been our teachers. They have helped us continue to develop and refine our approach to online teaching, as well as the model we use to develop and teach our classes. How to develop online learning communities has been the focus of our work since we delivered our first online course in 1993. More and more often, we are asked to consult to educational institutions where distance learning programs have been implemented but have not had successful outcomes or are not satisfactory to those involved, or with institutions that have begun to use online learning but wish to make their courses more interactive and to include a learning-community approach. Many institutions are lured by attractive software packages or by the prospect of reducing costs and increasing their student population through the use of distance education. These can certainly be benefits. However, focusing on these elements and ignoring what it takes to learn in this environment can be expensive mistakes.

In this book we share our approach—as well as our successes and our difficulties—with our colleagues who wish to deliver online learning more effectively. The book is designed to be useful to anyone engaged in the process of online work, be they academics, group facilitators, or those working in networked organizations or delivering corporate training programs online. It is written both for faculty who have been teaching online and wish to discover new ideas to incorporate into their practice and for those who are embarking on this journey. It will help new faculty make the transition from the face-to-face classroom to the virtual classroom and more fully understand the new approaches and skills they will need if they are to be successful. It will also help veteran faculty who have been teaching online to improve their practice by focusing on community-building skills to enhance the delivery of their classes. Others who will find the book useful are department chairs and deans responsible for the development and delivery of online offerings, those responsible for faculty and instructional development, and instructional designers who are working with all of those groups in order to make the transition to online teaching work.

This book is not about technology per se. Neither is it about the use of computer-assisted instruction, wherein a student interacts only with a software package installed on a computer, an approach often used in corporate training settings. We are concerned with software and hardware only as vehicles in the creation of an environment that is conducive to learning. The process of teaching and learning through the creation of an online community is our concern. We have gleaned from our experience a number of techniques and approaches that work well in online courses, which we now apply in every class we teach. We present these techniques, along with examples and questions to consider, to help with their implementation. Because we teach in the social sciences, our own examples and cases emerge from that discipline. However, we are including examples provided by our colleagues who teach in the sciences, computer science, mathematics, and humanities to help illustrate our approach in those disciplines as well. We also encourage readers from disciplines other than the behavioral sciences to seek out colleagues across the country who are teaching classes online. Instructors teaching online frequently make their materials available on the Internet, welcoming comments and questions about their courses and experiences. At the end of the book, we provide some resources that instructors can use to assist them in finding some of these courses and to assist them in developing their own courses.

As academic institutions continue to move toward the use of online media to offer courses and programs, as well as to develop fully virtual universities, instructors must be trained and supported. We cannot assume that all faculty, regardless of how well they perform in the classroom, will be able to make this transition easily, just as we cannot assume that all students will fare well. This book will make a significant contribution to the discussions and struggles that frame the ongoing transition to and delivery of online courses. We offer suggestions that can help pave the way to and enhance well-planned and effective online distance learning.

ORGANIZATION OF THE BOOK

As in the first edition, the book is divided into two parts. Part One lays the foundation for the learning-community approach to online learning. Chapter One begins to explore the issues involved in teaching and learning when learning leaves the classroom and moves into the online environment. It also introduces our framework for online teaching. Chapter Two looks at the importance of building community in the online environment. Extensive material on the role of social presence in forming and maintaining community has been added to this chapter. In addition, we include discussion of the link between social presence, the achievement of learning outcomes, and student satisfaction with the online learning process. The chapter differentiates for the reader a traditional model of pedagogy from a model that will lead to success in the online classroom. Chapter Three has been retitled and reorganized. It looks at the need to recontextualize what we commonly refer to as community and explores in more detail the issues that we have discovered to be key and that need attention in the online classroom. These key issues have emerged from our teaching and consulting work; consequently, we include dialogue from our classes to illustrate each issue. Chapters Four and Five tackle some of the more concrete issues of time, group size, cost, security, and technology as they pertain to online teaching. The discussions about time have been updated, and the material on cost and security are new to this edition. Chapter Six discusses the roles that faculty and students take in the development of the online learning community, as well as presenting some learning theory that supports their roles online.

Part Two presents a practical guide to creating an online learning community that will lead to an effective teaching and learning experience. Chapters Seven through Ten provide practical applications and include discussion of the importance of collaboration and the transformative learning process that occurs online. More specifically, Chapter Seven offers suggestions for creating an appropriate syllabus, setting objectives and learning outcomes, negotiating guidelines, setting up the course site online, gaining participation and student buy-in for the process, and accounting for presence in the online classroom. Some updated examples have been used in this revised chapter to illustrate the application of the community concept to courses outside of the social and behavioral sciences and to better apply these concepts to today's online classroom environment. Chapter Eight describes practical techniques for stimulating collaborative learning among participants. It presents ways to promote and facilitate relationship building and personal process, thus further supporting community development and the establishment of social presence. Chapter Nine explores a critical component of online learning—transformative learning, which is learning about how we learn through the use of technology, learning about the technology itself, and, most important, learning about ourselves through the online learning process. The chapter shows how to incorporate this process stream into the context of the online course. Chapter Ten focuses on an important concern of most educators—how to assess and evaluate results. This chapter discusses student assessment, appropriate assignments for assessment purposes, as well as the importance of aligning assignments, expectations, and assessment. Finally, the chapter discusses course and program evaluation. To close the book, Chapter Eleven summarizes and reviews the keys to successful online learning. In addition, it discusses the ramifications of this work for teacher training and some recent applications of the community concept to the larger academic institution. The case examples, vignettes, and questions for consideration in all of the chapters will help readers bring the material alive and apply it successfully in their own online classes.

Included throughout the book are student posts to various types of discussions in online courses. Some of them are from our original work and some are newer posts from our online classes. It amazes us that despite the number of online courses we have taught and the number of students we have worked with, their reflections regarding online learning are so similar. Therefore, if a student quote from the original work captures the essence of what we hope to illustrate, we have left it in place. As in the past, we have deliberately left the quotes untouched. Except for paring them down to manageable size and updating the content a bit, we have not edited them for grammar and have, as usual, asked the publisher to refrain from doing so. We have found in our experience of online teaching that commentary on or editing of student posts creates a type of performance anxiety that results in reduced participation. Just as most instructors would not think to correct the grammar of a student who is verbally contributing in a face-to-face class, we would not correct the spelling or grammar in a post, as this is the equivalent of speaking in class. Because an instructor who is venturing online needs to be prepared to receive unedited posts from students, we have deliberately chosen to leave the ones we present as they are. The increasing amount of time that our students spend online has brought with it a new language of online terminology. Although this is not appropriate terminology to be included in course papers or projects, it does make an appearance in discussion postings and instructors need to be prepared for their response to it. This shift in thinking represents but one of the numerous shifts instructors need to make as they enter the online classroom.

Online education is dynamic and ever-changing. Even though we have been at this for a while, we believe that online education is yet in its infancy, with far more change to come in the not-so-distant future. In this updated edition, we have perhaps captured and discussed the issues as they exist today. However, advances in technology and society will continue to bring new challenges to an evolving field. Even so, this book should help instructors face today's challenges more effectively.

May 2007

Rena M. Palloff
Alameda, California
Keith Prat
Pineville, Missouri

ACKNOWLEDGMENTS

A book such as this, which describes a collaborative learning process, could not have been completed in isolation. We wish to acknowledge a number of people who contributed to the development of our work. We continue to be deeply grateful to Fielding Graduate University—its faculty, staff, and students—for starting us on this path and continuing to support us along the way. Not only did we begin our collaboration at Fielding but we were also encouraged to begin our research into this new territory while the university worked to gain a more solid footing in online and distance learning. Thanks to Judy Kuipers, president of Fielding, Anna DiStefano, provost, and Charles McClintock, dean of the School of Human and Organizational Development. Thanks especially to Judy Witt, dean of the School of Educational Leadership and Change, who championed our idea for a certification program in online teaching entitled "Teaching in the Virtual Classroom." Thanks, Judy, for helping us find our way home.

We wish, once again, to acknowledge the "pioneers"—the Elcomm group—who were the first contributors to our research in the area of building community online. We continue to have contact with many of them; they have become our lifelong friends. We also continue to be grateful to our wonderful students for their enthusiastic participation in our online classes, their willingness to allow us to use some of their posts in our books, and mostly for teaching us more than we could ever hope to teach them. We also thank our faculty colleagues with whom we have interacted both online and in training programs and conferences—you are our inspiration! We are extremely grateful to David Brightman of Jossey-Bass, who is an ardent supporter and good friend. Thank you, David, for taking on this project in the first place, for believing in us, and encouraging us to update and revise this work. Thanks as well to David's editorial assistant, Erin Null, for her assistance and support and for helping us find all those pesky old files.

Finally, but definitely far from least, we wish to acknowledge and express our gratitude and love for Gary Krauss and Dianne Pratt, as well as the rest of both of our families. Thanks to all of you for putting up with both of us. We could not have done this without you.

THE AUTHORS

Rena M. Palloff and *Keith Pratt* are managing partners in Crossroads Consulting Group. Since 1994 they have collaboratively conducted pioneering research, consultation, and training in the emerging areas of online group facilitation, face-to-face and online community building, program planning and development of distance learning programs, faculty development and coaching for online teaching, and planning, management, and supervision of online academic programs. In conjunction with Fielding Graduate University, they developed, direct, and are core faculty in the Teaching in the Virtual Classroom academic certificate program designed to assist faculty in becoming effective online facilitators and course developers.

Rena Palloff has consulted extensively in health care, academic settings, and addiction treatment for well over twenty years. She is faculty in the masters' degree program in Organizational Management and Development (OMD) at Fielding Graduate University, as well as in the School of Educational Leadership and Change. She is also adjunct faculty at Capella University in the School of Human Services. In addition, she has taught classes on organizational behavior and management and leadership on an adjunct basis for the International Studies Program at Ottawa University in Ottawa, Kansas, and in various sites throughout the Pacific Rim, and was core faculty in Holistic Studies at John F. Kennedy University.

Dr. Palloff received a bachelor's degree in sociology from the University of Wisconsin-Madison and a master's degree in social work from the University of Wisconsin-Milwaukee. She holds a master's degree in organizational development and a Ph.D. in human and organizational systems from Fielding Graduate University.

Keith Pratt began his government career as a computer systems technician with the U.S. Air Force in 1967. He served in various positions, including supervisor of computer systems maintenance, chief of the Logistics Support Branch, chief of the Telecommunications Branch, and superintendent of the Secure Telecommunications Branch. After leaving the air force, Dr. Pratt held positions as registrar and faculty (Charter College), director (Chapman College), and trainer and consultant (The Growth Company). As an adjunct faculty member at Wayland Baptist University and at the University of Alaska, Dr. Pratt taught courses in communications, business, management, organizational theories, and computer technology. He was assistant professor in the International Studies Program and chair of the Management Information Systems Program, main campus and overseas, at Ottawa University in Ottawa, Kansas, and served as associate dean of distance learning at Northwest Arkansas Community College. He currently teaches online at Fielding Graduate University, Wayland Baptist University, Northcentral University, and Baker University.

Dr. Pratt graduated from Wayland Baptist University with a dual degree in business administration and computer systems technology. He has an M.S. in human resource management (with honors) from Chapman University, a master's degree in organizational development, a Ph.D. in human and organizational systems from Fielding Graduate University, and an honorary doctorate of science from Moscow State University.

Building Online Learning Communities

PART ONE

The Learning Community in Online Learning

chapter ONE

When Teaching
and Learning
Leave the Classroom

In the last ten years, significant change has occurred in online learning. Once viewed as a less rigorous, softer, easier way to complete a course or degree, faculty now realize that the time involved in the development and delivery of a high-quality online course is substantial, and students are now realizing that completing courses and degree programs online is hard work. There is no longer a need to spend time defining what online distance learning is or is not; it is now commonplace in higher education and is gaining popularity in the K–12 arena as well. Ten years ago, we were trying to decide what constituted distance learning and asked questions such as, "If the class meets face-to-face two or three times during the term, is that a distance learning course?" Today we know that distance learning takes several forms, including fully online courses, hybrid or blended courses that contain some face-to-face contact time in combination with online delivery, and technology-enhanced courses, which meet predominantly face-to-face but incorporate elements of technology into the course. In addition, academic institutions are experimenting with time schedules that depart from the traditional semester or quarter in order to more effectively deliver online classes.

It is not unusual now to see six-week intensive courses or courses with flexible start and end dates. If we examine all the ways in which distance learning is occurring now, it is possible to state that almost every course delivered via some form of technology is a distance learning course. There is one important element, however, that sets online distance learning apart from the traditional classroom setting: *Key to the learning process are the interactions among students themselves, the interactions between faculty and students, and the collaboration in learning that results from these interactions.* In other words, the formation of a learning community through which knowledge is imparted and meaning is co-created sets the stage for successful learning outcomes.

Ten years ago, the notion of building community online was seen as "fluff" or just one more thing an instructor might pay attention to in the delivery of an online course. However, much research has been conducted in recent years regarding the importance of community in an online course and in online teaching in general (Garrison, n.d.; Rovai, 2002; Rovai and Jordan, 2004; Shea, Swan, and Pickett, 2004; Wenger, 1999) and, further, into the concept of social presence, defined as the ability to portray oneself as a "real" person in the online environment (Gunawardena and Zittle, 1997; Picciano, 2002; Richardson and Swan, 2003; Rovai and Barnum, 2003). The findings of these research studies and others have supported our notion that the key to successful online learning is the formation of an effective learning community as the vehicle through which learning occurs online. Adams and Sperling (2003) note that the community building process embedded in online courses has helped transform teaching and learning in higher education. Some of the changes they describe for students include greater availability and accessibility of information, engagement of different learning styles, and promotion of increased responsibility for teaching and learning. The changes faculty are experiencing include greater accessibility to and availability of information but also encompass the development of new skill sets for teaching and the need to rethink pedagogy, redefine learning objectives, reevaluate assessment, and redefine faculty work roles and culture.

We also see these changes in a number of college classrooms today, not just in online classrooms. And we continue to learn more about how people learn. Carol

Twigg (1994b) indicated that many students are concrete-active learners, that is, they learn best from concrete experiences that engage their senses. Their best learning experiences begin with practice and end with theory (Twigg, 1994b). Many instructors, seeking to improve their practice and the learning outcomes for their students, have incorporated active learning techniques such as working collaboratively on assignments, participating in small-group discussions and projects, reading and responding to case studies, role playing, and using simulations.

These practices transfer well into the online classroom. However, instructors need to be diligent and deliberate in ensuring their success. When learners cannot see or even talk to each other, the use of collaborative assignments becomes more challenging but far from impossible. (We offer suggestions for implementing collaborative learning techniques in the online classroom in Chapter Eight.)

Learning in the distance education environment cannot be passive. If students do not enter into the online classroom—do not post a contribution to the discussion—the instructor has almost no way of knowing whether they have been there. So students are not only responsible for logging on but they must also contribute to the learning process by posting their thoughts and ideas to the online discussion. Learning is an active process in which both the instructor and the learners must participate if it is to be successful. In the process, a *web of learning* is created. In other words, a network of interactions between the instructor and the other participants is formed, through which the process of knowledge acquisition is collaboratively created. (See Chapters Eight and Nine for a discussion of collaborative learning and the transformative nature of the learning process.)

Outcomes of this process, then, should not be measured by the number of facts memorized and the amount of subject matter regurgitated but by the depth of knowledge and the number of skills gained. Evidence of critical thinking and of knowledge acquired are the desired learning outcomes. Consequently, cheating on exams should not be a major concern in an effective online environment because knowledge is acquired collaboratively through the development of a learning community. (The assessment of student performance in this environment is discussed in Chapter Ten.)

Institutions entering the distance learning arena must be prepared to tackle these issues and to develop new approaches and new skills in order to create an empowering learning process, for the creation of empowered learners is yet another desired outcome of online distance education. Successful online teaching is a process of taking our very best practices in the classroom and bringing them into a new, and, for some faculty, untried, arena. In this new arena, however, the practices may not look exactly the same.

Take, for example, a recent discussion with a professor in a small college where a distance delivery model was being implemented for a master's degree program. A software program was chosen and a consultant hired to install it on the college's server. There it sat for almost a year until the college decided to begin using it more extensively. Because of our expertise in faculty training and development for the delivery of distance education programs, we were consulted about the best way to improve a program that was not working very well. The professor informed us that the software had been used by a couple of instructors for a couple of courses. However, with further inquiry, we discovered that a course syllabus had never been posted online in any of these courses; nobody knew that an extensive faculty handbook for course development and delivery was embedded in the software. All they had been doing was using this potentially powerful software package as an e-mail system rather than for creating a distance learning environment. Was distance education and learning really happening here? No, of course not. So what does it take to make the transition from the classroom to the online arena successfully? What are the differences we face in this environment? And finally, what issues do we need to be concerned with? We answer the last question in the next section through a discussion of the issues and concerns related to online education. The answers to the other questions follow in subsequent chapters.

ONLINE ISSUES AND CONCERNS

When instructors begin to use technology in education, they experience a whole new set of physical, emotional, and psychological issues along with the educational issues. Many of these issues relate to the development of social presence. As we struggle to define ourselves online, we may experience emotions and try out behaviors that have not been part of our repertoire. The new issues also include the physical problems that can be experienced as the technology is used extensively, such as carpal tunnel syndrome, back problems, headaches, and so forth. Psychologically, students and faculty can become addicted to the technology. In fact, there are now centers devoted to the study and treatment of Internet addiction. Students and faculty can begin to fantasize and experience personality shifts while online, and their minds can drift. They may have a difficult time setting reasonable boundaries and limits around the amount of time they spend online. We have not had to address these issues in the traditional classroom, but we must do so as we teach online because they affect the ways learners interact with each other and with course material. In the traditional classroom, if a student experiences mind drift it may not be noticeable to the instructor or to the other students in the class. The student may be physically present but psychologically absent. In the virtual classroom, however, if a student drifts away, that absence is noticeable and may have a profound impact on the group.

Online learning has brought a whole new set of issues and problems into academics; as a result, instructors and their institutions have had to become more flexible and learn to deal with these problems. Professors, just like their students, need the ability to deal with a virtual world in which, for the most part, they cannot see, hear, or touch the people with whom they are communicating. Participants are likely to adopt a new persona, shifting into areas of their personalities they may not have previously explored. For example, an instructor, like a student, who suffers from performance anxiety in the face-to-face classroom may be more comfortable online and more active in responding to students. A colleague of ours who has wanted to teach for several years and who feels that he has a contribution to make is very nervous about entering a classroom and facing a group of students. He has been offered several opportunities to teach because of the expertise he would bring to a learning situation, but he has resisted. When offered an opportunity to teach online, however, he accepted readily, acknowledging that the relative anonymity of the medium feels more comfortable for him. The idea of being able to facilitate a discussion from the comfort of his home office was very appealing to him, whereas doing the same thing face-to-face was intimidating. However, the opposite may also be true: an instructor who does well face-to-face may not be successful online. We were told the story of an accounting professor who was extremely personable in his face-to-face classes. To assist students in memorizing difficult concepts, he would compose songs and play them in class, accompanying himself on his guitar. He was approached to teach online but resisted strenuously because he did not feel he could adequately transfer his musical approach to accounting to the online environment, even with the use of attached audio files. His first attempt at online teaching was not well-received by students and he decided not to continue with online teaching. Just as all instructors are not successful in the classroom setting, not all will be successful online. It takes a unique individual with a unique set of talents to be successful in the traditional classroom; the same is true for the online classroom. The ability to do both is a valuable asset in today's academic institutions.

STUDENTS ONLINE

Some attributes make students successful online when they are not in the face-to-face classroom. For example, what about the introverted student? Will such a student, who does not participate in the face-to-face class, blossom in the virtual classroom? Research conducted by one of us indicates that an introverted person will probably become more successful online, given the absence of social pressures that exist in face-to-face situations. Conversely, extroverted people may have more difficulty establishing their presence in an online environment, something that is easier for them to do face-to-face (Pratt, 1996).

The Illinois Online Network (2006) describes the characteristics of successful students in distance education programs:

- Open-minded about sharing life, work, and educational experiences as part of the learning process
- Able to communicate through writing
- Self-motivated and self-disciplined
- Willing to "speak up" if problems arise
- Able and willing to commit four to fifteen hours per week per course
- Able to meet the minimum requirements for the program (that is, this is not an easier way to meet degree requirements)
- Accept critical thinking and decision making as part of the learning process
- Have access to a computer and a modem (and, we add, at least some minimal ability to use them)
- Able to think ideas through before responding
- Feel that high-quality learning can take place without going to a traditional classroom (para. 2)

Nipper (1989) described the successful learner in an online environment as a "noisy learner," one who is active and creative in the learning process. This and other, similar references led many to believe that distance education is best applied to and seen as most successful in the arena of adult education. However, more high schools, colleges, and universities are using this delivery method with all groups of students regardless of age or level of educational experience. Should we expect that all students will succeed in this environment? Although a student who is unsuccessful in the face-to-face classroom may do well online, it is unrealistic to expect that all students will do well. When a student does not perform well, as evidenced by lack of participation, he or she should be given the option of returning to the face-to-face classroom. This should not be considered a failure but simply a poor fit. Changing to another delivery medium is not usually an option in the face-to-face classroom; there may be no other alternatives. The online classroom provides an alternative that may be useful for some students.

In our experience, online distance education can successfully draw out a student who would not be considered a noisy learner in the traditional classroom. It can provide an educational experience that helps motivate students who appear to be unmotivated because they are quieter than their peers and less likely to enter into a classroom discussion. Take the example of an Asian student, Soomo, who participated in one of our online classes on the topic of management and organizational theory. He introduced himself to the group in the following way. We have not changed his writing; we wanted his struggles with language to be apparent.

> And one of my problems, it's my responsibility, English is not my native language so I'm still struggling with learning English. I'll try hard but everyone's consideration will be appreciate regarding this matters in advance. I'm also see myself with introvert style. And feel uncomfortable to talk by on line.

By his own admission, he was generally a quiet member of face-to-face classes. Although he wanted to share, his struggles with English and the extroverted nature of his classmates left him silent, though actively listening to discussion. As our online course continued, his posts to the discussion were frequent and indicated a depth of thought. The following is his contribution to a discussion of *Reframing Organizations* by Bolman and Deal (2003):

> My understanding for the human resources frame is that this frame focuses on the fit between individual and organization. In this point of

view, I can think about the "manager's job and the organization theory." The potentially disastrous consequences can be avoided, however, if the manager commands a sound knowledge of the organization theory. This theory can help him or her make quality decisions and successfully influence others to carry them out. It can help improve decision quality by making the manager aware of the various components of organization theory. To understand how they fit together as an explanation of the activity of the organization provides a perspective for seeing a decision's consequences. . . . . Better quality decisions coupled with more effective implementation through better understanding of individual and group behavior can bring improved performance to the organization. I think it's important that a manager (management group) ensure that its members have exposure to organization theory.

Personally, I don't like the word "Frame." Because it means, in other words, "easy to break." Some organizational changes are incremental. They entail incorporating new technologies with existing missions and strategies. Organizational growth and redirection may also be incremental, but not necessarily. Other organizational changes are frame breaking. The risks are high, and events happen quickly. This usually means a change in the organization's goals and operations. Organizational start-ups and mergers are likely to be frame-breaking experiences.

Most of this student's contributions to the discussion throughout the course were of this nature. He received feedback from other students regarding the thoughtfulness of his contributions and his ability to help them look at ideas in another way. Generally quiet and concerned about his language skills in a face-to-face classroom, this student was able to overcome all of this in the online environment and make significant contributions to his own learning as well as to that of his student colleagues.

MAKING THE TRANSITION AND ESTABLISHING PRESENCE

The following is from a graduate student.

On Monday I had a mini-meltdown all on my own. I was really missing the body language cues and the time lag in the conversation was frustrating. I was very aware that I am working with a bunch of people who are obviously high functioning with lots of expertise. I wanted to be able to contribute at a comparable level and wondered if I was up to the task. I also wanted to respond quickly to all the links while juggling too many other responsibilities. I took a deep breath, looked at the humour in the situation and went to bed! *Cheryl*

This quotation, posted by a graduate student to an online course, is representative of some of the struggles that may occur as the transition is made from the face-to-face classroom to an online environment where interactions among learners are expected. When teaching and learning leave the classroom, many elements are left behind and new expectations emerge.

Picture a classroom on a college campus. As the time for class approaches, students begin to gather. They may arrive individually or in small groups. They begin to talk to each other, possibly about the class or about activities, friends, and life outside the classroom. When class ends, students gather again in the hallways, on the grounds of the campus, down the street at a coffee shop, or in the student union in order to make personal connections, create friendships, and simply socialize. In the online classroom, as it is configured currently, instructors and students are predominantly represented by text on a screen. We cannot see the facial expressions and body language that help us gauge responses to what is being discussed. Unless we are working in a synchronous virtual classroom situation, we cannot hear voices or tones of voice and thus may have difficulty conveying emotion. As Cheryl indicated in her post, it is difficult for some students to establish a sense of presence online. Instructors and their students become, in effect, disembodied. In a face-to-face situation, we are able to convey in a multitude of ways who we are as people. How does one do that online? How do we help the other participants get to know us; likewise, how do we get to know them so that we have a sense of the group with which we are communicating? How does an instructor teach in this environment? How do the participants in the online classroom become re-embodied? In Chapter Two, we explore the important concept of establishing presence in much more detail.

One way to help create presence, however, is through the use of *threaded discussion*—a series of posts displayed in outline form in the discussion area of the online course. Although many instructors use course management systems to deliver course content, some are still confused by the use of threaded discussion. They are not sure about how to use it effectively and so simply avoid it. We discuss the importance of threaded discussion throughout this book and provide examples of its use as well. Exhibit 1.1 shows one of the ways in which people can connect online, illustrating how threaded discussion can be used to mediate the somewhat disembodied nature of online learning and the consequent need for techniques to personalize and humanize the course. The exhibit shows the instructor posting a series of discussion questions and students responding both to the questions and to one another (the students in the discussion are fictitious).

Although the graphical interfaces contained in current software packages devoted to online distance education are helping to create a more interesting and stimulating environment in which to work by allowing posting of photos, brief video introductions by the instructor, or creation of Web pages that present a profile for a student or instructor, they are still predominantly textual. Many who write about distance education have expressed concern as to how participants make more "human" connections while continuing the learning process.

Nipper (1989), a relatively early writer on online distance learning, discusses the need to create a sense of "synchronous presence" and reduce the social distance between all participants. Presence can be defined as the degree to which a person is perceived as "real" in the online environment. The concept of presence has triggered numerous research studies and has been correlated with increased learner satisfaction with online courses and a greater depth of learning (Picciano, 2002; Richardson and Swan, 2003; Rovai and Barnum, 2003). Rovai and Barnum (2003), as well other researchers, note that the interaction of the instructor with the learners together with the development of highly interactive course activities helps increase the perception of learning online. Picciano (2002) cautions, however, that interaction and presence are not one and the same: "Interaction may indicate presence but it is also possible for a student to interact by posting a message. . . . while not necessarily feeling that she or he is part of a group or a class" (p. 22). This caution is one that we, too, have presented to the faculty we have trained to teach online: simply getting students to talk to one another is not sufficient. Instead, there needs to be a focus on establishing human-to-human contact before the interaction involved with course content begins, a means by which presence can be established. Richardson and Swan (2003) found a correlation among presence, student learning, and satisfaction with online courses but have determined that there is a paucity of research about presence online. They suggest that this is an area meriting more study and discussion. We present our own thoughts about the importance of social presence online and how it affects community building in Chapter Two.

Even though in most online distance learning courses students have the luxury of logging on to the course site whenever it is convenient for them (known as asynchronous communication), Nipper (1989) suggests that it is important to somehow create the sense that a group is working together in real time. Rarely will that group of people be online at the same time unless synchronous communication (also known as chat) is built into the course design. However, an attempt to form connection and community online through asynchronous threaded discussion allows participants to feel, when they enter a discussion forum in a course site, that they have entered a lively, active conversation.

Nipper states that the need for social connection is a goal that almost supersedes the content-oriented goals for the course. Students should gather online, just as they do on the campus of a university. To accomplish this, they must establish a sense of presence online, thus allowing their personality to come through to others in the group. This sense of presence, along with the relative anonymity of the online medium, may create a sense of freedom, allowing otherwise unexplored parts of their personality to emerge. Such exploration can be fostered by encouraging students to post introductions along with their fears and expectations for the process or, when possible, to create a homepage that others in the group can visit. Some course management applications allow for the creation of a homepage, complete with graphics and links to other sites on the Internet that are favorites of the person who created the page. This is a wonderful way for students to let others in the group know who they are and how they might connect with each other.

As online communication deprives us of some of the physical cues of communication and allows for or even demands more self-generated cues that affect our behavior, it also adds dimensions that otherwise would not be present (Pratt, 1996). For example, the availability and number of personal interactions via computer is limited only by time and access, not by distance. We can create, cultivate, and maintain social relationships with anyone who has access to a computer. Connections are made through the sharing of ideas and thoughts. How people look or what their cultural, ethnic, or social background is generally becomes irrelevant in this medium, which has been referred to as the "great equalizer." The increasing popularity of sites such as Friendster and My Space offers evidence of the search for social connection online. Although they are not online learning communities, these sites do provide social outlets for students outside of the online classroom.

The relationships formed online may, in fact, be more intense emotionally as the physical inhibitions created by face-to-face communications are removed. Social psychologist Kenneth Gergen (2000) believes that these interactions can continuously alter who we are: "One's identity is continuously emergent, re-formed, and redirected as one moves through the sea of ever-changing relationships" (p. 139).

In the traditional face-to-face classroom, the quality and intensity of social relationships is simply not as much of an issue. The traditional model of pedagogy allows for the instructor as expert to impart knowledge to students, who are expected to absorb it. How students interact socially is not generally a concern. Many instructors have begun to realize that the traditional lecture model is not the model of choice for today's more active learners and have begun to adapt their teaching methods accordingly by including techniques such as small-group activities and simulations. Campuses are working to develop both residential and discipline-based learning communities because of the power they hold in facilitating a culture of lifelong learning (Fleming, 1997; Smith, MacGregor, Matthews, and Gabelnick, 2004). In the online classroom, it is the relationships and interactions among people through which knowledge is primarily generated. The learning community takes on new proportions in this environment and consequently must be nurtured and developed so as to be an effective vehicle for education.

THE SEARCH FOR KNOWLEDGE AND MEANING IN THE ONLINE CLASSROOM

Young children today are being weaned on interaction with various forms of media. Involved in everything from video games to the Internet, our youth are coming to expect more active ways of seeking knowledge and entertainment. Two studies, conducted by the Kaiser Family Foundation (2005) and the Pew Internet and American Life Project (Lenhart, Madden, and Hitlin, 2005), note that approximately 87 percent of youth between the ages of twelve and seventeen are online and also using other forms of technology, such as cell phones and gaming technology. In addition, youth are engaging with social networking sites on the Internet, such as My Space and Friendster. Adults, including educators, however, are for the most part newcomers to this technological arena. As a result, something of a technological generation gap is emerging. Writers examining this gap note that the technological changes sweeping our culture have left education largely unchanged. A rift has opened between how education is viewed and delivered in the classroom and how we are beginning to obtain knowledge in our society. The Pew report notes, "Students report that there is a substantial disconnect between how they use the Internet for school and how they use the Internet during the school day and under teacher direction. For the most part, students' educational use of the Internet occurs outside of the school day, outside of the school building, outside the direction of their teachers" (Levin, Arafeh, Lenhart, and Rainie, 2002, para. 3). Parents report that their children rarely read books or go to the library to complete assignments. Instead, Internet searching and use of sites such as Wikipedia are the means by which students complete homework and school assignments. Although the use of the Internet has grown among adults as well, adults often need additional training along with a shift in thinking and practice in order to successfully use the Internet for academic purposes. Consequently, a gap exists between our youth and those who are attempting to teach them—a gap that is not only forcing adults to become more technology-savvy but also to explore different theories and means by which to deliver education online to youth, whose expectations for learning have changed.

Recent theories in educational circles that attempt to bridge this gap, such as constructivism and active learning, posit that learners actively create knowledge and meaning through experimentation, exploration, and the manipulation and testing of ideas in reality. Interaction and feedback from others assist in determining the accuracy and application of ideas. Collaboration, shared goals, and teamwork are powerful forces in the learning process. Group activities, simulations, and the use of open-ended questions are but a few of the activities used to achieve these goals. Learners interact with knowledge, with the learning environment, and with other learners. The instructor acts mainly as a facilitator of the learning process. This is the essence of self-directed learning: it empowers learners—independent of the instructor—to follow those interactions wherever they may lead. Jonassen and others (1995) discuss the outcome of this form of teaching and learning. They note that the facilitation of learning environments that foster personal meaning making, as well as the social construction of knowledge and meaning through interactions with communities of learners, is preferred to instructor interventions that control the sequence and content of instruction. In other words, the educational process is learner-centered, with the learners taking the lead and determining the flow and direction of the process. Weimer (2002) notes that in order for this form of teaching and learning to occur, the balance of power between teacher and student needs to change. She comments that instructors have always held the power but that this power relationship needs to be reexamined. Instructors still retain the responsibility for teaching, but the decisions involved in learning really belong to students. By empowering students to take charge of their own learning process, learner-centered, constructivist teaching can emerge.

PUTTING THE PIECES TOGETHER

With community as a central feature in online courses, what other elements are needed to enable a learner-focused, active learning process? Unlike campus-based or residential learning communities that focus on curriculum as a unifying feature, allowing both students and faculty to come together in meaningful ways (Laufgraben, Shapiro, and Associates, 2004), the online learning community is the means by which the curriculum is delivered. Consequently, although the purpose for creating the community is the curriculum, there are other important elements that must be present in order for the community to form. Preece (2000), in describing online communities that are not focused on learning, notes that there are four basic features that must be present in order for community to form: *people, purpose, policies,* and *computer systems.* We believe, and Preece concurs, that this is not sufficient for the development of online *learning* communities, however. Two additional elements must be present in an online learning community: the collaborative learning and reflective practice that are necessary for transformative learning to occur (Palloff and Pratt, 2003). (We further discuss transformative learning in Chapter Nine.)

Our more recent thinking about the elements that must be present in order for online community to form have continued to evolve. We now organize them into three groupings—*people, purpose,* and *process*—and believe that the outcome of a well-constructed, community-oriented online course is *reflective/transformative learning.* Within the realm of community, however, are a number of elements. Exhibit 1.2 is a graphic representation of our model of online learning communities and their impact on learning.

Although we clearly need people in order to create a community, what is not so obvious is how people express who they are online. Thus, social presence becomes a critical element in community building. The instructor models the development of presence through his or her guidance and facilitation of the course, and empowers students to take on the continued job of community building and the exploration of content. Establishing guidelines as a starting point in the online course serves as a means by which the group defines shared goals and purpose. Other issues that affect the definition of purpose for the group include practical considerations such as time (including the time involved in working in an online course

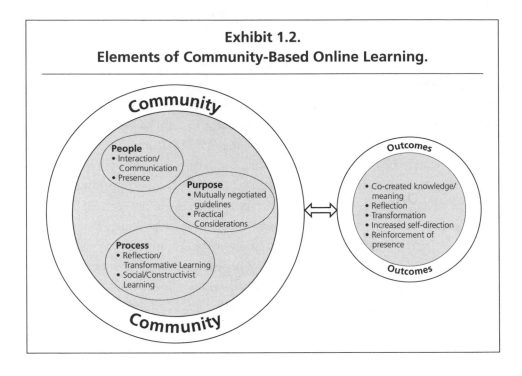

Exhibit 1.2.
Elements of Community-Based Online Learning.

Community

People
• Interaction/
Communication
• Presence

Purpose
• Mutually negotiated
guidelines
• Practical
Considerations

Process
• Reflection/
Transformative Learning
• Social/Constructivist
Learning

Outcomes

• Co-created knowledge/
meaning
• Reflection
• Transformation
• Increased self-direction
• Reinforcement of
presence

Outcomes

Community

and time management issues), the size of the group, and the ability to create a sense of safety and security. The process of online learning becomes a bit more complicated. Interaction and collaboration are critical to community development; without them, there would clearly be no community. The inclusion of collaborative activity and teamwork helps increase the level of communication and interaction in the class. Finally, the social constructivist context wherein the group works together to actively create knowledge and meaning becomes the vehicle through which learning occurs online and is a critical component of the process of online work. All of these elements work together to create the online community; none is any more or less important than the others.

Looking at the full picture of community-based online learning shows us that a more active learning model is the model of choice for this environment and will support the desired course outcomes. Given the limitations of access to the student population, as well as such elements as time and distance, the instructor has limited control over what is being learned and how. And because learners are left to some degree to their own devices, it is up to them to make sense of the body of knowledge associated with the course being delivered. The instructor supports this process through the development of the course itself, use of collaborative assignments, facilitation of active discussion, and promotion of the development of critical thinking and research skills. The outcome is an environment rich in the potential for collaborative learning and the social construction of meaning, as well as transformative learning and reflective practice. As we proceed through the book, we explore each element of the model in depth; as such, the model becomes an organizing mechanism for our look at online community building.

NEW APPROACHES, NEW SKILLS

What leads to successful outcomes in online classes? Is it the mode of teaching or facilitation? Is it the norms established or the guidelines for participation? Is it the level of education of the group? Is it the ability of the instructor to act as a facilitator during the process of delivering the course? All of these factors come together to create success in this medium. When teaching and learning leave the classroom, it is up to the instructor to create an effective container within which the course proceeds by posting goals, objectives, and expected outcomes for the course, initial guidelines for participation, thoughts and questions to kick off discussion, and assignments to be completed collaboratively. Then it is time to take a back seat of sorts and gently guide the learners in their process by monitoring the discussion and entering it to prod participants to look at the material in another way or to gently steer the conversation back on course if it should stray. This is not a responsibility to be taken lightly and requires daily contact and presence with the learners online. Often the instructor finds that he or she must be present and active more in the beginning of the course and then can gradually pull back as the learners take the lead. Collison, Elbaum, Haavind, and Tinker (2000) note that good facilitation on the part of the instructor becomes apparent when the learners, on their own and with one another, begin to use the types of interventions the instructor might use: "If you've done a good job of laying the support framework for pragmatic dialogue, the participants begin . . . to facilitate their own dialogue" (p. 203). Along the way and especially at the end of the course, then, the instructor incorporates peer feedback on assignments into the evaluation of student progress, which can later be figured into a grade.

What we are suggesting is a different way in which to deliver a course. In our observation, many online courses still are typically content- and faculty- or facilitator-driven, just as they are in the face-to-face classroom. In many ways they perpetuate an old model of teaching and learning, wherein participants produce pieces of work that are to be assessed and commented on by an expert. There is discussion and feedback, but it relates to the work that has been presented by the expert. The framework we offer in this book, by contrast, is more free-flowing and interactive. Participants generate a bibliography of readings beyond the assigned text through their own research and interaction with their peers; they negotiate guidelines for participation based on direction from the instructor; the instructor creates a structure that allows students to venture into areas previously unexplored. The work that students create in the process may be shared online and peer feedback on the work encouraged. This is truly an empowering, mutual learning experience, akin to the synergy that can occur in the classroom when an instructor energizes students by allowing them to fully immerse themselves in content and follow the resulting paths of inquiry wherever they might lead. The following sections show what a framework for successful online teaching should contain.

Access to Technology and the Knowledge to Use It

In order to successfully conduct classes online, make sure that participants have access to and familiarity with the technology to be used. Comfort with the technology (both hardware and software) contributes to a sense of psychological well-being and thus a greater likelihood of participation. It is also important to pay attention to the learning curve involved in the use of the technology by participants, as well as faculty or facilitators. This should be incorporated into the learning process. (We explore this more fully in Chapter Five.)

Guidelines and Procedures

A set of guidelines should be generated by the instructor as a first item of discussion in an online course. The guidelines and procedures should be loose enough to allow for some debate and discussion, open to some degree of negotiation (that is, how a student receives a grade is not negotiable, but due dates might be negotiable), and generated partly by the participants, particularly as they apply to how students will interact with one another; in other words, students should be encouraged to develop a common set of ground rules for interaction. Imposed guidelines that are too rigid will constrain discussion, causing participants to worry about the nature of their posts rather than to simply post freely. In larger classes, small discussion groups or work teams can be created wherein guidelines can be discussed and negotiated. Good, respectful "netiquette," however, should be encouraged regardless. (In Chapter Seven, we provide suggestions and examples for the development of this type of class, including some sample syllabi that have been successfully used online.)

Participation

Buy-in from the participants is essential. Participants must first agree to minimum participation standards and understand what they are committing to. Minimum levels of participation should be established and agreed upon in order to create a high level of discussion. In some cases, an initial face-to-face session can be held that will establish a sense of being part of a group and thus serve to support participation. When this is not possible, and it often is not, initial online contact must include attempts at group development before moving into content. We like to refer to this as Week Zero, or the important community-building week that precedes the actual start of the course. For example, the instructor may ask that all participants post an introduction. This may be followed by the instructor posing open-ended questions, possibly around the establishment of guidelines or that relate to the students' previous experiences with the content to be studied. Continued attention to these issues must be included throughout the course. (We continue our discussion of these issues in Chapter Two and throughout the book.)

Collaborative Learning

In order to be successful, classes conducted in an online environment must create an equal playing field. In other words, there must be equality of participant-facilitator and participant-participant interactions. The most powerful experiences are those in which interaction occurs throughout the group instead of between one participant and the facilitator within a group setting. The best facilitation is through modeling the methodology, that is, by acting as a group member who is contributing to the learning process. (We discuss these issues further in Chapter Eight.)

Transformative Learning, or Learning About Learning, Technology, and Oneself

A critical outcome of online learning is the learning that occurs through the use of the online medium itself. Participants must be given the opportunity and space within the context of the class to explore how this learning environment is different for them. They need to discuss the fears and insecurities, as well as the successes and surprises, associated with the online medium. Transformative learning moves a student from someone who takes in information to a reflective practitioner involved with the creation of knowledge. (We discuss this issue extensively in Chapter Nine.)

Evaluation of the Process and Student Assessment

Finally, it is important to encourage participants to provide feedback to each other on an ongoing basis as well as to the instructor about their experience in the course. Given the nature of the online environment, it is also important to pay particular attention to the issue of student assessment. How will student performance be assessed? How do we evaluate the success of the course or lack thereof? Is the online program meeting the needs of the participants? Because we are promoting the use of a collaborative environment in the teaching process, collaboration must also be incorporated into the process of assessment and evaluation. And because we are attempting to create empowered learners as a desired outcome, self-evaluation is also an important component. (We return to this important issue in Chapter Ten.)

IMPLICATIONS

The keys to the creation of a learning community and successful facilitation online are simple: *honesty, responsiveness, relevance, respect, openness,* and *empowerment.* When faculty create a virtual environment for participants in which these elements are present, group members can feel safe in expressing themselves without fear of how they will be perceived, allowing for active, rich discussion. The implications are that as educators and facilitators we must be able to create an atmosphere of safety and community in all of our learning settings, whether they are electronic or face-to-face. Students or participants must be able to speak and debate their ideas without fear of retribution from any source and should be encouraged to explore and research topics that may not be an explicit part of the curriculum or agenda. Instructors and facilitators should act as "playground monitors" or gentle guides while participants "play in the sandbox," developing the norms and rules as they go. Facilitators and participants must become equal partners in the development of an online learning community, as it is the participants who are the experts when it comes to their own learning.

If we can facilitate this occurrence in the online environment, we will be well ahead of what has traditionally occurred in the face-to-face or virtual classroom. Ideally, this will encourage us to engage in best practices in both environments. In fact, many instructors comment that their face-to-face teaching, as well as that of their colleagues, has improved and become more innovative, active, and creative as the result of teaching online.

Finally, many current models of distance learning maintain a traditional student-teacher relationship in interaction with a set curriculum. Our experience of online facilitation shows us how much further we are capable of traveling into the unknowns to explore new worlds of online learning. The development of community as a part of the learning process helps create a learning experience that is empowering and rich. It is essential to impart the importance of this process to faculty in order to maximize the use of the online medium in education. Without it, we are simply recreating our tried and true educational model and calling it "innovative," without fully exploring the potential the online medium holds. We now move on to a more thorough discussion of what we mean by community online and the importance of social presence in that online community.

Recontextualizing Community

*To know someone here or there with whom you can
feel there is understanding, in spite of distances or
thoughts expressed, can make of this earth a garden.*

Goethe

M. Scott Peck (1987) makes a powerful statement about community that is often quoted:

We know the rules of community; we know the healing effect of community in terms of individual lives. If we could somehow find a way across the bridge of our knowledge, would not these same rules have a healing effect upon our world? We human beings have often been referred to as social animals. But we are not yet community creatures. We are impelled to relate with each other for our survival. But we do not yet relate with the inclusivity, realism, self-awareness, vulnerability, commitment, openness, freedom, equality, and love of genuine community. It is clearly no longer enough to be simply social animals, babbling together at cocktail parties and brawling with each other in business and over boundaries. It is our task—our essential, central, crucial task—to transform ourselves from mere social creatures into community creatures. It is the only way that human evolution will be able to proceed. (p. 165)

More recent research on the application of community concepts to education support Peck's thoughts. Wenger (1997), a well-known author in the area of communities of practice, notes that the value of education is in social participation and that education should first be addressed in terms of the identities of the participants and the means of belonging to the group. In other words, who we are as social beings drives learning, and the social aspects of learning are the most important. Consequently, those connection points, better known as community, become extremely important in creating a sense of belonging. We further believe that through the creation of a sense of shared values and shared identity, that sense of belonging emerges, and the result is a sense of community in the online class.

Online community has been defined in the literature in many ways, but these definitions often include several common elements or themes, including the ability to build mutual trust, a connection of the spirit, a sense of belonging, a sense of membership, a sense of support, and an ability to share in the educational journey together (Shea, Swan, and Pickett, 2004). More than simply a common meeting or networking space online, such as My Space or Friendster, which have been frequented by younger students (much to the dismay of their academic institutions due to some of the inappropriate activity that goes on there and the mistaken sense that casual connection equals community), the learning community in an online course allows for mutual exploration of ideas, a safe place to reflect on and develop those ideas, and a collaborative, supportive approach to academic work.

Prior to the exploration of online communities, when we thought about place-based community or community groups, the concepts of *differentiation* and *membership* were relevant factors. People seeking commonality and shared interests formed groups and communities in order to pursue the interests that distinguished them from other groups. In addition, communities were generally considered to be place-based, and it was generally believed that to form community, one needed to meet the other members of that community face-to-face. The small town or neighborhood in which you lived was your community. Adherence to the norms of that community allowed you to maintain membership. Expressing your uniqueness as a person was at times problematic because of the need to adhere to those norms (Shaffer and Anundsen, 1993).

Because community is no longer simply a place-based concept, we are seeing it recontextualized and are even applying the concept of place-based communities to online communities. For example, a colleague of ours, Dorothy Ward of Delgado Community College in New Orleans, comments that the creation of community in an online class is much like a neighborhood because the class community would fit within the larger concept of community at the institutional level. In other words, the institution forms the larger community and, when attention is paid to community building in an online class, each class becomes a neighborhood within that community. Wenger and his colleagues (Smith and Doty, 2003) have also used the neighborhood concept in the development of training programs conducted through CPsquare, a site devoted to the study of communities of practice by participating in a community of practice. In CPsquare's training courses, participants enter a community that is made up of smaller "neighborhoods" (or interest groups or domains) and even smaller "households" (small discussion groups). The groups can choose to work around their "kitchen tables" for private discussion, and public discussion occurs on the "front porch." Another example is Second Life, a virtual reality site in which participants or organizations can buy land, build structures, and use avatars, or graphic representations of themselves, to travel around the community and interact with other community members. We find this an interesting way to recontextualize the notion of community online. We return to a discussion of this concept later in the book.

THE IMPORTANCE OF COMMUNITY

Carolyn Shaffer and Kristin Anundsen (1993) talk about our human yearning for a sense of belonging, kinship, and connection to a greater purpose. Changes in the makeup of our families, neighborhoods, and towns have increased that longing, because we are not as easily able to identify with something we can call a community. Our communities today are formed around issues of identity and shared values; they are not necessarily place-based (Palloff, 1996).

Shaffer and Anundsen (1993) define community as a dynamic whole that emerges when a group of people share common practices, are interdependent, make decisions jointly, identify themselves with something larger than the sum of their individual relationships, and make a long-term commitment to well-being (their own, one another's, and the group's).

Because of the requirement, perhaps, to place the needs of the group above those of the individual, some people fear entering into a community because they assume in doing so that they must submit to the will of a group. According to Shaffer and Anundsen, however, the need for connectedness—for community—does not necessarily mean giving up autonomy or submitting to authority in order to become part of a group. Instead, creating a community is a mutually empowering act—a means by which people share with each other, work, and live collaboratively. In the past, we assumed that involvement in community was determined by where you lived (your home town or neighborhood) or determined by your family or religious connections (identification with a country of origin or religious organization). Involvement in community today means making a conscious commitment to a group. Shaffer and Anundsen refer to this as *conscious community*—meaning community that emphasizes the members' needs for personal growth and transformation, as well as the social and survival aspects of community. This aspect is part of what differentiates community from social networking spaces such as You Tube or My Space.

COMMUNITY ONLINE

With the advent of all forms of electronic communication, from the Internet to cell phones, it has become difficult to determine exactly what is meant by the word *community*. Just like the word *family, community* is a word that is now extensively used, perhaps because of the increasing sense of isolation that many people feel in today's world. Communities have spun off into many types, with many varied attributes. Entry into a virtual community, and maintenance of membership in that community, entails a very different process and may, in fact, be more difficult for some people to achieve. Steven Jones (1998) notes that the creation of an online social world is dependent upon the degree to which people use the Internet to invent new personas, to create or recreate their own identities, or a combination thereof.

Jones's early description of online identity refers to what is now termed *social presence*—the person we become when we are online and how we express that person in virtual space. An earlier study by one of us entitled the *Electronic Personality* (Pratt, 1996) supports the notion that one's personality changes when interacting with technology. Introverts, who tend to have more difficulty establishing presence in person, may become more extroverted and establish presence more easily, whereas extroverts, who easily establish presence in person, may have more difficulty connecting with others online. Our work has shown that for this electronic personality to exist, certain elements must manifest:

- The ability to carry on an internal dialogue in order to formulate responses
- The creation of a semblance of privacy both in terms of the space from which the person communicates and the ability to create an internal sense of privacy
- The ability to deal with emotional issues in textual form
- The ability to create a mental picture of the partner in the communication process
- The ability to create a sense of presence online through the personalization of communications (Pratt, 1996, pp. 119–120)

Thus each person creates his or her own virtual environment, in a sense, that allows his or her electronic personality to emerge. People who are introverts are more adept at creating a virtual environment because they can process information internally and are less outgoing socially. It is more comfortable for an introvert to spend time thinking about information before responding to it. It is more difficult—but not impossible—for extroverts to interact this way, perhaps because they have less need to. Extroverts tend to feel more comfortable processing verbally and in the company of others. "Extroverts choose higher levels of noise in a learning situation and perform better in the presence of noise, while introverts perform better in quiet" (Ornstein, 1995, p. 57). Consequently, the introvert may have less difficulty entering the virtual community, whereas the extrovert, with a need to establish a sense of social presence, may have more trouble doing so (Pratt, 1996). Both of us have personally experienced this phenomenon. Keith, an introvert, is uncomfortable in face-to-face social situations but feels very comfortable entering groups online and expressing himself, whereas Rena, a strong extrovert, experiences just the opposite. As mentioned, this difference relates to the ease with which the introvert or extrovert can establish social presence. The use of online communities such as Second Life for the delivery of online classes may change this picture, however, by providing "noisier" spaces that make use of graphic three-dimensional avatars and voice, as well as the use of text.

This ability to create a virtual space is not without unintended consequences, however. The relative sense of anonymity provided by the text-based online environment may encourage the emergence of aspects of the personality that may not otherwise exist face-to-face (Pratt, 1996). Because they are not face-to-face with others, people may feel freer to express hostility, anger, or judgment, for example, which can lead to difficulties within the community. Mutually agreed upon behavioral and communication guidelines become critical in community development and also support the emergence of social presence.

THE ELEMENT OF SOCIAL PRESENCE

The concept of social presence is not new. Short, Williams, and Christie (1976) defined social presence as the degree to which a person is perceived as "real" in communication that is conducted via the use of some form of media. They felt that the degree of presence developed was attributable to the particular media in use. However, more recent studies of social presence as it relates to online learning have noted that the medium has little to do with developing a sense of presence. Lombard and Ditton (1997) note that the emergence of social presence depends to a varying degree on how well participants fail to acknowledge or are able to ignore the presence of the medium. Instead of media, it is participant behavior online that appears to have a greater impact on the development of presence (Polhemus, Shih, and Swan, 2000). When there is a high degree of interaction between the participants, the degree of social presence is also high, and vice versa (Stein and Wanstreet, 2003).

Social presence is something we rarely consider in the face-to-face classroom. When students can see one another within a physical space, we simply assume that presence will occur; students will develop a sense of who their colleagues are simply by being around them. When active and collaborative learning are part of that face-to-face environment, a sense of social presence is more likely to occur naturally through that interaction. Picciano (2002) cautions that simple physical presence may not be enough, however.

> A student's physical presence in a face-to-face course assumes that she or he has a sense of belonging to the class or group of students enrolled in the course. He or she listens to the discussion and may choose to raise a hand to comment, to answer or to ask a question. Furthermore, the same student may develop a relationship with other students in the class and discuss topics related to the class during a break, at the

water fountain, or in the cafeteria. However, this is an assumption and not always true. (Picciano, 2002, p. 22)

Online there is greater possibility for a sense of loss among learners—loss of contact, loss of connection, and a resultant sense of isolation. Consequently, attention should be paid to the intentional development of presence. We present strategies for doing so at points throughout this book.

Social presence has been correlated with learner satisfaction online (Gunawardena and Zittle, 1997), as well as a sense of belonging to a community (Picciano, 2002). Garrison, Anderson, and Archer (2003) believe, as we do, that in order to form community online, a sense of social presence is required among participants. Although many researchers have attempted to measure means by which social presence can be identified in various media (Garrison, Anderson, and Archer, 2000; Gunawardena and Zittle, 1997; Polhemus, Shih, Richardson, and Swan, 2000; Short, Williams, and Christie, 1976; Tu and Corry, 2002), there has been little agreement on how that might occur. What it looks like and its characteristics, however, are more easily discerned. Polhemus and others (2000) note that some of the indicators that social presence has emerged in an online class include the use of personal forms of address, acknowledgment of others, expression of feeling, humor, social sharing, and the use of textual paralanguage symbols such as emoticons, font colors, different fonts, capitalization, and symbols or characters for expression. These indicators correspond with our own thoughts about the indicators that provide evidence that community has formed in the online class:

- Active interaction involving both course content and personal communication
- Collaborative learning evidenced by comments directed primarily student to student rather than student to instructor
- Socially constructed meaning evidenced by agreement or questioning, with the intent to achieve agreement on issues of meaning
- Sharing of resources among students
- Expressions of support and encouragement exchanged between students, as well as willingness to critically evaluate the work of others

Given the close connection between social presence and the development of the online community, it becomes important for instructors to be knowledgeable about the various aspects that comprise it. In addition, social presence plays an important role in coalescence and the online community.

COALESCENCE AND BELONGING ONLINE

Just as there is a strong connection between the development of a sense of social presence and the formation of community online, so is there a strong connection between presence and coalescence. As already noted, presence is the ability to present oneself as a real person online. Students in an online class, feeling themselves to be real persons, are likely to want to connect with another real person. Picciano (2001) states, "Students who feel that they are part of a group or 'present' in a community will, in fact, wish to participate actively in group and community activities" (p. 24).

Coalescence, defined as the formation of that sense of group or community, can be sometimes instantaneous, especially if a group comes together with a strong interest, for example a political campaign or a common problem. But it sometimes takes prodding and deliberate action on the part of the instructor and other students for coalescence to occur. For a coalesced community to be functional and exist for any extended period, coalescence must also take place over a period of time.

What many educators are beginning to realize is that the way the online medium is used depends largely on human needs, meaning the needs of both faculty and students, and that these needs are the prime reason that electronic communities are formed. As previously mentioned, Wenger (1999) notes that the social aspects of education are the most important. In some respects, these educational communities may be more stimulating, interesting, and intense for those involved with education because they bring together people with similar interests and objectives, not just people who connect casually, as we find in other areas of the Internet.

Can the community-building process in online groups be complete without the group meeting face-to-face? Although face-to-face contact at some point in the community-building process can be useful and further facilitate community development, it is not likely to change the group dynamic initially created online. It is possible to build community without it. In our own experience, we have found that an initial face-to-face meeting can be helpful to orient students to the online environment and technology in use. What we did early in our online teaching was to hold brief one- to two-hour meetings to introduce students to one another and the technology. Once the online course started, students tended to quickly forget those initial face-to-face meetings; it was as though they had never occurred. Our experience has shown us that unless the initial meeting extends over a period of days and includes intentional activity geared toward community building, it is not likely to be effective. In fact, having periodic face-to-face meetings throughout the term in a predominantly online course can actually detract from the online work; what tends to happen is that posting to the discussion will drop off as a face-to-face meeting approaches, and then it will take time to build again.

Beginning the formation of online communities without face-to-face contact demands greater attention up front to issues of policy and process. Shaffer and Anundsen (1993) feel that what they term *conscious community* can be created electronically through the initiation of and participation in discussions about goals, ethics, liabilities, and communication styles—that is, the norms by which the group will operate. Consequently, just as norms would be negotiated in a face-to-face group or community, the same needs to occur online. In fact, in the online environment, collaboratively negotiated norms are probably even more critical because they form the foundation on which the community is built. Agreement about how a group will interact and what the goals are, also known as establishment of guidelines or a group charter, can help move that group forward. In a face-to-face group, assumptions are made but not necessarily discussed, such as rules that one person will talk at a time and that a person should ask to be recognized before speaking. In an online group, we can make no assumptions about norms because we cannot see each other. Therefore, nothing should be left to chance, and all issues and concerns should be discussed openly. The following excerpt illustrates how community can emerge in this environment. This particular group had no face-to-face contact until well after their class ended.

> I have never seen anything develop quite like this. Endings, beginnings, break-ups, new-flowering love, blues, backaches, and the wonder of it all! I have been touched by so many of your messages and in such diverse ways that I confess to feeling unable to respond appropriately to each without risking the appearance of insincerity—or multiple personalities. Each response would seem to call for a different emotional driver. *Mel*

Or take another example:

> As a book lover, on one level this seminar is like reading a favorite novel. Each day I pick up the book . . . and join the characters in the evolution of the story. Just as I become emotionally absorbed into the people and ideas of a good novel, I have become absorbed into the seminar. *Claudia*

Numerous discussions and sites on the Internet are related to the virtual community—how it is formed and the elements that compose it. Many agree on some basic steps that must be taken in order to build such a community:

- Clearly define the purpose of the group.
- Create a distinctive gathering place for the group.
- Promote effective leadership from within.
- Define norms and a clear code of conduct.
- Allow for a range of member roles.
- Allow for and facilitate subgroups.
- Allow members to resolve their own disputes.

Taking these steps can foster connections among members that are stronger than those in face-to-face groups. The following excerpt from one author's dissertation journal gives credence to the quality of relationships that can be formed online when these connections do occur. This was written following a face-to-face session concerning the development of a dissertation proposal.

> As I continued to struggle with my concept, I found myself directing my comments, discussion, and attention increasingly toward Marie. It wasn't that she, above the rest, understood my concept any better. It was that I felt confident that she really understood *ME* based on our previous online connection. That gave me comfort and the confidence to struggle on.

RECONTEXTUALIZING COMMUNITY

From our discussion thus far, it is clear that the growth of the Internet and its popularity are having a significant impact on how people interact, as well as how they define and contextualize notions of community. Societal and scientific advances and discoveries, along with technological development, have given us different approaches to issues that are deeply embedded in our attempts to interact. Students from elementary school through graduate school are now using more forms of communication technology than ever before. A recent article that appeared in the *San Francisco Chronicle* (May 14, 2006) notes that adults, who did not grow up with all of this technology, tend to pick and choose what they will do online. However, younger students, who have grown up in the middle of a technological revolution of sorts, have been bombarded with various forms of technology and tend to use them all. E-mail and text messaging are commonplace, especially among younger students. Blogging (or Web Logs), which started out as political journalism online, are now being used by many people for running commentary on their own lives. Blogging sites have emerged on the Internet, allowing people to create Web logs and visit those of others. Sites such as My Space or Friendster are promoting opportunities for younger people to connect online and are being frequented to a great degree by younger students, sometimes raising great concern on the part of adults about what goes on there. But does familiarity with all of these forms of technology assist younger students to form community in online classes? Our opinion is that it does not. Younger students are bringing their casual use of technology into the online classroom, creating a challenge to the academic setting and a need for institutions and instructors to provide instruction and orientation about what it means to use these technologies for academic means and for forming a learning community. Some young people are finding that it is becoming too much for them; that is, too much sharing of personal information online on a daily basis is becoming exhausting for them (Lee, 2006). This does not bode well for the involvement of younger students in online learning communities.

Embedded in the process of communication, whether it is through e-mail, text messaging, or chat, is the fact that we live in and search for community. Many of our attempts to communicate are, at core, attempts at community building—a search for the commonality that connects us. Our basic need to connect on a human level has not only affected the development of electronic communication but, conversely, has also been affected by it. This accounts for the popularity of sites such as My Space, Friendster, and even Second Life. Our relationships are far more complex because of our increasing network of associates and are enhanced by postmodern technological developments. Our communities and neighborhoods are now virtual as well as actual, global as well as local. Our technology has helped create a new form of social interdependence, enabling "new communities to form wherever communication links can be made" (Gergen, 2000, p. 213).

Linda Harasim (in Shell, 1995), a professor of communications and writer in the areas of computer-mediated communication and distance learning, states that the words *community* and *communicate* have the same root, *communicare*, which means *to share.* She goes on to say, "We naturally gravitate towards media that enable us to communicate and form communities because that, in fact, makes us more human" (p. 1). Certainly, online communication is one such medium. It has helped shrink the globe while dramatically expanding the parameters of what we call our communities. It is important, at this point, to begin to discuss what is meant by *community* and why this is important to the process of education and learning online.

The social-psychological literature is full of material about group development. The literature about the development of community shows parallels to that process. One of the best-known writers in the areas of group and organizational behavior has referred to these stages as forming, norming, storming, performing, and adjourning (Tuckman, 1965). First, people come together around a common purpose. This is the forming stage. Then they reach out to one another to figure out how to work toward common goals, developing norms of behavior in the process. Not uncommonly, conflict may begin as members grapple with the negotiation of individual differences versus the collective purpose or objective (storming). However, in order to achieve group cohesion and to perform tasks together, the group needs to work through the conflict. If attempts are made to avoid it, the group may disintegrate or simply go through the motions, never really achieving intimacy. Just as in face-to-face groups, the conflict phase is an essential element that the group must work through in order to move on to the performing stage. Our work with online groups has shown us that these groups go through the same stages as face-to-face groups and communities, even if they do not work together face-to-face. But how do online groups deal with these phases without the benefit of face-to-face contact? A study conducted by Johnson, Johnson, and Smith (1998) compared the Tuckman model of group development to other models in a group of online graduate students. They found that the Tuckman model, with its task orientation, appeared to most accurately describe how the group developed, including the team's ability to engage in conflict online.

Linda, I love your creative approach to inviting conflict and controversy into the room. I wonder if there is a way to reframe the concepts with different language, as it is my sense that the words conflict and controversy have a negative or repulsive kind of charge to them. I am a huge believer in the generative power of conflict, but notice that whenever I visit with people about it they tend to recoil at the mere mention of the word. I'm not sure what an alternative might be but just thought I'd put that out there as food for thought. *Tim*

Sproull and Kiesler (1991) talk about the difficulties that distributed work groups have in achieving consensus when no face-to-face contact occurs: "When groups decide via computer, people have difficulty discovering how other group members feel. It is hard for them to reach consensus. When they disagree, they engage in deeper conflict" (p. 66). They seem to be suggesting that the conflict is a bad, undesirable thing. Ian Macduff (1994), in his article on electronic negotiation, states that there is greater potential for conflict to emerge in electronic discussion than in face-to-face discussion due to the absence of verbal, facial, and body cues and to difficulty in expressing emotion in a textual medium. However, he sees great potential in the resolution of conflict through the use of electronic media, especially if norms and procedures for conflict resolution are established and used. The study by Johnson and others (1998) noted that conflict in online classes does not seem to stem from the completion of the tasks or assignments in the class. Instead, it seems to stem from an unwillingness to participate, poor group planning of activities or assignment completion, and disagreements between group members. In other words, it is the social aspects of group study that breeds conflict and appears to need attention up front as the guidelines for the class are developed so as to minimize this potentially detrimental effect.

So if conflict is not such a bad thing, and if it is necessary in order to achieve group cohesiveness and intimacy, why do so many fear it and attempt to avoid it, especially in the online medium? And how do we as educators establish norms and procedures for resolving conflict in this virtual community of online learning?

One of the concerns about conflict online is that with the absence of face-to-face contact and cues, many people feel less socially constrained. In a face-to-face situation, people tend to choose a number of options for dealing with conflict.

They may avoid it altogether or confront the situation directly. Although this may be done in anger, it is best done within the confines of what we would consider to be socially appropriate behavior. We see the same conflict choices being made online, but because the conflict is being handled through the transmission of written messages, with the possibility of timing and sequencing becoming a problem, resolution of conflict in this medium takes patience and work. In an online classroom, another member of the group may step in as a mediator to facilitate this process.

In one of our earliest online class experiences, which was devoted to exploring the topic of creating online community, conflict occurred between two members of the group, mainly because of the sequencing and timing of messages. Communication was out of sync, which led to a flaming incident, that is, an angry personal message was publicly posted. One of the group members involved in the conflict responded as follows:

> When I read that last message, my heart sank. That's it. I'm sorry. I can't go on. This is one of those places where this medium simply hasn't sufficient dimensionality for me to express what I want and to feel comfortable that my meaning has gotten across. I feel the need for those subtle physical and psycho-social signs that are so much a part of face-to-face communications. *Mel*

He was opting to pull away from and avoid the conflict. However, another group member stepped in to mediate and offered the following:

> I'm having a hard time understanding all the heat around defining community. . . . .I realize that the purpose of this seminar is to debate issues around community and to define what the intersection is between the "human" and "virtual" communities. I also realize that we will disagree on what those elements and definitions are and that sometimes that disagreement will get heated. That's fine with me. But can we agree to establish a norm that we won't make it personal? I think that if we can, we may move through some of the conflict into some really important ideas about what comprises community. *Claudia*

The working through of this conflict helped create an extremely strong connection among the members of the group, leading to a positive learning outcome.

In a face-to-face classroom, conflict may also emerge as a part of a disagreement over ideas. Generally, opening the classroom environment to the debate of ideas is seen as positive; it provides evidence that students are engaging with the material. And although conflict can become heated to the point that the instructor needs to intervene, for the most part it is manageable in the classroom context. However, conflict is not considered part of a community-building process in a traditional classroom. Although it can contribute to learning outcomes, it is not a critical component of the learning process.

In an online learning community, conflict contributes not only to group cohesion but to the quality of the learning outcome. Therefore, instructors in the online environment need to feel comfortable with conflict; they may actually need to trigger it or assist with the facilitation of its resolution. And they should applaud its appearance.

However, there is a danger in unresolved conflict in this medium. If an instructor fails to intervene or fails to support the attempts by other students to resolve a conflict, students will begin to feel unsafe and participation in the online course will become guarded and sparse. In addition, the direction of communication will change, with students directing their posts to the instructor and not to the other members of the group. We experienced this in one of our online courses. A participant became angry about what she perceived to be a lack of participation by the other group members. This was not revealed online but was told to one of us in a phone conversation. Very quickly we noticed that this student's posts were being directed toward us, without comment or feedback directed toward the other participants. Without naming anyone in the group, we simply restated the group guideline that all students should provide feedback to each other online. The result was a rather surprised message from the student in question containing an apology to the group for not being open with them about her concerns and for withholding feedback from them. Given this unique aspect of the virtual community, let us turn now to a discussion of its importance in online education.

COMMUNITY IN THE VIRTUAL CLASSROOM

What does all of this discussion of community have to do with education and online learning? If we reconsider our discussion in the previous chapter of the paradigm for learning online, which involves a more active, collaborative, constructivist approach, the link between the importance of community building and online learning becomes clearer. The principles involved in the delivery of distance education are basically those attributed to a more active, constructivist form of learning—with one difference: *in distance education, attention needs to be paid to the developing sense of community within the group of participants in order for the learning process to be successful.* The learning community is the vehicle through which learning occurs online. Members depend on each other to achieve the learning outcomes for the course. If a participant logs on to a course site and there has been no activity on it for several days, he or she may become discouraged or feel a sense of abandonment—like being the only student to show up for class when even the instructor is absent. Without the support and participation of a learning community, there is no online course.

Instructors who do well online promote a sense of autonomy, initiative, and creativity while encouraging questioning, critical thinking, dialogue, and collaboration (Brookfield, 1995). In a face-to-face learning situation, this can be accomplished through the use of simulations, group activities, and small-group projects, as well as by encouraging students to pursue topics of interest on their own (Brooks and Brooks, 1993). A sense of community in the classroom might be helpful to this process but is not mandatory to its success.

Students in a face-to-face classroom see each other and work together in the same physical space, getting to know each other better through that process. How can we make that happen when most contacts consist of text on a screen? In fact, we cannot make the process happen instantaneously. It must be facilitated. One way community can be developed is through the mutual negotiation of guidelines regarding how the group will participate together. Beginning a course by posting introductions and encouraging students to look for areas of common interest is a good way to start. Instructors in this medium need to be flexible—to throw away their agendas and a need to control in order to let the process happen and allow for the personal agendas of the learners to be accommodated. This may mean that the discussion will go in a direction that does not feel completely comfortable to the instructor. But rather than cut it off abruptly, the instructor should gently guide that discussion in another direction, perhaps by asking an open-ended question that allows the learners to examine that interaction.

We must be able to make space for personal issues in an online course. This should be done deliberately and fostered throughout the course. If this space is not created, it is likely that participants will seek out other ways to create personal interaction, such as through e-mail or by bringing personal issues into the course discussion. Some participants, however, when finding the personal element missing, may feel isolated and alone and, as a result, may feel less than satisfied with the learning experience. Cutler (1995) notes, "Social presence in cyberspace takes on more of a complexion of reciprocal awareness . . . of an individual and the individual's awareness of others . . . to create a mutual sense of interaction that is essential to the feeling that others are there" (p. 18). To enable the emergence of the personal element, we set up a space in the structure of our online classrooms, a cyber café of sorts, to enable this to happen. (We explore this further when we discuss techniques for building foundations for the course in Chapter Seven.) The development of community thus becomes a parallel stream to the content being explored. It is given its own equal status and is not seen as something that "mucks up" or interferes with the learning process. Harasim, Hiltz, Teles, and Turoff (1996) state: "Social communication is an essential component of educational activity. Just as a face-to-face school or campus provides places for students to congregate socially, an online educational environment should provide a space, such as a virtual cafe, for informal discourse. The forging of social bonds has important socioaffective and cognitive benefits for the learning activities. The virtual cafe should be primarily a student space and not be directly tied to the curriculum" (p. 137).

But are all online classrooms active, constructivist learning environments? Do all distance education programs use active and collaborative tools and approaches to learning? Unfortunately, the answer is no. We continue to see many distance education programs in which the instructor posts lectures and attempts to control the learning outcomes by directing and dominating the process. We have also seen many instructors who continue to use multiple-choice and true-false exams as the only measures of learning. Many of these instructors are forced to bow to pressure from their universities, which are unwilling to let go of old methods of pedagogy and student assessment or do not understand how that could be done. Many of these universities are also facing pressure from accrediting agencies that do not understand the forms of teaching and learning that work best in this environment. We have heard many online instructors complain about the absence of interaction among their students or about the lack of response to questions they posed online. With further exploration, we usually find that either these instructors were posing closed questions that did not stimulate discussion or the instructors were dominating the discussion, thus not allowing the process to be learner-focused. (We discuss the differences between forms of questions in Chapter Eight.)

PARTICIPATION AND DESIRED OUTCOMES IN THE ONLINE CLASSROOM

Clearly, an online learning community cannot be created by one person. Although the instructor is responsible for facilitating the process, participants also have a responsibility to make community happen. We have already established that the learning process in the online classroom is an active one. Therefore, in order for students to be considered "present" in an online class, they must not only access the course site online but must make a comment of some sort. Many course management systems in use today allow the instructor to see whether a student has logged on, where in the course they have visited, and for how long. In other words, if students are "lurking," meaning that they are reading but not posting, the instructor will know and can intervene to encourage participation.

Instructors often establish guidelines for minimal participation, making it more likely that students will engage with their colleagues and to facilitate the community-building process. This expectation of participation differs significantly from the face-to-face classroom, where the discussion can be dominated by one or more extroverted students, giving an illusion that the class is engaged. The ability to think before responding and to comment whenever the student wishes helps create a level of participation and engagement that goes much deeper than a face-to-face discussion might. As one of our students describes it:

> It seems that we as students have been more willing to talk and discuss the issues at hand than we probably would inside the classroom. I feel this is so for two reasons. One is that we have time to concentrate on the question and think, whereas in the class you are asked and immediate response is in need. Two, we can discuss openly and not have to worry about failure as much. If you post something that is not right, no one has said this is wrong but instead we give encouragement and try to guide each other to find the right answer. *Brandi*

In addition, because we are working in a primarily text-based medium, in the absence of visual and auditory cues participants focus on the meaning of the message conveyed. As a result, ideas can be collaboratively developed as the course progresses, creating the socially constructed meaning that is the hallmark of a constructivist classroom in which an active learning process is taking place. This ability to collaborate and create knowledge and meaning communally is a clear indicator that a virtual learning community has successfully coalesced.

It is certainly possible, in this environment, to foster the development of a community wherein very little learning occurs but strong social connections exist among members. It is for this reason, among others, that the instructor needs to remain actively engaged in the process in order to gently guide participants who stray, coaxing them back to the learning goals that brought them together in the first place. It is the development of a strong *learning community* and not just a social community that is the distinguishing feature of online distance learning. The desired outcome, then, is the formation of a learning community through which knowledge about the content can be conveyed and the ability to collaboratively make meaning from that content can be achieved.

We have described what the online learning community looks like and how it functions, as well as its importance in the online learning process. We have also discussed the importance of the instructor in facilitating the community's development. However, we have not yet discussed the numerous issues that are likely to surface as that community is forming; neither have we described the need for instructors in this environment to be aware of those issues and to facilitate the discussion about them once they emerge. The acknowledgement and discussion of these issues support the development of social presence in the online community, that is, the ability to portray oneself as a real person and to perceive the same in one's learning colleagues. In the following chapter, we explore these topics in detail, along with the contribution each makes to the development of the online learning community.

The Human Side of Online Learning

When we discuss community building online, we are really concerned with humanizing a "nonhuman," technological environment and creating a learning community in the process. As we attempt to build an online community, human issues will emerge, whether we expect them to or not. In a traditional classroom setting, an instructor may not know that a student is struggling with the end of a relationship or a chronic illness in the family unless the student volunteers that information. In the virtual classroom, however, in order to create community, it is critical to make room for the personal, the mundane—in other words, everyday life.

Certain issues surface time and again as we build learning communities while delivering classes online:

- The need for human contact
- Connectedness and coalescence
- Shared responsibility, rules, and norms
- Roles and participation
- Shadow issues (those elements we choose not to face) and other psychological issues

- Ritual as the psychological expression of community
- Spiritual issues
- Culture and language
- Vulnerability, ethics, and privacy

This chapter addresses each of these issues in turn. We include excerpts of dialogue written by our online participants as they dealt with these concerns.

For example, among the numerous psychological issues and questions that emerge, what is the impact of electronic communication on our perceptions of others? How well do we establish social presence and how well do we project ourselves as real people who happen to be communicating through text? How do we negotiate the ways in which we will communicate? What happens when personal boundaries are crossed? How will we know if we have crossed personal boundaries, what can we do about it if that occurs? Discussions about psychological issues and particularly spiritual issues are often considered controversial and even volatile when they occur in a face-to-face classroom, let alone in the online classroom. In presenting the psychological and spiritual issues embedded in the online community, we are not suggesting that instructors need to become counselors or spiritual advisers for their students. We are suggesting, however, that our participants' attempts to connect in the online arena will cause these issues to surface. We need, therefore, to acknowledge and recognize psychological and spiritual issues when they emerge, as they are core issues in the formation of community.

We value rugged individualism in our culture. But our intense holding of this value may be part of what causes emotional and psychological distress (Peck, 1993; Ornstein, 1995). So our search for community and the solace we find there is in part our need for connection, interdependence, intimacy, and safety—psychologically and spiritually speaking. Fear is what keeps us from experiencing a high level of connection with others—fear that we will lose ourselves in the process, that we will be rejected, that we are fakes, that we are just not good enough. Our isolation is a major contributing factor to psychological and spiritual unease or illness (Peck, 1993). Connection, through community, friendships, therapy, and so forth, is a means to achieve well-being (Shaffer and Anundsen, 1993). Being accepted and supported for who we are is the psychological and spiritual benefit of community.

Engaging in online community does bring with it some complications, however. Sproull and Kiesler (1991) state: "When people perceive communication to be ephemeral, the stakes of communication seem smaller. People feel less committed to what they say, less concerned about it, and less worried about the social reception they will get. . . . By removing reminders of a possibly critical audience, electronic mail induces people to be more open" (p. 42). The up side of this is that "social posturing and sycophancy decline. The disadvantage is that so, too, do politeness and concern for others . . . reduced social awareness leads to messages characterized by ignoring social boundaries, self-revelation, and blunt remarks" (p. 39). Craig Brod, a psychologist, takes a particularly pessimistic view of the impact of electronic communication on a social-psychological level. He feels that as our computer use increases, we are "diminishing and altering our sense of self and of others, creating new barriers to what we long for: intimacy, continuity, and community" (Shaffer and Anundsen, 1993, p. 133). As we previously established, however, direct attention to community building online can break down these barriers, allowing for a new sense of intimacy and connection.

It is difficult but not impossible to convey feelings online, especially anger. Depending on the kind of community developed and whether it involves both face-to-face and virtual contact, expectations about how messages are received are somewhat different. In other words, when both face-to-face and virtual contact occur, participants assume that since they have met one another in person, others will understand the intent behind their words in exactly the way they mean them to be understood. So to some degree, participants are less cautious about what they say in print because they think everyone knows and understands them. Further, in completely textual communication, the relative anonymity of the medium, as noted by Sproull and Keisler (1991), tends to loosen the sense of what is acceptable in communication and creates a sense that all is fair game. This delusion can cause pain and conflict, as it is impossible for people we have met only briefly or only virtually to truly know us and what we stand for unless a deep level of connection is promoted and sustained and a commitment made by members of the group to work through differences.

Virtual contact offers many advantages to the shy or reclusive person, who can sit at the computer and interact with people without all the "hassles" of making physical or visual contact. People desiring virtual isolation can simply refuse to respond or interact with other participants. Certainly, this can become a problem when options for socialization are limited to contacts made through electronic communications or when expectations are that a student will participate in an online class. However, we have found that those of our students who are shy in social settings learn something about social skills by interacting in an online course. We have seen this increase in social skills begin to carry over to face-to-face classrooms. One of us had the experience of working with a student both in an online and a face-to-face class during the same academic term. Describing herself as shy and reclusive to the online group, the student also noted that it was becoming easier for her to interact with members of the group when she met them in other social or classroom situations. Her participation in the face-to-face class increased as she continued to interact with the online group and receive positive feedback for her contributions to the course.

THE NEED FOR HUMAN CONTACT

The removal of visual and verbal context cues in online communication can be both beneficial and detrimental. Textual communication is a great equalizer, promotes a sense of relative anonymity, and can prompt us to be more thoughtful about what we say online or, conversely, can free us up to say things we might not say face-to-face. But the issue of isolation can also be a factor when communicating online. Although we create connection while online, the risk of isolating ourselves from face-to-face contact in the process does exist.

Students who do not do well online attribute this to not being able to see their instructor or classmates, hear what they have to say, or actively engage in verbal conversation. They describe "missing" this form of contact. The advent of virtual classroom technologies that allow for synchronous, real-time interaction as well as the ability to use voice-over in those settings or to add an audio or video file to an asynchronous online course helps to some degree to mitigate this problem. However, in the absence of audio and video, which are not yet widely used for a number of reasons that we discuss later in the book, paying attention to those students who seem to be having trouble making contact is important. Reaching out to the more "silent" students online and inviting them into the conversation can help. The longer a student is absent from the conversation, the more difficult it will be for that student to connect. Sometimes a phone call or an e-mail is all it takes to bring someone back in.

I "hear" "tones of voice" in messages I read, from either strangers or friends who communicate in this medium. In some case they are remembered tones of voice (those I "know"), in other cases they are imagined tones of voice (those I don't know). *Mary Ann*

We have had more than one student post an introduction in an online course but then we hear nothing further, leaving the other students wondering what happened to him or her. One student, who had dropped out of a course with no explanation, finally contacted us to say that her expectation after she posted her introduction was that the others would respond to her personally and make comments about what she had said about herself. When that did not happen, she became discouraged and disappeared, reluctant to respond even to our inquiries about her intent to continue. This was an important lesson to us as instructors, and since then we have learned that the one place where we respond to every student post is at the beginning of the course as students are introducing themselves. In so doing, we welcome them into the newly forming learning community and model that behavior for the other students. We do not want to see someone leave the group because he or she felt unacknowledged.

However, the same phenomenon can occur in face-to-face groups. People simply drop out or away for whatever reason, and a core group continues. Usually in a face-to-face group situation, although perhaps not in a classroom, people who leave are asked to come back and say goodbye to the group or may be asked to send a note or e-mail to say goodbye. The physical presence or absence of someone in a face-to-face group is noticeable, whether they participate verbally or not. In an online setting people can disappear more easily; their absence is noticed but is easier to ignore than an empty chair would be. It is also easier to be a silent member in a face-to-face group. People know that you are present even if you are not speaking. In our online groups, however, silent members just are not there. As instructors, we can use the software to track their presence; however, if they are simply "lurking" in the course, they are not contributing to the development of the group or the exploration of content.

When members do not participate or respond to messages-it might be they are too busy, overwhelmed, ambivalent, apathetic, or whatever, but it can be construed as a mode of control in the sense that we don't know why they aren't joining us. *Cyd*

Beaudoin (2001), in his study on student lurking, noted that it is still possible for students who lurk to do well on course assessments such as tests, quizzes, and papers. Picciano (2002) asserts, however, "Students who feel they are part of a group or 'present' in a community will, in fact, wish to participate actively in group and community activities" (p. 24). It is important for instructors to pay close attention to which students are posting messages and which are not. Because the success of the course depends on participation by all members, instructors should remind students about their responsibility to participate, either by posting messages to that effect on the course site or through individual contact.

We have been in online learning situations where people were "listening in," whether or not they made their presence known. Participants simply ignored their presence, which is easier to do when the listener is unseen. An observer in a classroom is noticed by the students attending the class; an observer in an online classroom is easily ignored because he or she does not participate in the discussion and, hence, is not "seen."

We have found that even when students know they are being observed in the virtual classroom, their willingness to share on a deeply personal level is not affected. One of us was teaching a class where students were sharing openly their concerns about the program in which they were enrolled. Unknown to them or to the instructor, the chair of the department began observing in order to evaluate instructor performance. Once this information was shared with the students, it did not alter their participation or the nature of their contributions, although they did share some concern about how they might be received. Nonetheless, it is important for instructors to provide an explanation to participants when someone will be listening in but not participating in the discussion and to allow discussion of this issue if it makes anyone uncomfortable.

> Participation is essential if we are to learn of and from each other. It isn't simply a matter of arbitrarily choosing to participate or not-this is a collective, or better collaborative, effort REQUIRING conversation and reflection. To be truly collaborative, we must all participate. *Cyd*

CONNECTEDNESS AND COALESCENCE

As we have discussed, connectedness and coalescence of the group in the online classroom does not happen instantaneously; time and encouragement are needed from the instructor. Although it can begin with the discussion of mutually agreed upon guidelines for the course, the need for connectedness does not necessarily mean giving up autonomy or submitting to authority or to the group. Instead, connecting should be a mutually empowering act. This sense of connectedness and coalescence can lead to an increased sense of knowing one another, or social presence, through the shared experiences of struggling with course material and the medium together; connectedness also comes through conflict and through learning to learn in a new way.

> I'm not someone who connects easily with "strangers". Small talk is my downfall. I wrote in my article "An Introvert's Guide to Networking" that I need a reason to call my mother. So I find reasons. I suppose in some ways you could say I have a phobia about face to face contact. Until I have some reason to connect, something to connect about. I may have passed each of you in the [university] "halls," but without SOMETHING that connected us, probably just said hello. Now we have a common experience to talk about. *Theresa*

As students struggle together to navigate the online course or to understand the content, coalescence happens. It is a gradual understanding that they are experiencing something larger than themselves. It is greater than the sum of the parts and creates a stronger whole that is a learning community.

> This has been a delightful course. Through whatever serendipity was operating, the participants brought together a lovely spirit of engagement, mutual respect, love of learning, and great professional and personal diversity. This was most evident in the virtual collaboration involved in constructing our group handbook project. Everyone and everything seemed to fall together in a natural and positive way—though in my experience such teamwork is not 'natural'. It comes through the maturity, wisdom, and selfless commitment of each participant to the greater whole. So I am deeply grateful for my colleagues and all that they brought to the course. *Barrett*

SHARED RESPONSIBILITY, RULES, AND NORMS

Our model of the online learning community and how it develops pays attention to the topics of shared responsibility, rules, and norms. These elements compose the purpose of our work together, the policies through which we will accomplish our work, and the processes by which we will work together. We share the responsibility for the development of the group through participation. The rules need to be fluid, and in fact, there should be few actual rules; instead, there should be guidelines by which we will interact with one another and some boundaries around that interaction. For example, there should be guidelines about professional communication (or "netiquette"), how often students will participate, and possibly even due dates for when that participation should occur. The only real discussion many of our groups have had around ground rules was regarding participation and norms, specifically how much and how often. Our groups did not always agree on this. It seems, at times, that we as facilitators have different expectations for participation than the group does. Consequently, it is important to openly discuss these issues when the group first convenes. This can be done by sharing a set of faculty guidelines or expectations at the start of a course and then asking students to comment on and agree to them. This forms a contract for learning.

Norms emerge in these groups as the process moves along. Frequently, we find groups discussing issues of openness, honesty, and safety as norms we commonly hold and that need to be reinforced. As a group, we may also discuss our goals, communication styles, and the liabilities of this type of communication. These discussions help create a community that evolves emotionally and spiritually and that provides a safe, intimate, and cohesive space in which we can openly share our thoughts and feelings while learning from each other. Few norms of this sort are mandated or established at the beginning of our classes; participants usually agree to norms of openness, honesty, and confidentiality. Norms around levels of participation will be established up front by us and discussed by the group. The other norms emerge as the group progresses.

> Communicating interactively needs tools, processes, and roles/responsibilities to synthesize a variety of opinions, to seek out the silent voices, and to keep it all moving. It has been a challenge for [our university] as it seeks to do more [electronically]; it is a challenge for business; it will be a challenge for our towns and government. *Claudia*

> It is very important to establish a virtual environment with norms, purpose, and values. In that sense I don't think it is any different from establishing a healthy human environment. It needs to be seen as safe for everyone to enter and participate. The voices must be heard, the individuals respected. *Claudia*

ROLES AND PARTICIPATION

As for roles, the instructor as designated facilitator serves a number of functions, from organizer to cheerleader to imparter of information. Participants, too, take on roles. The literature on work groups interacting through technology suggests that task and process roles do emerge in these groups (McGrath and Hollingshead, 1994). We have found in our groups that there is always a participant who attempts to keep things moving when the discussion lags, or one who attempts to mediate conflict or who looks for other members when they have not been present in the discussion for a few days. The emergence of these roles is an indicator that community is developing, that members are beginning to look out for one another and to take care of the business of the course as well. (We offer a much more extensive discussion of roles and their importance in online learning in Chapter Six.) In a traditional classroom, leadership will emerge from one or several students in the group. This, too, represents a way in which students connect and look out for each other.

> I can see how the groups in this virtual class are being created already. Of course, we have our formal groups but certain informal groups are being formed. We have all started to develop roles, too. Who are the ones that have a lot to say, who are the ones that just comment on what the other people say and add insight, who are the ones that get a lot out of the book, or the ones that have personal experiences? *Carmen*

SHADOW ISSUES: THE ISSUES WE SIMPLY DON'T WANT TO FACE

Community can provide all of the psychological benefits we have been discussing. But speaking from a Jungian perspective, community also has a shadow side—elements that are "buried" and unconscious—elements we do not want to face. Some of those are a tendency to promote "groupthink," that is, the subtle and not-so-subtle pressure to conform in thought and action. This kind of oppression can be devastating on a psychological level. When one is experiencing that kind of pressure, the result can be feelings of unease, not belonging, not feeling safe—feelings of being an outsider. There is a tendency to keep quiet and just feel uncomfortable when a loud, vocal group is speaking for the community or group. After a while, one may speak out and risk ostracism or leave. If this is occurring in an online classroom, some students who are uncomfortable will simply drift away and possibly drop the course whereas others may become very vocal and angry. A Native American student with whom one of us was working in an online class was struggling with traditional academics and questioning his ability to do academic work. A very capable student, his frustrations became "louder" as the term progressed, prompting other students to contact him offline via e-mail and also to contact the instructor. Reaching out to him individually was important; it did not solve the problems he faced in a university setting, but it did calm things a bit for him and the other students by allowing him another channel of expression of his concerns.

It may be difficult for an instructor to reengage students who feel they cannot share their thoughts with a very vocal group. When this occurs, it is important for the instructor to intervene and make space in the process for more silent members. Just as an instructor may call on a quiet student in a face-to-face setting, the same may be necessary in the online group, particularly to support a student with a dissenting opinion.

Another shadow issue in community is the relative anonymity that the medium provides. Because students cannot see reactions through facial expression when something is said, they can sometimes be less cautious about what they say and how they say it. Somehow, this creates a sense that they are only communicating with their computer and are not responsible for what they say. Although we have mentioned that this can be a good thing from the standpoint of the introverted student, it also can create a situation in which the usual and customary rules of behavior go by the wayside. One of us was teaching an online class in which a fairly dominant student became confused and frustrated. She lashed out publicly on the discussion board, and when the instructor attempted to intervene with her, she refused any attempts at private conversation. Finally, she was removed from the class until she was willing to work out her differences. In another example, in a class on social change, a student got into a heated discussion with another student regarding gun control. The exchange seemed to be a simple difference of opinion until the student who objected to gun control posted a picture of himself in the course depicting him with all of his guns surrounding him. He then challenged all of the students in the group to comment on his picture. The instructor intervened privately with him to let him know that this behavior was inappropriate and that the picture needed to be removed and apology made to the group. He had not even considered that anyone would get upset with this behavior and complied immediately, stating that even his wife hated that picture of him. In a face-to-face classroom, neither of these incidents would have been likely to occur. The student who was upset with the instructor would probably have approached the instructor after class and discussed her issues. The person who objected to gun control would probably not have brought his guns to class for "show and tell"—at least we hope not! These examples show, however, that because students are unable to see the reactions of their peers, it is possible that, for some, inappropriate behavior may result. When this occurs, it is important for the instructor to intervene so as not to reduce the level of safety that other students need to feel in the learning community.

OTHER PSYCHOLOGICAL ISSUES

From a technological point of view, psychological well-being may depend on the hardware and software environment. If a person feels comfortable with those two components, then the environment is likely to feel safe and secure. But the opposite could be true if the hardware or software environment changes or is difficult to navigate. This can also cause physiological problems, such as eyestrain, back problems, headaches, and stress, all of which can have psychological results. We have known class participants who, because of the hardware or software being used, felt frustrated and unhappy with the entire online experience. We have also experienced software changes at various universities and saw attrition from courses and programs as a result. This is not to say that software changes should not occur. Instead, it is important to plan and prepare for these changes by introducing students to them in advance and offering training and the chance to ask questions prior to implementation.

Risk taking for the purpose of connecting with others appears to be the main psychological issue facing those in communities, whether online or face-to-face. Consequently, instructors must be cognizant of the psychological issues that could affect the success or failure of an online class. Just as in the traditional classroom, attention must be paid to students who seem overly stressed or who express a significant degree of painful emotion in their posts. Although instructors want to encourage students to take risks and to post ideas that might be considered different or controversial, it is important to strike a balance and intervene if a student appears to be in psychological trouble.

I find myself now part of the [group] and psychologically involved. And yet, I feel the walls and bounds between us. Out of courtesy and respect, we don't probe each other too much. We often take safe positions. I read that some of you are going through some pain, yet I don't know how to reach out through this medium. I feel safe in communicating with you all, yet I do not (yet) feel a strong individual connection with any one of you. I know you are out there and willing to support. But, we each have to be responsible for taking the first step—to ask for help, to share a problem or an achievement. I suspect inclusion and a psychological connection come only when we each decide to jump in and get involved. There are some interesting questions here about personal responsibility in community. *Claudia*

RITUAL AS THE PSYCHOLOGICAL EXPRESSION OF COMMUNITY

Phil Catalfo (1993) wrote about his experiences on the WELL (Whole Earth 'Lectric Link), one of the earliest attempts at online community. He related a story about John Barlow, who was the lyricist for the Grateful Dead. Barlow was apparently doing an interview on "small towns, real and virtual" and said that "cyberspace villages like the WELL would never become real communities until they could address sex and death in ritual terms. Marriages and funerals are the binding ceremonies in real towns . . . but they have a hard time happening among the disembodied" (Walker, 1993, p. 169). Phil Catalfo disagreed, and so do we.

On more than one occasion we have had to deal with the death of a faculty member or student as an online class was in progress. Participants have created a mourning ritual that included a forum through which feelings and memories could be shared. When possible, we have, with the consent of the group, printed those postings and shared them with the families of the group members we lost. Through these forums, we clearly celebrated in ritual terms what it means to be human. In addition, it is not uncommon for students to post regarding the illness or death of a loved one. The response is usually an outpouring of support for the community member. The following was posted in response to the death of a faculty member:

The night I read about Ari's death, I sat and stared at the computer while tears flowed down my face. His death came less than a week after I lost a close colleague. It hit me hard. I felt a sensation of disbelief flow through me like a lightening bolt. Though I will later suggest that computers themselves do not embody a spirit, they certainly did during that mourning period. I could not have gotten through Ari's death without the [online] "memorial." *Theresa*

As a result of the sudden death of a student participant at the start of one of our classes, we created a memorial forum online. The posts were printed and read at the student's funeral by one of us and were given to her family, who were amazed at the depth of feeling being expressed by her student colleagues. The following is an example of one of the posts to the memorial forum:

For the past week or so, I have contemplated how the loss of one of my classmates will affect me or if it even would. I have a hard time dealing with death whether it be somebody I never met before or someone that was extremely close to me. I lost my father a year ago and one of my best friends in August. I'm not sure if these have an effect on the way I feel about the loss of Pam or not but this is how I feel. . . . Pam was a challenge to me. She was not a student that accepted what a professor said and took it as the truth. She challenged every idea to the fullest. I remember that in most of my classes if we were discussing something then Pam would always bring in articles from the Wall Street Journal or somewhere that she had read about the issue. I can only imagine how hard it is to try and be a non-trad student, to get along with all of these teenage or older kids that try and blow everything off (the things that seemed so important to Pam). Although I never tried to reach out and meet Pam, I learned two things that I feel were very important to her. First of all, I truly learned how important Pam's degree was to her. Especially from the lecture our class got the first day in HR Admin. and the way she applied herself to everything, I knew that Pam was proud of the fact that she was at school and accomplishing something that she wanted to do for herself. Secondly, Pam lived and loved for her daughter. There were many times in classes that she discussed something about her daughter or just related about her in a story. She posted about her in her biography in this class. I could just tell that she was always thinking about her and cared for her so much. Death is a tragedy no matter how it occurs. I am saddened by the loss of a classmate that I had in all four of my classes this semester and thankful for the simple lessons that my short occurrences with her taught me. God works in mysterious ways and although sometimes his plans confuse me, I am going to bed praying tonight that Pam rests in peace happily by his side. Who knows, maybe she is meeting some of my past and learning something about me. Rest in Peace, Pam. *Carmen*

It is also important to celebrate accomplishments and positive occurrences in ritual terms. For example, members of the university's track team participated in one of our online courses. When they won a significant victory, we celebrated online by acknowledging the win and encouraging others to do the same. We have also celebrated marriages, births, and other significant achievements during the course of an online class. Celebrating these rituals is an important expression of community.

SPIRITUAL ISSUES

The importance of ritual in an online class is related to spirituality because part of the expression of the human spirit is through ritual. When we first thought about spirituality and online learning communities, it almost seemed like an oxymoron. However, we do feel that spirituality enters the online community in more than one way and thus enters the virtual classroom.

First, given that online communities are essentially human communities, they are also essentially spiritual. One of the key words here is *essentially,* as we feel that the spirit is the essential energy that drives and connects us all. That is, it is an unseen force that is greater than all of us and works through us. Everything we do as humans, including our interaction with technology, is spiritual. John December (1997), in a special focus issue of *CMC Magazine* devoted to spirituality online, stated that "if we confine our study of CMC [computer-mediated communication] to only a perspective which assumes a technological, social, or cultural basis for phenomena [we] will miss part of the essence of human experience online" (p. 1).

Although we are not specifically referring to religion in this discussion, the spiritual nature of the online learning community does prompt some students to discuss their religious beliefs as they relate to the course. We had one student who began to quote from the Bible to support his posts in a class. As an instructor-facilitator of this process, it is important to accept and accommodate this as a dimension of the spirituality of the medium and the online group. As we have consulted with and trained faculty for online work, concern has been expressed as to the appropriateness of quoting scripture or the Bible in an online course. Although it is not a concern for religiously based institutions, this can become a concern in public or private institutions that do not have these affiliations. Religiously based institutions will consciously incorporate religious ritual into an online course, such as through the use of prayer to kick off the week's discussion. We teach in institutions that do not have religious affiliation, but we have allowed the use of Bible and scripture quotations if they directly connect to the course. In a course on mind-body healing in a nonreligious institution, one of us allowed students to create a prayer circle at their request. The use of the circle was completely voluntary; students could post a request for prayer for themselves or for friends or family who were ill. They supported their request by citing recent research studies supporting the use of prayer in healing. Since this aligned with course content, it seemed appropriate, and other students did not object.

Spirituality and consciousness are closely intertwined. Our spirituality helps increase our level of openness and awareness. The increasing openness with which participants communicate in an online class is spiritual. We find the power of groups, whether face-to-face or electronic, intensely spiritual. For us, the experience of spirituality goes back to connectedness. The connection between people, however that may happen, touches a spiritual core.

> This seminar will be long over and we will all be off onto other tasks. It feels sad to me. If part of being in community is a sense of caring and interest in each other, then, for me, a piece of that is already here. I may not have a visual picture of all of you to draw on, but after reading several messages from each of you, there is a sense of personality and spirit that comes through. *Claudia*

Again, it is important for instructors to make room for the spiritual in an online course, although its emergence is likely to vary depending on the course content and nature of the course. Students frequently express a sense of wonder and amazement at the depth and nature of the interaction that occurs online. In so doing, they are commenting on the spiritual nature of their connections with one another.

CULTURE AND LANGUAGE ISSUES

An instructor must be sensitive to the variety of cultures in today's online classroom. It is not uncommon to have students from all over the globe in one class, whose varying needs and concerns must be accommodated. In some cultures, it is considered inappropriate for students to question the instructor or the knowledge being conveyed through the course. The co-creation of knowledge and meaning in an online course, coupled with the instructor's role as an equal player in the process, may prove to be a source of discomfort for a student from such a culture. Conversely, a student who is part of a more communal culture, where group process is valued, may feel uncomfortable in a course in which independent learning is the primary mode of instruction. This student may actually feel more comfortable with the creation of a learning community in the online class. Culture also relates to the issue of spirituality. In some cultures, the expression of spirituality is well accepted, whereas in others, it is a private matter. The instructor's job, then, in responding to the cultural needs of a diverse student population involves seeking out, to whatever degree possible, materials that represent more than one cultural viewpoint or, when this is not possible, encouraging students to bring such resources to the online group. Creating flexible assignments and task completion structures can also assist with this process. Asking students to share from their cultural perspective assists not only that student but also increases the cultural sensitivity of the group. Recognizing the different ways in which students might respond to instructional techniques online and being sensitive to potential cultural barriers and obstacles are means by which the online classroom, and thus the online learning community, can become more culturally sensitive.

Language is also a concern, particularly when students such as Soomo, whom we introduced in Chapter One, are uncomfortable with their language skills. This is particularly true of nonnative English speakers in courses in which English predominates but is also true of those students who are not comfortable with their writing skills. The instructor needs to pay close attention to these students, refer them for writing assistance when necessary, and take care not to correct their writing in public. We would not necessarily correct a student's spoken contribution in a face-to-face classroom, and this situation would be the equivalent. It is important to make space for all contributions to the online community.

VULNERABILITY, ETHICS, AND PRIVACY

Any social interaction—any attempt at connection—involves making ourselves vulnerable. We risk rejection, pain, and misunderstanding when we reach out to others. But as we have established, the benefits of connection far outweigh the risks. Privacy is a major issue in community. How much do we need to share about ourselves in order to connect, and how much can we legitimately retain without jeopardizing the essence of community? To some degree, this is an issue of personal comfort, but some guidelines around sharing personal content should be established. In a recent online faculty development session, an ice breaker activity was introduced by some of the participants. The result was some deep personal sharing on the part of some of them. Although we were very comfortable with the level of sharing and did not feel that anything inappropriate had been disclosed, it made a few participants uncomfortable, and a discussion of this issue ensued. The end result was an awareness that the instructor needs to establish his or her own sense of boundaries and communicate that to students so as to help them set boundaries around what they share in class. This can be done publicly if it will not shame the participant for sharing, or privately if a boundary has been significantly crossed.

> For me, it appears in postings that discuss frustration with the process, frustration regarding timeliness, lack of response to request for negotiation, and request for revisiting norms. For me, personally, part of it is navigating this on-line environment—how do I build relationships when we're not face-to-face? How are group members perceiving me and am I getting my points across effectively when I can't see body language? Is it okay for me to be vulnerable and really let group members see who I am? Will I be accepted? (This last part is becoming less of an issue for me, but still exists to a small degree.) *Shelli*

Privacy issues emerge in community in other ways. For example, in face-to-face or telephone interaction, we can have relatively private conversations. We can also feel somewhat sure that a message sent directly to someone's mailbox in e-mail communication is relatively private. However, there are no assurances of privacy when we communicate in the virtual classroom. Several writers have noted that people communicating on bulletin boards frequently act as though their contributions are private and are shocked and hurt when they discover the reality. It is similar to holding a cell phone conversation in a public place. We never know who might be listening. Often we advise caution to both students and instructors online. One suggestion that is often made is to avoid posting something you would not want your mother to read or that you would not want to see on the front page of the *New York Times*. Although that suggestion is made in jest, establishing norms of caution in an online class is nonetheless important. In addition, it is often appropriate to establish norms of confidentiality. We both teach in a program in which corporate executives are students. They often discuss a norm of confidentiality relative to their posts, because they do not want private company information shared outside of the group. Some have taken to providing a pseudonym for their company in order to further protect privacy.

The question of ethics opens an area of discussion that is frequently controversial. Because this area is so new, the ethics around how communication happens are still being debated. There are many places, both in the online classroom and around the Internet, where the notion of ethics comes into play. Those who have used e-mail systems at work probably have many stories about both ethical and unethical uses of e-mail. Increasingly, we see articles appearing in journals, newspapers, and on the Internet discussing this subject, along with discussion of e-mail monitoring in the workplace and spyware programs that allow others to see what websites someone is visiting online. University administrators are being pressured to confront these issues and set standards around them because of the increase in unacceptable and even illegal uses of e-mail on campus (McDonald, 1997). Mary Sumner (1996) categorizes the social and ethical problems in this medium as abuse of public computing resources. Included in her list of abuses is tying up open-access workstations, disk space, network printers, and other shared resources; invasion of privacy, such as gaining unauthorized access to other people's electronic mail by breaking passwords or spoofing; and improper use of computer systems, including harassment, commercial use of instructional facilities, and misrepresentation of user communications. We revisit these issues in Chapter Four as we discuss practical considerations for online interaction.

Sexual issues are another unavoidable concern in electronic communication. Common abuses in this area may include someone posing as a person of a different sex, sexual innuendos in textual communications, and sexual harassment. One instructor reported to us some of her experiences with online courses, one of which was interrupted by a "peeping Tom." Students who were participating and sharing some fairly personal material were angry and felt violated when this person revealed himself to the group in an inappropriate way. Although course sites are generally password-protected, it is possible for an intruder to enter. Despite the fact that observers may be present or others may be able to access the site, the group constructs an illusion of privacy, which allows them to continue to share openly with one another (Pratt, 1996).

No online classroom is truly private. Usually, system administrators, department chairs, deans, and directors of distance learning have access to the site in order to work with technical or other problems that may arise. As part of a peer review system or training program for new faculty who want to teach online, many institutions have asked faculty to shadow one another in an online course. Finally, another student can hack into a course, as the student just mentioned was able to do. Consequently, instructors and students need to think carefully about what to share or encourage in an online class, and strong norms must be established for those who have legitimate access to courses for what materials can be carried out of the course without the consent of the participants. The goal should be to establish a balance between open dialogue and caution. If an instructor feels that a participant's posts are too personal or too open, it is important to contact that student confidentially to discuss the issue. In addition, it is important for instructors to report any breaches of security in the system immediately so that the integrity of the course is maintained. Finally, material posted by students in the course should not be used by either the instructor or the institution for any reason without the express consent of the student. The student's intellectual property, which takes the form of his or her contributions to an online course, must be respected.

The encryption of messages is the most reliable means of assuring privacy online, but it is rarely employed in an academic setting. When the issue of privacy is addressed directly, the vulnerability of participation becomes evident, as uncertainty remains about how and whether contributions will be used by others. Although this uncertainty should not stop instructors and students from using the Internet for educational purposes, it does raise fairly significant issues that must be addressed as a virtual community is developing. Members must know that their communications are not secure and that they must use good judgment in what they share. Boundaries, therefore, may be more important online than they are face-to-face, and they must be adhered to and enforced.

Guidelines for the appropriate use of course material should be posted at the beginning of the course with a request for clarification and discussion to ensure that participants understand the importance of this issue. Inappropriate use of materials, e-mail, or access to the course must be addressed by instructors quickly and directly so as to maintain the norm of safety and acceptance within the group. If an instructor or a participant becomes aware that information posted to a course site has been quoted elsewhere without permission, for example, this breach must be directly confronted. If it comes to the instructor's attention that a member of the group is being stalked by another member, this must also be confronted and stopped, even if it means removing a student from the class. If a student drops the class, access to the course site must be denied through deactivation of his or her password. These are concerns we rarely have in a face-to-face classroom situation, but they become critical to the creation of a safe course site that facilitates the development of an online learning community.

> Privacy is an interesting topic to me. I am a very private person in person. Yet I have been conversing with you about my fears and insecurities and life choices. And though I do intend my words for those who have been responding, I am aware that this is a public place where there are silent readers who now may know me a lot more than I know them. *Theresa*

Privacy, ethics, vulnerability, and boundaries are all closely related issues in the online community. Attention to these issues helps create a foundation that supports the purpose for being there and the purpose of the work together, as well as reinforcing the creation of a safe and secure environment in which to work. In the next chapter, we look at these and other issues from a practical standpoint.

FINAL THOUGHTS

Online education requires more than a software package that allows an institution to offer coursework online. In any setting, whether academic, organizational, or corporate, it is *people* who are using the machinery that makes the course go. The human element, therefore, will inevitably play a role in the electronic classroom, particularly as we work toward the *purpose* for being together online.

Human concerns should be welcomed into the classroom, not feared, and should be worked with as they emerge. The human issues in a developing online learning community create a level of challenge to the instructor that might not be present in the face-to-face classroom. The physical distance between members in the community pushes instructors to be creative in how they cope with difficult students who are not participating or those who are violating the privacy of the group. The fact that the course is being conducted online does not limit the instructor to resolving all of these issues online. All means of communication, including the telephone and face-to-face meetings, need to be employed in order to address concerns and deal with problems. The lack of face-to-face contact means that the sense of group in an online learning community can be fragile, especially as it is forming. The group can disintegrate quickly when problems occur.

Consequently, what is most critical for the instructor, even when playing a facilitative and nondirective role in the learning community, is to stay abreast of developments within the group and to act decisively and quickly when necessary. In the next chapter, we reconsider these human concerns plus two more practical elements that affect the people and the work of online distance education: time and group size.

Practical Considerations in Online Learning

In the previous two chapters, we discussed some human issues that arise as we form an online learning community. We also noted that online learning communities do not just happen but need to be created with good planning and forethought. Consequently, there are some practical considerations that must be taken into account if the class is to be successful. Included in these are *time, size, cost,* and *security.* Another consideration is the software used for the class, which we discuss in Chapter Five. The success or failure of an online endeavor depends on getting these practical considerations right.

ABOUT TIME

Concerns about time relate primarily to the amount of time required for participation on the part of both students and faculty. In this section, we discuss several of the concerns related to time: asynchronous and synchronous environments, time offline versus online, time constraints, and time management.

Asynchronous and Synchronous Environments

Online classes can be conducted either synchronously (real-time virtual classrooms or chat) or asynchronously, meaning that postings are staggered. Our preference, based on our experiences with online teaching, is for the asynchronous environment. It is the creation of community in that environment to which all of our previous discussion relates. The asynchronous environment allows participants to log on to the class or discussion at any time, think about what is being discussed, and post their own responses when they wish. However, recent advances in synchronous technology, as well as increasing skill with its use, are helping us see the benefits of this form of technology in community building and the delivery of an online class.

The challenge of conducting a synchronous meeting or class session is to coordinate time with a dispersed group and to facilitate in such a way that all "voices" are heard. Although many groups ask for the ability to have synchronous discussion (chat capability), we find that skill is needed on the part of the facilitator for productive discussion or participation or it will disintegrate into simple one-line contributions of minimal depth and wander off topic. It can replicate the face-to-face classroom in that the participant who is the fastest typist will probably contribute the greatest amount to the discussion, thus becoming the "loudest voice" in the group. In addition, contributions may end up out of sync; a participant may respond to a comment made several lines earlier but be unable to post that response immediately due to the number of people posting or the speed of the connection to the discussion. Some newer forms of technology, such as virtual classroom technology, have helped mitigate some of these concerns. Finkelstein (2006) notes that to make synchronous interaction and the use of virtual classrooms effective, an agreement must be struck between the instructor and participating learners. The instructor, in arranging the synchronous session, has determined that this is the optimal means by which to engage with learners in exploring content, in essence making the commitment not to waste learner time. Learners agree to minimize the distractions around them as they work synchronously and to use the time meaningfully.

If the group is internationally distributed, time differences become critical, as does the impact of culture on communication. Careful determination must be made of whose time zone will be used to conduct synchronous sessions. If students are located simultaneously in Europe, across the United States, and in Asia, as we have experienced in some of our classes, the challenge to hold synchronous sessions increases. Often the students themselves will resist using chat to communicate with one another in these circumstances and will remind their peers that time zone issues are a concern when the possibility of holding a chat session is raised.

Synchronous communication has become popular with those who need to conduct meetings with distributed work teams through technologies such as WebEx. Again, however, time zone concerns are crucial. We were asked to consult to a human resources staff person for a large multinational company that used a distributed team format. The manager of an internationally distributed team within the company was baffled when a Japanese member resigned. Upon investigation, she discovered that the team member was required to drive for two hours in the middle of the night in order to get to the office to participate in a synchronous team meeting. However, because it was not appropriate for him to complain to a superior, given his cultural background, he felt that his only option was to resign. Conversely, we worked with an agri-business firm located in the central part of the United States, Canada, and Mexico. In this case, the use of synchronous technology for training was useful because all participants were in the same time zone, thus creating ease of access and minimal inconvenience. As online distance learning programs attract an increasingly international market, educators will need to consider the impact of time and cultural differences on the conducting of courses.

The managers of an educational program being conducted completely online told us recently that they were resisting the addition of chat capability for their students because of concerns about time. Because the students in the program were globally distributed, theirs was a logistics concern. How would they be able to conduct a class meeting synchronously, given that their students were all over the world? On whose time schedule would these meetings be conducted? Would the schedule be determined by the instructor? The students? Whose time zone would win out? Although these may seem like small, petty issues to some, they become critical when an instructor or a participant is asked to get up in the middle of the night to participate in a class discussion. Certainly, this would reduce the quality of participation and thus erode a developing sense of community in the group. These are certainly not insurmountable concerns—rotation of times for meetings or multiple meetings might help overcome these challenges—but the point is that they need to be considered carefully.

Another concern in synchronous communication is the ease with which members can become confused and overloaded if guidelines for participation are not established at the start. As discussion occurs in real time, members may not be able to keep up with the pace established. In an attempt to deal with this problem, many virtual classroom applications for synchronous communication include ways to signal for recognition—much like raising a hand in a face-to-face classroom.

Although this helps create order out of possible chaos, it does not help stem a sense of overload as the discussion proceeds. Consequently, the facilitator should stop periodically and check to see whether there are questions from silent members or to break up the flow a bit. Finkelstein (2006) likens the role of the facilitator-instructor to a host at a successful dinner party. A good host prepares for his or her guests to arrive, welcomes them, assesses their mood and needs, helps them feel included in the conversation, and facilitates connection and conversation between them. Given that the synchronous virtual classroom most approaches what goes on face-to-face, he notes that it is easy to fall into an "autopilot" mode when working synchronously and forget that the learners are even present.

We do not mean to condemn synchronous communication, however. It clearly can be a dynamic and challenging setting in which to meet and can be especially useful in facilitating brainstorming and whiteboarding sessions. (*Whiteboarding* is writing or drawing on a shared screen.) A recent example of effective use of synchronous media has been Delgado Community College's Summer Institute. Devastated by Hurricane Katrina in 2005, Delgado, located in New Orleans, has had to turn to the use of online classes in order to continue to serve its student body. The number of online courses being delivered by the institution has grown dramatically since the storm, and faculty have been anxious to receive training to improve course development and delivery. Prior to the storm, Delgado held a two-week, on-campus institute focused on the use of technology in the classroom. However, with staff, faculty, and students dispersed and with the new focus on online delivery, a decision was made to hold a one-week institute online. The response by faculty to this idea was extremely positive, and a one-week course that contained asynchronous discussion assignments for participants along with live webcasts and synchronous chat sessions was delivered. A week of real-time, synchronous sessions would have been exhausting for all participants, but the combination of asynchronous and synchronous delivery created variety, as well as time for participating faculty to catch their breath.

As the Delgado example conveys, the key is to choose the appropriate synchronous media in an online course and to pay particular attention to good facilitation skills to make it effective and worth the time and effort it takes to arrange it. Designing a one-week institute clearly takes a great deal of time and effort. However, there are simple ways to include synchronous media in an online course. One of us uses chat regularly to hold online office hours or to set up a question and answer session for students. Chat can be a useful adjunctive tool in a predominantly asynchronous online class, but for it to be successful, the number of students participating should be small, the concerns and time zones of all participants must be considered, and guidelines for equal participation must be established in advance.

In asynchronous classes, members have the luxury of time. Postings can occur at the convenience of the participants, allowing them time to read, process, and respond. However, because participants can take their time, asynchronous classes need to take place over a much longer period, which should be factored into the planning. What might have been a weekend workshop may have to be stretched over one or two weeks to allow for full participation. The amount to be discussed in one week during a semester course may need to be pared down to manageable size in order for all participants to have an opportunity to read and respond. This is not to say that due dates and guidelines should not be established; we routinely set due dates for discussion postings in order to help students manage their time. Having the luxury of time does not mean letting things slide.

> I really enjoy being able to do my work whenever I want to. Along with the flexibility it also gives me a sense of responsibility. *Jason*

Time Offline Versus Time Online

As we conduct our classes and training sessions about online teaching, one reaction is always expressed by several members of the audience: surprise about the amount of time it takes to teach a course online. Many instructors, institutions, and students mistakenly believe that this mode of teaching and course delivery is easy. We have found the opposite to be true. An instructor for an online course cannot simply post material and walk away for a week. If that happens, the instructor may log on to find a flurry of posts and questions and may have difficulty appropriately reentering the conversation. The same, of course, is true for students.

One of the greatest institutional concerns that we have encountered in the last few years is instructor accountability. There is concern that some instructors are simply posting discussion questions and then do not log back into the course as the discussion is occurring to monitor progress or offer input and feedback. We find that we need to check the course site at least once a day, if not more, in order to respond quickly to student posts, offer advice or suggestions, or simply make our presence known and felt. We do, however, recommend setting boundaries around instructor time. The fact that an online classroom is open and available twenty-four hours a day, seven days a week does not mean that the instructor is also available during all of that time. Instructors need to factor in time off as well as reasonable response times and communicate those to students at the start of the course. For example, students should know response times to e-mail, such as twenty-four to forty-eight hours, and to the grading of assignments, such as seven to ten days, as well as how often the instructor intends to log on and participate. We encourage instructors to take at least one day off per week from their online courses. If that day is a set day per week—for example, we both take off on Saturdays—then that can be communicated to students early on with notation that e-mails will be returned and questions answered on the instructor's return.

One thing we have learned, however, is that giving students too much information about time away makes them anxious. We both travel extensively and always leave home with a laptop computer in order to keep up with classes. This is one of the benefits of online learning: it is portable. However, when we have kept students abreast of our travel schedules, we have found that it will almost certainly result in some negative comments on final course evaluations, such as, "She was away too much or too busy to pay attention to us." It is interesting that if students perceive that the course is being delivered from the instructor's home or office on campus, they do not seem to worry about how busy the instructor may be. But when the course is being delivered from a hotel room, their perception changes. Consequently, we have become more cautious about sharing travel schedules or other information regarding potential interference with time online and have only done so in urgent situations, such as illness or inability to log on.

Students also need to be responsive and involved, as we have discussed previously, and to inform the instructor and their peers should they need to be away from class. As one of our students stated:

One thing I must say with this group as compared to my classes last quarter, you have to check in more than the required two times a week. . . . . I found that when I came on-line there were so many long postings and so many rich thoughts that it was hard to respond to soooo much. So my answer is to try and come on-line more often. *Cindy*

Another student commented:

To some degree it's easier to drive to a class every Wednesday night for three hours or to spend all weekend in class. At least you know that the time is designated and finite. This class, on the other hand, goes on 24 hours a day, 7 days a week. This makes it so much harder to know when to "go to class" so to speak. I thought this would be an easier way to take class. I was wrong! *June*

Instructors in the online arena will find that the time needed to deliver this type of class is two to three times greater than to deliver a face-to-face class, especially as they develop and deliver a course for the first time. Exhibit 4.1 illustrates this difference. It is an accounting of time by one of us in the online delivery of one week of a class, Basic Addiction Studies. The class was a graduate-level class that normally met once a week for two-and-a-half hours. The instructor needed to cancel a class and could not reschedule it, so she conducted the class online for a week. The twenty-three students participating were divided into four discussion groups. All of the groups were discussing the same topic. Students had varying levels of comfort with technology, although the instructor was very comfortable with it. This was the first experience in online learning for most of the students; very active discussion ensued.

Although the amount of time involved with the delivery of one week of instruction may seem daunting, the level and quality of participation on the part of students helps surmount any feelings of being overwhelmed that might result. In addition, as both instructor and students become acclimated to the online environment, both develop time-saving devices that help them be more efficient with their time. The first time an instructor delivers a course will be far more time consuming than the third or fourth delivery of the same class, even with updates and modification. Regardless of the amount of time an online class takes, there is nothing more exciting than to log on to a course site and see groups of students actively engaged with the material. We find it energizing and exhilarating, although the amount of work involved cannot be minimized.

Additional Time Issues

Increasing amounts of online time can contribute to issues now noted in the literature on online learning, such as addiction to being online and information addiction. Frequently referred to as information overload or "infoglut," information addiction actually goes beyond what we ordinarily think of as overload. In an overload situation, students and faculty may be inundated with so much poorly managed information that they feel they simply cannot keep up.

Exhibit 4.1.
Time Comparisons of an Online versus Face-to-Face Class for One Week.

Instructor Activity	Face-to-Face Class	Online Class
Preparation	2 hours per week to:	2 hours per week to:
	Review assigned reading	Review assigned reading
	Review lecture materials	Prepare discussion questions and "lecture" material in the form of a paragraph or two
	Review and preparation of in-class activities	
Class time	2 1/2 hours per week of assigned class time	2 hours *daily* to:
		Read student posts
Follow Up	2 to 3 hours per week for:	Respond to student posts
	Individual contact with students	2 to 3 hours per week for:
	Reading student assignments	Individual contact with students via e-mail and phone
		Reading student assignments
Totals for the week	6 1/2 to 7 hours per week	18 to 19 hours per week

Note: Time involved with online classes is related to a number of variables such as the number of students enrolled in the class, the level of comfort with the technology on the part of both the instructor and the students, the encountering of technical difficulties, the degree to which discussion is an expected part of class activity, and the types of activities in which students are engaged.

Harasim and others (1996) report on this negative aspect of learning online and student reactions to it: "Students report information overload, communication anxiety in relation to the delayed responses in an asynchronous environment, increased work and responsibility, difficulty in navigating online and following the discussion threads, loss of visual cues, and concerns about health issues related to computer use" (p. 15). A typical reaction to overload is to retreat. If a student disappears from an online class, overload may be the culprit. This needs to be investigated with the student so that appropriate course management techniques can be implemented. Frequently, students who are new to online learning call us asking for assistance in taking in and responding to the amount of information being generated within a course. Providing tips on how to read and respond often helps. Generally, we advise these students to log on just to read what is newly posted. Then we suggest that they log off to spend time reflecting on what they have read and to compose their own comments. Once that has been completed, we advise them to log back on to post their responses only. This helps students manage their time as well as deal with the information contained in an online course in "chunks" rather than all at once.

With information addiction, however, the opposite of overload occurs. Participants may begin to "binge" on e-mail exchanges or contributions to the course site or just to being online. A sense of urgency develops, coupled with frustration when others do not respond in kind. Inflammatory messages may be the result. Participants experiencing information addiction may, but will not always, sense that they are somehow out of control. Their need to spend time online takes over and goes beyond what would appear to be the norm. They may ignore family, work, and classes to spend time on the Internet (Young, 1998). Frequently, as with any other form of addiction, they do not recognize the extent of their problem; the instructor may need to intervene and help them manage the time they spend online. Although this may seem far-fetched to some, L. Dean Conrad and Perry Crowell (1997), in their article "E-mail Addiction," describe this means of communication as both a blessing and a curse. If not properly managed, addiction to the medium can lead to becoming less effective overall. The American Psychological Association, in its 1997 annual conference, also recognized this problem by presenting a diagnosis based on research conducted by Kimberly Young (1998), which they term *pathological Internet use* or PIU. Those suffering with PIU are said to spend in excess of thirty-six hours per week online and to experience some of the symptoms mentioned earlier.

Conrad and Crowell (1997) present a "12–Step Program" to regain control. Many of their suggestions would be useful to a participant in an online course who is struggling with issues of information addiction:

- Set a specific time each day to read and respond to messages rather than doing it throughout the day.

- Wait to respond to a message that upsets you and be careful of what you say and how you say it.

- Never say anything that you could not tolerate seeing in print on the front page of your local newspaper.

- Establish clear priorities for dealing with messages and categorize messages by importance and need to respond (pp. 4–5).

The instructor's response to all of this should be course management techniques, such as good organization of the course site and presentation of material in manageable pieces, along with sensitivity to the signals that students may be giving regarding their inability to keep up. Good course management includes the use and enforcement of participation deadlines. For example, students may be told that a discussion opens on Monday and that their first post in response to the discussion questions is due by Wednesday and their responses to their peers by Friday. Creating deadlines such as these creates boundaries in a setting where boundaries are difficult to determine, assists the students in scheduling and managing their time, and helps reduce anxiety. Exhibit 4.2 lists some of the time concerns that may arise and techniques for dealing with the concerns.

Instructors must be prepared to help students manage their time online to avoid both overload and the potential for developing addiction to the medium. On a more positive note, however, students who use the medium appropriately find that it can help them develop the research skills needed for other classes, become more responsible in their study habits, and be better able to manage their time overall.

> I do spend a LOT more time on line. Not only for this class, but I find myself using the Internet more for my other classes as well. *Carmen*

Time Management

Clearly, the need to be involved to a greater extent in these classes creates a greater need for time management. Part of what participants need to learn from an online class is how to divide their time into tasks: reading the assigned material to prepare for the online discussion, reading the contributions of other students and preparing one's own, participating in small-group work, and completing the other assignments for the course. The instructor can assist with this process by assigning reading material in manageable pieces, attempting to enforce time limits on the discussion of a particular topic by locking discussion forums or using the selective release features built into many course management systems, and

Exhibit 4.2.
Course and Time Management Techniques.

Concern	Instructor Response
Minimal or no participation on the part of one or more students due to information overload.	**Personal contact to determine cause.** **Suggest setting a time daily to log on in order to read only.** **Print messages from course site.** **Set two additional times per week to respond. Prepare responses in word processor and copy and paste to course site.** **Assist in management of outside reading for the course.**
Information overload due to poorly managed or poorly organized information.	**Make sure that students are posting to the appropriate discussion forums and correct if necessary.** **Add discussion forums if necessary to separate and organize material.** **Present outside reading in manageable amounts.** **If class is large, divide the group into smaller discussion groups.** **Establish time limits on discussion of topics (such as one or two weeks per topic)**
Communication anxiety	**Personal contact to reassure student.** **Supportive response every time the student posts until anxiety is reduced.** **Ensure that student is comfortable with the technology being used.** **Encourage preparation of posts in word processor and copy and paste into course site rather than posting on the spot.**

(continued)

Exhibit 4.2.
Course and Time Management Techniques *(continued)*

Concern	Instructor Response
Lack of participation due to technical difficulties	Personal contact with student to provide instruction and coaching on the technology in use.
	Contact with systems administrators to resolve technical problems that are out of student or instructor control.
	Availability of technical support for participants.
Reduced participation due to concerns about privacy and exposure	Personal contact with students to determine nature of concern and encourage participation.
	Supportive responses to student posts to reduce anxiety and encourage participation.
	Plug any security leaks immediately by working with systems administrators and changing passwords if necessary.
Excessive posting accompanied by irritation with others who cannot "keep up"	Personal contact with the student to assist with course management and to provide feedback on participation.
	Suggest only one time daily for logging on.
	Limit posts to two per week.
	Limit length of posts.

establishing participation guidelines. In addition, student anxiety about the perceived need to respond immediately to course material can be minimized through good time-management techniques.

Some of the suggestions we have made to students who are having difficulty with time management and course management in general are as follows:

- Log on to the course site with the intention of downloading and reading only.

- Print new messages, if possible, to allow time to review them in a more leisurely fashion.

- Once messages have been read and reviewed, formulate a response to be posted. Do not feel as though an immediate response is necessary in an asynchronous environment.

- In order to be more thoughtful about responses, prepare them in a word processor and then copy and paste them to the course site. If hard disk space is at a premium or if a lab computer is being used, copy your responses to a disk, CD, or flash drive for use later on.

These suggestions tend to allay student fears about what constitutes good participation while providing them with a more organized and thoughtful way to approach the course. An additional benefit of this approach is that it can help minimize the potential of lost work due to Internet time-outs or other problems with technology. Also, they reduce some students' tendency to respond off the tops of their heads, thus improving the quality of their responses; the possibility of conflict and flaming is reduced as well.

Time Constraints

A final consideration in the issue of time, as it relates to online courses, is time constraints. Frequently, because instructors are teaching online courses through institutional structures, they are expected to fit these courses into existing time frames, such as quarters or semesters, although many institutions are now experimenting with variations such as six- and eight-week intensive courses. This can be somewhat constraining or inhibiting in that an online course frequently takes on a rhythm of its own. It may start out somewhat slowly, as students work out any technical problems they may be experiencing and begin to feel out the parameters of the course and to know each other. We then frequently see the course take off for a time, with students contributing at a very high level and responding to each other with great frequency. The course may then begin to wane around midterm, particularly as students begin to grapple with the expectations and demands of their other face-to-face or online courses. Consequently, preparation for exams and term papers may slow down the interactive process, which may force the instructor to take a much greater facilitative role as the quarter or semester progresses, when we would expect the opposite to be true. After the midpoint of the course, we are likely to see a flurry of participation, particularly toward the end, as students ask questions about course completion, post final assignments to the course site, and are asked to reflect on and process the experience as a whole. It is interesting that in most cases, as the course progresses, there tends to be less need for the instructor to actively participate in the online discussion past the midpoint. As students form their learning community, they look more to one another for feedback and feel less need to depend on the instructor. Some instructors have difficulty with this, as they feel that they have lost control of the process. And some institutions have difficulty with this, because they feel that the instructor is not doing his or her job. We feel, however, that this diminishing dependence on the instructor is very positive and shows that a solid learning community has formed. One of us facilitated a class that was so highly interactive that instructor participation was actually seen by the students as an intrusion. The students told the instructor, in this instance, that they would invite his participation if they needed it and asked him to otherwise monitor and only jump in if it was necessary from his point of view. Although we have never seen this happen in another class, it is an indicator that a very strong community had formed and was progressing well through the course as a result.

Another unrelated but interesting time constraint is the expectation of many institutions that instructors maintain office hours. An instructor who maintains an office on campus and is teaching both face-to-face and online classes may not find this particularly challenging. But how is this accomplished when the office is virtual? If students are geographically dispersed, as many are in online courses, or the instructor is adjunct and not available on campus, this can be a challenging restriction. Certainly, it is important for instructors to make themselves available by phone to students in an online course or they can set up weekly synchronous chat sessions and invite students to participate as needed or to set an appointment to meet in the chat room. These are by far the simplest solutions. The establishment of telephone office hours, telephone appointments, or chat time can serve the same function as face-to-face office hours.

One accounting instructor with whom we worked a few years ago came up with a particularly creative solution to this dilemma. She established online office hours in an asynchronous environment. She notified students that she would be checking the course site every few minutes on Monday evenings from 9:00 P.M. until 10:00 P.M. and on Thursday evenings from 9:00 P.M. until 9:30 P.M. The Thursday office hours happened to coincide with the time that the television show *Seinfeld* was on in her area and she told her students that she would be watching *Seinfeld* in between the times that she checked the course site. What quickly happened was that all of the students began watching *Seinfeld,* checking the course site, interacting with the instructor and also with each other, discussing what was happening in the television show in one area of the course site and posting questions for the instructor in another area of the discussion board. Not only did this solution create the opportunity to have questions answered by the instructor during her office hours, but it also deepened the sense of community within the group. This was a particularly interesting and creative means by which to accomplish this, given that the course was a statistical methods course—a subject that would be challenging in terms of creating an online learning community.

At a recent distance learning conference, a nursing instructor shared an interesting story related to time and time constraints—a story that we have heard from many other instructors as well. She found that her class time online was not being respected by others in her department. If she logged on to her course site while in her office at the university, others did not seem to respect that she was actually teaching a class. Colleagues would come into her office and ask to speak to her. Someone would interrupt her and ask her to do something or ask whether she was interested in having a cup of coffee. Her eventual response to these interruptions was to close her office door and post a sign on it that read, "In class. Please do not disturb." Her colleagues respected the closed door, and she was able to have uninterrupted time in which to focus on her class.

What is most important in considering a means by which to hold "office hours" and have the dedicated time for an online class is that instructors delivering online courses do not have the luxury of going on vacation for a week or two, at least not without a laptop! Their continuous presence, guidance, and availability to the participants is critical to successful course outcomes. These elements must be acknowledged and respected by administrators and colleagues in order to provide the support instructors need to successfully teach in this arena.

GROUP SIZE

Closely related to issues of time are those of group size. Group size is of major importance in an online classroom because it relates to the ability of the instructor to maintain some modicum of control over the process without subjecting participants to information overload.

If a synchronous meeting or class is being conducted, the group should be small enough to allow for full participation and to prevent information overload. Groups that are too large can be overwhelming for the instructor and the participants; five to ten is an ideal number. Asynchronous groups, however, can be much larger. As many as twenty or more participants can have a successful experience in an asynchronous setting. However, the success of a large group depends on the skill of the instructor as facilitator, his or her knowledge of the course management system and online facilitation, the content being discussed and explored, and the means by which that exploration occurs. A recent ASHE Higher Education Report notes that the best argument for establishing class size is instructional philosophy and instructional design. Although cost efficiency is a concern, it should not be the driving influence in establishing class size (Meyer, 2006).

If participants are expected to post papers for discussion, for example, having a smaller number of participants or staggered posting dates would better facilitate that process. In addition, a large group can be broken into small groups or teams for the purposes of completing assignments, having discussions, or conducting evaluations, thus promoting an environment in which collaborative work is necessary. Small group leadership can be rotated among the students and an area can be created in the course in which the leaders report on group discussion weekly. Again, the nature of the course and the types of assignments given must be taken into account when creating this type of structure. Smaller groups are necessary if papers are to be written collaboratively or if online presentations are to be prepared, for example, for presentation to the larger group. However, one caveat is not to create groups that are too small. We have found that groups smaller than five tend to lose energy and have difficulty maintaining a discussion. If there is uneven participation among the members, this can become an even more difficult issue.

Creativity on the part of the instructor is necessary to promote the best use of group size. The educational level of the participants and the course content play a role here as well. In many of our graduate-level classes, we ask students to research and complete papers that are posted online and then facilitate a discussion with their peers on that content. This creates the basis for discussion that allows the participants to go far beyond the designated course content. With an undergraduate course, however, we may stay closer to the textbook but create smaller groups or teams to complete projects and work together on case studies that may or may not be presented to the large group. Discussion takes the form of responses to questions posed to the entire group; questions are related to the material being read in the textbook.

Regardless of the means by which group management is attempted, issues related to group dynamics and the potential for unequal participation must be considered. Whether working in a large group or in smaller teams, the dynamics of the online group and the process through which it develops is similar to face-to-face groups. Therefore, the instructor should monitor that process and jump in as facilitator when necessary. When smaller groups are created within a larger class or group, each group should be asked to appoint a team leader or, if the group project is to span a number of weeks, to rotate facilitation. That person then becomes responsible for facilitating the interaction within the team, with the understanding that help can be requested from the instructor if that becomes necessary. Other roles may be assigned as well, a topic we will discuss later in the book. In the guidelines that we create for our online classes, we always ask group members to be willing to work out any issues or differences online. We do this to minimize outside discussion that may be harmful to the development of a working group. If members are gossiping or having what we like to call "side dishes" or side conversations that may not be supportive of what is happening in the group, it frequently will show up in limited participation in the group and an unwillingness to work collaboratively.

Although we tend to stay out of the small group discussions, we do monitor them for participation, and the student leader for the week can invite us into the discussion if there are issues that need our attention. Brookfield and Preskill (2005) note that the assignment of small group discussions is not a means by which the instructor can "opt out" of facilitation. Instead, the instructor should take the opportunity to model good discussion skills and monitor the small groups. In so doing, the instructor is asking students to do no more or less than he or she would do.

It is important to stress that group members have a responsibility to each other; they also depend on each other for the successful outcome of the course. One means of ensuring that participants work together, as we have previously discussed, is to establish participation guidelines at the outset. This still may not solve the problem of unequal participation, however. Harasim and others (1996) describe the problem as follows: "A potential benefit of learning networks is that each student can participate equally in class discussions and activities; however, each student may not put in the same volume or quality of material. Differences based on student interest, ability, availability, or other considerations affect the upper and lower levels of participation. . . . some students may dominate or others refuse to participate" (p. 228).

Because of the issue of unequal participation, it is important to include participation levels in whatever form of evaluation is undertaken to measure student outcome. We have had team members evaluate each other's participation and contributions to the class within guidelines. For example, the team leaders can assign a grade for participation each week to the members of their team. That grade is then reported to the instructor, who evaluates it for fairness and may make some modifications if he or she deems necessary. In addition, we will ask each member of the group to submit a self-assessment, which we take very seriously as we assess student performance.

COST AND OTHER ADMINISTRATIVE ISSUES

Linda Harasim and her colleagues (1996), when discussing the online classroom, state: "The change in the concept of time that an instructor spends with students will present an even bigger challenge for the administrator. The time and effort an instructor expends becomes a linear function of the number of students in a class. Administrators can no longer economize on educational effort by increasing class size. The instructor can no longer adapt to class size by allowing less time for individual interaction with the students" (p. 232).

Clearly, the idea that the larger the class, the greater the return cannot be applied to the online classroom, a conclusion supported by the ASHE Report (Meyer, 2006). Given the amount of time needed on the part of both faculty and students to make the class proceed successfully, limiting class size when delivering courses in this medium is the key. A survey conducted by RAND (reported in the *Economist*, May 10, 1997) indicates that courses delivered via the Internet can help cut central administrative costs while reaching out to more students who are beyond the confines of the university. Given the lower costs involved in delivery, universities can afford to keep class sizes small without reducing the revenues from these classes. The survey further suggests that offering these types of courses is having an impact on how universities are organized. This study does not factor in the costs of course development or course revision, however, nor does it look at the costs of student and faculty support as a course is delivered (Meyer, 2006). These factors must be taken into account to determine the true costs of delivering online courses and programs. One way that institutions are coping with developmental costs is through scalability. Through good use of instructional design and the development of courses that can be delivered to a larger number of students, development costs are minimized. These methods will not eliminate delivery costs (that is, faculty salaries), however, or the costs to support students and faculty online. Nonetheless, good training is needed to assist faculty in becoming better facilitators, and flexible instructional design allows them to customize a course as needed.

This discussion of the cost of online learning does raise a larger issue regarding course fees and faculty compensation. Many universities are charging the same fees for both face-to-face and online classes. We have heard students complain about this, stating that because the course does not cost the university as much to deliver, their fees should be reduced. Students do not see the costs involved with online learning because they are not physically attending a class where the instructor is present. Consequently, students in this environment must see a high degree of faculty involvement and presence in order to feel that they are getting what they paid for. In addition, they need adequate technical support. Costs involved with this mode of delivery include licenses for the software in use, servers to house the software, course development, faculty training for both course development and course delivery, faculty pay, technical support, securing and maintenance of the system, and much more. Most of these costs are hidden from student view but are very real to university administrators, and they need somehow to be accounted for in budgets for online programs. Meyer (2006) notes that it is important to distinguish between the services used by campus-based and online students and to communicate to students how those differences impact fees.

Another critical cost factor is faculty pay. A summary of studies in the ASHE Report (Meyer, 2006) indicate that the faculty time required for online classes is *greater* than that required for face-to-face teaching, although pay for that work may not be commensurate. Some of the additional tasks for faculty involved in online teaching are receiving and responding to a greater number of e-mails, researching new knowledge to assist with the development and revision of courses, learning to use software, facilitating the class, holding more office hours, and grading student work. Some institutions pay faculty less for teaching online because of the absence of travel and designated class time, along with the smaller group sizes. However, when we have discussed this issue with faculty who are teaching online, the feeling is that because they are required to be available every day for a particular class and are actually doing more work in the preparation and delivery of the class, salaries for this form of teaching should be higher. A study regarding institutional support for distance teaching (Wolcott and Haderlie, 1997) reports that faculty are more motivated to participate in distance learning programs when this is included as part of their teaching load and not considered an add-on. However, the ASHE Report indicates that many faculty are being asked to teach online in overload situations. Consequently, in addition to a full load of face-to-face classes, they may be asked to teach one or two online courses. According to Wolcott and Haderlie, motivation increases when faculty feel they are adequately compensated for the amount of work required. Faculty feel less motivated to teach in distance mode when they do not feel supported by the institution or recognized for their efforts in this arena. The study states: "The amount of work required, together with the time involved to adapt instruction for distance delivery and to learn new skills associated with the technology, posed significant barriers to participation when added to an already heavy workload" (p. 15).

In fact, the provision of distance learning options may not be less expensive for the institution. Although the institution saves money on the use of classroom space, the costs we mentioned earlier that include the technology, transmission, maintenance, infrastructure, production, support, and, of course, personnel all need to be factored into the mix. What we are really looking at, then, is the allocation of resources, both tangible and intangible. The tangible resources are the hard costs such as hardware, software, and faculty salaries—items that have a specific cost attached and can be clearly budgeted. The intangible resources are elements such as training and support.

The Instructional Telecommunications Council of the American Association of Community Colleges completed a survey regarding faculty compensation in distance learning courses. What they found was a range of compensation formulae among the institutions surveyed from no additional compensation, to added pay after a seat maximum, to elimination of enrollment ceilings, to per-head compensation for remote students. Some institutions offered a stipend for course development, the addition of preparation pay for the first class, or reduced enrollment for the first class (Salomon and others, 1997). Again, given that many institutions are still finding their way in the arena of online learning and much research still needs to be done on actual costs of delivery, as well as effective compensation schemes, it will take time to sort out a formula for appropriate fees and salaries. If the RAND study is correct and the very nature of our academic institutions continues to change as the result of the implementation of distance education, institutions will no longer be grappling with the issues of cost, fees, and compensation; they will become a way of life. As with the pedagogical methods we have discussed, old forms of determining fees and salaries must make way for newer ones that factor in time and group size, course development, facilitation, and support—issues that are very much a part of the delivery of distance education.

ONLINE SECURITY

In recent years, online security has become a major concern. In the past, we worried only about the potential for compromised passwords or the possibility that a hacker might access a course site. Although these problems still exist, others have been added to the growing list. Viruses are proliferating on the Internet, as are spyware and adware programs that monitor keystrokes and websites visited. But in addition to these somewhat obvious hazards, according to López de Vallejo (2002) there are three major areas of concern in securing online courses and programs: security of hardware, information, and administrative functions. Hardware security includes the security of the network on campus and relates to the actions of the users within the network and potential intrusion of those outside of the network. Information security includes the computers that access the university network as well as the communication that goes on between users. Administrative security includes protecting the privacy of users. There are prevention measures that apply to all three. However, in discussing the security of the online learning community, it is the security of information and administrative functions that are primary.

The use of antivirus software, personal firewalls (as well as institutional firewalls), and anti-spyware programs by both faculty and students, as well as careful monitoring of passwords and limited use of personal information in the course, can help secure the information that is transmitted as part of an online course and also address administrative concerns. The Family Education Rights and Privacy Act of 1974 (FERPA) provides guidelines for the type of personal information about students that can be shared:

- Name
- Address
- Phone number and e-mail address
- Dates of attendance
- Degree(s) awarded
- Enrollment status
- Major field of study

Although we cannot imagine a student requesting that his or her name not be used in an online course, other information, such as phone number and address, can only be shared with permission. It is permissible to ask students to provide that information, but is within the student's rights to refuse to provide it to the online instructor. The sharing of e-mail addresses is fairly common practice in order to establish an account in the software used for the online course, but students should be asked for their consent to do so.

In addition, the inclusion of guidelines regarding the use of information posted can be helpful. For example, a group may establish a guideline that anything posted in the course is considered private information and may not be shared without the express consent of the person who posted it, thus helping to create a sense of security and privacy that promotes the development of the learning community. This guideline applies to the way in which faculty or the institution uses information or content after the course ends as well. All of the student quotes in this book, for example, have been used only with the written consent of the students who posted them.

We continue our discussion of administrative issues relative to the delivery of online courses in the next chapter as we explore the technical issues involved with online teaching. Yet to be explored are issues related to the choice of appropriate technology, the development of an institutional infrastructure, and the support and maintenance of that infrastructure.

Managing the Relationship to Technology

The technology available for conducting classes and meetings online generally involves the use of software that is either intranet-based, meaning that students use software to access a closed network on a remote server, or Internet-based. Several types of course management software, as well as meeting or conferencing software, are currently available; they vary in terms of features and ease of use, and allow for anything from brainstorming sessions to long-term discussion, as well as the use of graphics, audio, and video. Virtual classrooms and desktop video conferencing are also developing technologies, enabling participants to hold face-to-face or voice sessions over the Internet, thus adding real-time audio and video to the mix. Recent developments such as wireless networks on campuses and in coffee shops, podcasting and vodcasting (or the broadcasting of multimedia material, such as music or lectures, that can be accessed via a computer or an MP3 player), and the use of handheld computers and cell phones have made access to online courses easier but also more challenging.

Will these newer technologies and ever faster access to courses have an impact on the development of the online learning community? We assume that they will—to what extent remains to be seen. However, some of these impacts are already emerging. Wireless and some other technologies assist learners in connecting with one another and the instructor from just about anywhere, thus enabling learners to stay current in their courses while traveling or attending to other life responsibilities. The downside is that these technologies increase immediacy, meaning that expectations for instant response grow as the speed of connections increases. As a result, as we discussed previously, it becomes much more critical for instructors to set firm boundaries around their own time as well as to assist learners in managing their time. We have already established that the development of community takes time. With increasing speed and just-in-time, on-demand learning, such as that delivered in a podcast or vodcast, opportunities for connection between people decrease, thus potentially weakening a sense of community.

Many of these technologies, although they allow for increased ability to deliver robust content, also return us to older forms of pedagogy. As mentioned, podcasting, or the creation and delivery of a Web-based broadcast or broadcast series, allows an instructor to deliver a lecture or a series of lectures to learners anytime and anywhere. Donnelly and Berge (2006) describe the benefits of podcasting as the ability to deliver voice content on demand, thereby allowing an opportunity for increased learner control over what is learned when and further allowing the learner to multi-task and time-shift as learning occurs. As we have established, however, the beauty of online learning lies in the ability to discuss content with one's peers. Certainly, podcasting can be used as one means by which content is delivered. But if used as the main means by which a class is conducted, it is likely to interfere with community building.

One form of technology that may, conversely, enhance the community-building experience is virtual reality. Online gaming programs such as Second Life are making their way into the academic arena. Academic institutions are purchasing space (known as islands) in Second Life and building virtual universities in those spaces. The program allows for the creation and delivery of online courses through the use of avatars (an icon or representation of a user) who interact in a three-dimensional digital world. The use of gaming technology is likely to move us away from the text-based online courses we currently experience and into a new mode of synchronous learning that does not necessarily involve a return to the lecture.

Regardless of the technology used, it should never serve as the driver of the learning process but should be viewed as the vehicle through which learning occurs. The risk in adopting the newer technologies is that the technology will move to the forefront of the learning experience and the more technology-savvy users will gain an advantage over those with less comfort or experience. The instructor also needs to be somewhat knowledgeable about it and comfortable enough to be able to help with problems. The instructor should also be able to configure the on-line course site so that participants find it easy to use and logical in structure. The advent of these newer technologies necessitates additional training for instructors so that they can effectively use them and support their students. The technology must be accessible to and usable by all participants. The most beautifully constructed site, complete with graphics, audio, and video, is useless to a participant working with older technology to access the site or limited experience with newer technologies. According to Whitesel (1998), "Technology does not teach students; effective teachers do. A virtual learning space that is effectively created by a competently trained instructor can deliver on the promises educators make to their students. It can help us deliver our content to a growing number of learners over a widely diverse geographical area" (p. 1).

It is not our goal in this chapter to discuss the various forms of technology available and their uses in distance learning. We are more concerned with developing an awareness of the role technology plays in the delivery of a course. Most important, the instructor or facilitator in an online distance learning environment must be continuously aware that people are connecting with them through a computer and that these participants are developing a relationship not only with each other but also with the technology itself. All of these relationships must be considered critical components of an online classroom.

THE RELATIONSHIP OF PERSON TO MACHINE

Many who write about distance learning and educational technology discuss the various types of technology that are available and how to use that technology in the process of developing and delivering a course at a distance. What the writers and software developers sometimes fail to consider, however, is that people interact with the hardware, the software, the process, and each other. These relationships create a continuous loop that embeds itself in and becomes part of the learning process. As a result of this loop, some of the participants begin to construct an alternate identity—the person they are when they are online—surrounded by a sort of impenetrable bubble. They create for themselves a sense of privacy that allows them to ignore the rest of the world (Pratt, 1996). This can be likened to new lovers out in public who have eyes only for each other. The rest of the world no longer exists for them.

Sherry Turkle (1995), in her book *Life on the Screen,* quotes a physics professor who describes this reality by stating: "My students know more about computer reality, but less and less about the real world" (p. 66). Turkle further states:

> When we step through the screen into virtual communities, we reconstruct our identities on the other side of the looking glass. This reconstruction is our cultural work in progress. . . . On the one hand we insist that we are different from machines because we have emotions, bodies, and an intellect that cannot be captured in rules, but on the other we play with computer programs that we think of as alive or almost-alive. . . . The Internet is another element of the computer culture that has contributed to thinking about identity as multiplicity. On it, people are able to build a self by cycling through many selves [pp. 177–178].

Although these statements may seem to demonstrate an occurrence of something known as the attachment phenomenon (or the attachment of person to machine) in the extreme, we do see evidence of it in the online classroom. We have had students who have named their computers. Some have even spoken of sleeping with their notebook computers while traveling. Some feel incapable of participating if their own personal computer goes down and do not seek out alternative means by which to connect to the course. More commonly, however, this attachment manifests itself through the alteration of human relationships, which include relationships with other participants in the course and with the instructor. Take the following bit of dialogue from one of our courses as an example:

> Here's a weird thought, but I just wondered if anyone else ever sensed it. Sometimes when I see some of the people out of this class I want to say something to them about the class or something but I feel like I can't because I need to e-mail them or put it in a forum. Is that totally dorky? Like, if I see Mason I am like so did you post, what did you think about this. But, if I see someone I don't really know like Mike or Rob, it is weird because I feel like I can only do it on-line. Is this just totally stupid or has anyone else experienced that? *Carmen*

Carmen I experience this a lot when I see you going into one of Mr. Schwartz's classes I want to have a long discussion with you, and sometimes we do when we are at practice during our free times. Yet I don't see hardly anybody on campus because I am not here! So the rest of you I could say I am not for sure how I would feel. *Stacy*

I know what you mean Carmen. I feel like the forums are a better place to discuss classroom things. I would feel kind of guilty if I only shared my thoughts with one person instead of posting it for everyone to see. Sounds strange, I know. *Jason*

This exchange illustrates how the attachment phenomenon relates to the developing sense of community in an online classroom. The exchange represents the establishment of boundaries around a protected space, with the members of the group sharing a common experience within those boundaries. However, at this stage of community development, participants are uncertain about the rules governing their interaction outside of that space. This type of exchange can lead to a deepening discussion among the members about the rules and norms of interaction both online and offline. We have seen this type of interaction not only between online learners, however. Instructors in some of our training sessions have also asked whether it is acceptable for an instructor in an online course to pick up the phone to talk to a student or to make a face-to-face appointment. When working online, many seem to feel that any form of communication other than e-mail or postings in the course forums constitutes a violation of the rules of interaction. Nothing could be further from the truth. Teaching or learning online should not limit forms of interaction. Conversely, it should open the door to other means by which to communicate.

The attachment phenomenon is not something to be feared but instead is an element that should be expected and taken into account as the course proceeds. In fact, a separate space should be created to allow it to happen. We have used a social space or café area or a discussion forum for reflections, which we create on a course site, as well as the other course discussion forums, to encourage the exploration of these relationships. We have also promoted the discussion of this phenomenon by posing questions that allow participants to discuss these issues without fear that they will be ridiculed. To illustrate this point, the example just presented occurred in response to questions posed regarding group behavior and team building online as a part of a course in organizational behavior.

An instructor or facilitator in an online setting will not bring these issues to the surface unless he or she feels comfortable with them and purposefully seeks out opportunities to do so. Such relationships are an important element of online communication and can affect the outcome of the learning process positively when they are encouraged. This exploration forms the basis of what we have termed a *double loop* in the learning process and is the foundation of a transformational learning process, which we discuss more fully in Chapter Nine.

Double-loop learning is a term offered by Chris Argyris (1992) to describe processes of organizational learning. He defines the differences between single- and double-loop learning as follows:

> Most people define learning too narrowly as mere "problem-solving," so they focus on identifying and correcting errors in the external environment. Solving problems is important. But if learning is to persist, managers and employees must also look inward. They need to reflect critically on their own behavior. . . . and then change how they act. In particular, they must learn how the very way they go about defining and solving problems can be a source of problems in its own right. . . To give a simple analogy: a thermostat that automatically turns on the heat whenever the temperature in a room drops below 68 degrees is a good example of single-loop learning. A thermostat that could ask, "Why am I set at 68 degrees?" and then explore whether or not some other temperature might more economically achieve the goal of heating the room would be engaging in double-loop learning [p. 84].

How does this concept apply to the use of technology and the relationship of the user to the technology in distance learning? When students are engaging in a learning process through the use of technology, they are learning not only course material but something new about the learning process and about themselves. The question becomes not "What have I learned about this course material?" but "What have I learned about this course material, what it takes to learn about it through the use of technology, and about myself in this process?" The learning process thus involves self-reflection on the knowledge acquired about the course, about how learning occurs online, about the technology itself, and about how the user has been transformed by his or her newfound relationships with the machine, the software, the learning process, and the other participants. The responses to these questions often provide some important evaluation data for instructors and the institution. The reflections take evaluation out of the realm of the popularity contest that Brookfield (1995) describes and helps learners to truly evaluate their learning process. The following example illustrates this point.

> I have got to say that this class has given me the opportunity to experience a lot. I [did] not use the computer for much but games. Now I think about it in a much different way. It is a learning tool. I have been able to research and expand my own ideas on many things. I have been able to question my own thoughts about many subjects. The ability to weigh my morals and judgements in regards to future lifetime experience will give me a strong basis for making decisions. It seems to have allowed me to express my thoughts without the fear of ridicule (that's a strong word) maybe non acceptance to a face to face encounter. Those have always been a [dis]quieting experience. I find that by posting on the computer I am able to accept the constructive criticism without out the facial or body criticism. This has been a good experience in all ways of manner. I have found that I have used the forum to warm me up to meeting and talking on-line to people across the world. It has open my ideas about many parts of the world. There is one thing though that you get hooked on this form of communication and like the others I can't wait to get on-line to find out what's happening. But still got to have baseball . . . that doesn't get put aside by the computer. Other things (maybe). *Mike T.*

The newer technologies to which students are exposed outside of the academic setting serve to complicate this process. Many younger students spend a great deal of time on instant messenger programs online (IM) or using cell phone text messaging for communicating with one another. The impact of this has been the development of a new language and means of communication that resembles shorthand. Such abbreviations as LOL (laughing out loud), BTW (by the way), and IMHO (In My Humble Opinion) and numbers substituted for words (2 for to, 4 to represent for, or 2morrow for tomorrow) are commonly used as a way to communicate quickly in IM or text. At times, that new, abbreviated language can find its way into the online classroom. In our own classrooms, we allow limited use of these abbreviations. Some use may be permissible in discussion postings that are of a more social nature. But in assignments or academic responses to discussion questions, we discourage and even prohibit their use. Although these practices are common among younger students, many adult students have not been exposed to them and are frankly confused by their use. Consequently, this is more likely to be an issue in secondary and undergraduate settings rather than in graduate-level classes.

Learning about the appropriate use of technology and its impact on the educational process becomes an important component of the learning process, as well as an outcome that we work toward. (We discuss the means by which to achieve this more fully in Chapter Nine.)

TECHNOLOGY AS A FACILITATIVE TOOL

Unfortunately, many academic institutions and instructors are swayed by the bells and whistles embedded in a fancy software package or the newer technologies and do not consider what the learner can receive and handle as part of the learning process. They want the ability to add audio and video to a course site. They want students to be able to engage in synchronous chat. They want to be able to use desktop video conferencing. The problem, of course, is that although these applications can be useful and greatly broaden the approach to a course, they are only good insofar as they can be used by the participants. Participants using older hardware or software or living in a remote area with a slow connection to the Internet may simply be unable to participate in a chat session or receive audio or video.

Although recent statistics have shown that approximately 55 percent of adults have access to high-speed Internet connections either at home or work (Horrigan, 2004), we still need to account for the student who does not have this level of access. We always need to take into account the person at the other end of the wire. The bottom line is that the technology should not drive the course. Instead, the desired outcomes and needs of the participants should be the deciding factors. Harasim and her colleagues (1996) state: "The real question . . . is not whether a course *can* be done online but what is the best media mix to achieve the goals of the course within the constraints of the available resources or geographic dispersion of the students. More fundamentally, how should the media be used? What approaches to teaching and learning are most effective in a computer networking environment?" (p. 24). As more and more courses are moved to the online environment, it is important to keep these questions in mind.

The issue, then, is how best to use the course management software developed to deliver the instructional material. When it is too complex, it can lead to frustration on the part of the user and frustration with the learning process. In addition, a complex software package would require that faculty be trained well enough to be able to develop and deliver the course, as well as act as a support person for the participants. Consequently, the course management system that is used should be

- Functional (posting course materials and creating discussion forums should be easy)
- Simple to operate for both faculty and participants
- User-friendly, visually appealing, and easy to navigate

We now explore these components in more detail.

Ease of Use

The software used for a course should be transparent. A participant should not have to spend time negotiating several steps in order to post a message or respond in a discussion. The software should be in the background, acting only as a vehicle or platform for course delivery. Furthermore, the focus should stay on the use of the software as a facilitative tool to reach the learner and to enable the learners to reach one another. The main concerns with hardware should be that the user has access to a computer, the ability to connect to the Internet, and a computer with enough memory and speed to allow for access to and navigation of the course site.

A means by which to evaluate the course software used is the absence of participant comments on the software. No comments in this area would indicate that the goal of transparency has been achieved. We expect some problems in the beginning of a course as participants become acclimated to the software and hardware. However, they should become adept at using the software quickly so as to get on with the more important aspects of the course. We have had student evaluations in which participants commented on the barrier that the software played in creating a successful learning experience. The following are examples of feedback we do *not* want to receive at the end of a course. This particular course was taught through an academic institution choosing to use software that was far from transparent or user-friendly. Problems with the software continued throughout the course, not only for the participants but for the faculty as well.

In terms of online learnings, I have learned that things will not always go the way they should but one must not give up when they don't. If I would have let problems with [the software] stop me from taking this class, I would have been the one who lost out. I'm glad I stayed through the electronic problems, through the storm, and even through the small class size. There was a great deal to gain from this class and I am glad that I was able to gain some of it, I feel I am the better for the experiences it held, both positive and negative ones. *Sandra*

Regarding my perceptions of strangeness-it has to do with many things-my trying to understand what taking an electronic course is all about-how it differs from traditional classes in the way information is exchanged, and knowledge is transferred-how it would have worked if the class had had more people and there were more interaction,-how things would have been if we hadn't had system problems in the beginning and if Sandra and Greg hadn't had their own computer problems. *June*

Although these students experienced system and software difficulties that interfered with the learning process to some degree, it is clear from these comments that some double-loop learning was an outcome. Because of their difficulties with the software, these students were put in the position quickly of assessing the impact of learning with and about technology. They learned that this is not the easier way to learn. One was happy to have had this experience and the other was not so sure. Regardless, a learning goal was achieved, although with more difficulty than we, as the course faculty, had hoped for or anticipated. When the technology is truly transparent, this goal can be achieved with far less pain.

Visual Appeal

The ability to create a visually appealing site does create greater interest on the part of the participants. The use of colorful banners, color within postings, and graphics helps keep students engaged. Exhibit 5.1 is an example of a course homepage with a banner created by one of us. The instructor provides information to the learners regarding the banners and uses them as an instructional device. They are told to watch for changes in the banners; when the banner changes, there is a new announcement or something new has been posted in the course. For learners who

are more visually oriented, this can be a useful way of keeping them up-to-date with the course. For others, it helps maintain interest and serves to further humanize the course site.

In addition to the use of banners and graphics, participants' ability to represent themselves visually on the course site allows them to express their personalities, ideas, and ideals, thus establishing their social presence. This can be done through the creation of student homepages or biographies, including pictures or some other graphic image that helps participants build an online presence. The simple use of photos with a bio also serves this purpose. This helps construct the relationships we described earlier to the machine, as well as to the software, the process, and to each other; all this contributes to the community-building process. Exhibit 5.2 is an example of a student homepage created for an online course.

When the only contact participants have with each other is virtual, they begin to create visual images for themselves about the other participants that may or may not be consistent with reality. Some faculty and students have described the

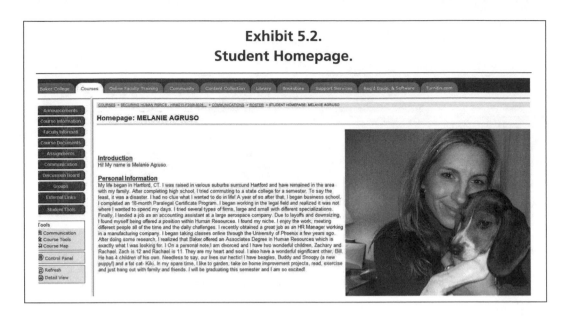

Exhibit 5.2.
Student Homepage.

advantage of having photographs of the others involved in a course available while interacting online. It is difficult for people to relate only to words on a screen. Having photos or visual images available helps embody others. The following examples describe this phenomenon.

> I'm not sure what the part is that scares me the most. Maybe it is the working with other people that you don't know or know that you can rely on. Maybe it is the fact that they will be these things on the computer that all you know about them is what they put in their bio. It is different with us now because we still see most of each other anyway. The trust factor I think just comes with getting to know someone which I would rather do in person. It is easier for this classroom because I know everyone already. (It's weird but it is really nice to see a picture of Dr. Palloff because then she is not just this complete stranger in the classroom.) *Carmen*

> Psychologically [this class] has played somewhat of a mind game in the sense that is this the true person that is talking and not the person being stated. In this particular situation where I know most of the students it is easier to tell but I feel that if I did not know the students then I would

have had a harder time understanding or maybe being so open with thoughts and ideas. *Rob*

Sometimes it is hard to deal with the idea of virtual people. I am glad that I know most of you so I can put a face with the posts. *Jason*

When students resist using photos, they can be encouraged to use an image that represents them. One of us had an experience where one student in a course was reluctant to post a photo but decided that an image would work well for her. She posted her image and the remainder of the group removed their photos and followed her in posting images instead. This became a strong community-builder for this group.

When a class involves both face-to-face and online contact, the issue of use of visual images diminishes. Participants are able to connect a face with the words appearing on the screen. However, face-to-face sessions are not always possible. Consequently, the ability to include pictures and visual images helps participants connect the words with a human being, thus humanizing the process and creating social presence. In addition, the ability to include graphic material helps keep them engaged.

EXCUSE US, WE ARE NOW EXPERIENCING TECHNICAL DIFFICULTIES

Because the software available for online classes is new to many users and is constantly changing, the possibility for encountering technical difficulties is very real. Many instructors have complained about the lack of participation among students, only to find that students could not access a course site. Although this can also be deemed a convenient excuse (and sometimes it is!), technical support must be available to help students log on, use the software, upload and download files, and so on, as well as help faculty who are experiencing their own difficulties and attempting to help students with theirs. Some of the types of difficulties that are beyond the control of a faculty member who has engaged in the best possible planning for a course are things such as the university's server going down, problems with an Internet service provider, and problems or "bugs" in the software that cause it to act in unanticipated ways. Problems that can be resolved by the faculty member or the institution need to be resolved quickly. Ideally, problems should be anticipated and resolved prior to the start of a course. When problems occur during delivery of a course, however, rapid response is essential to avoid serious participation problems.

We cannot assume that our students are adept to any degree with technology. Even students who spend a great deal of time sending text messages on cell phones, engaging in instant messaging, playing computer games, or using an MP3 player may not understand what it takes to navigate an online course. One technical support person gave us an extreme example of this when she told the story of a student living in a remote part of Alaska who was working on a doctorate through a distance learning program. She was attempting to talk him through some of his difficulties in accessing an Internet-based course and began to explain a command that needed to be typed in both capital and lowercase letters. The student asked, "How do I make a capital letter with this computer?" Should students who have so little knowledge of and ability with a computer participate in an online course? We emphatically say *yes*. Their participation can only increase their knowledge of, ability with, and facility in using technology. Rather than becoming upset or frustrated with the lack of technical expertise on the part of a student, faculty must remain helpful and flexible in order to enable the learning process around the use of technology. Institutions, however, should consider offering courses in basic computer skills to those students who need them or should have referrals to such courses at the ready.

Students are drawn to this mode of learning because it transcends distance and time constraints. However, this form of learning is likely to be totally new for them. We have had many phone conversations with students to enable them to become conversant with the software being used, as well as to allay their fears about participation online. When students have never interacted in a course through the use of technology, they are likely to hold some fears about how their messages are being received and interpreted by others. The fear can be paralyzing if intervention does not occur. Minimal or no participation on the part of a learner may be an indicator that "performance anxiety" has taken over. This, too, is an element of their developing relationship with the machine. Outreach from the instructor to assist the student in becoming more comfortable with posting can help. We have sometimes asked a student experiencing this form of anxiety to send a sample post to us via e-mail and we then respond to the post, generally with supportive feedback to enable the student to overcome his or her fear of posting. Often this works, but we have seen students drop out of an online course because this was a fear they simply could not overcome.

Psychologically, this class has been challenging. I am always worried about how my posts will be taken. Sometimes I worry so much about the syntax of my statements [that I also] worry about the context. *Jason*

Faculty need to be open to these questions and concerns and to regard them as opportunities for teaching. By doing so, faculty are enabling the double-loop learning process we have previously discussed; they are also encouraging new modes of expression and the ability to take risks in a new and sometimes intimidating environment. Our hope is that this type of learning will transfer into other learning arenas as well. But are students the only ones who experience technical difficulties and problems with this medium? Consider the following story:

We don't expect this to happen to us and become upset with our students who complain about technical difficulties. But, finally, it has happened to me. I had been traveling for 5 years with a workhorse of a notebook computer. Its only problem was its weight and that it could no longer really keep up with the demands I was placing on it. So, 3 weeks ago, I bought a brand spanking new Pentium notebook with all the bells and whistles. So what happens? Three weeks after I buy it, I take it with me to Malaysia. I am in the beginning stages of facilitating an online discussion which I really want to stay on top of, in addition to several hot, work-related issues that I have promised to stay in touch on. I arrive at my hotel, plug in the computer, turn it on, and discover that I have no display. I panic. I plug it into several different outlets and get the same response. I pull out the manual and pray that the trouble-shooting tips work. They don't. I'm jet-lagged, exhausted, upset, and angry. I decide that my only option is to go to sleep. The next morning, I wake up and as I'm reading the newspaper, I discover that there's a dealer for my brand of computer in the city I'm in. I call them, and shortly thereafter, me and my sick computer are in a taxi on the way to the shop.

When we arrive, the staff begins to ask questions about warranty. Of course, I hadn't thought to bring the sales receipt with me and what ensues are several phone calls to the States to get documentation faxed to me.

Then, the internal politics take over. Since this is a branch of a larger company, headquarters, which is 120 or so miles away, decides that they are the only ones who can do the warranty work. So off my computer goes via courier to HQ. Again I panic. What if it doesn't return in time for my departure? What if they can't fix it? As it turns out, both fears were justified. HQ suggested that the computer was so defective that I needed to just take it home with me and get a new one. Meanwhile, it didn't get back to me until about 2 hours before my scheduled departure.

So, how did I do what I needed to without a computer? Not very well. I sent faxes like a mad woman in an attempt to let people back home know why I'd disappeared from the virtual world. I found an internet cafe, which allowed me to access my e-mail but didn't really give me enough time online to teach my classes. Meanwhile, the discussion group back home simply faded away and I felt irresponsible and horribly inadequate.

This nightmare—a true story experienced by one of us—shows one of the down sides of online education. Although it is clearly the wave of the present and future, and many of us are working hard to stay on the crest of that wave, the fact that we are dependent on sometimes faulty hardware and software can make the ride more difficult than we have anticipated. Those words on a screen are currently our main connection to one another when working online. When we are unable to gain or maintain access, we lose.

On the up side, however, there is nothing more exciting than having the mobility that comes with this form of teaching and learning. One is not place-based. It is certainly possible to teach a class from halfway around the world and teach it well. The keys, however, are flexibility and adaptability. Institutions, faculty, and their students need to be willing to enter new territory and experience the unknown. They should not do so unsupported, however. Institutions, like their faculty, must engage in good planning in the delivery of online programs and courses and be willing to provide the level of support necessary to make the programs and courses a success. Anything less results in frustration on the part of both students and faculty, as well as a loss of confidence in the process of distance learning on the part of both. If institutions and faculty are unable or unwilling to make the commitment necessary to provide quality distance learning, they should not enter this arena.

Moving Teaching and Learning Online

In this chapter, we turn our attention to what makes teaching and learning successful online. At the end of this chapter, we discuss hybrid or blended courses, which utilize both online and face-to-face components, and consider the relationship of the learning community to that mode of instruction. We begin by examining the faculty functions that emerge in the learning process and roles students play in response to those functions.

EFFECTIVE TEACHING AND LEARNING IN THE ONLINE CLASSROOM

In previous chapters, we noted the change in the role of the online instructor from the central focus of instruction—that is, the source of information and knowledge—to a more facilitative role that allows learners to work together to explore course content. This approach encourages the learning process to be more learner-centered rather than instructor-focused. This shift in approach has led to some debate about how much control learners should have in the online learning process. Are we describing an approach that is learner-centered or learner-directed? Derrick (2003) notes that learning in the online environment requires a set of skills that is not usually associated with learning in traditional settings. Online learners are encouraged to be more autonomous, resourceful, and independent—

characteristics that are in keeping with a learner-centered approach. Weimer (2002) further notes that the learner-centered instructor focuses attention squarely on the learning process: what the student is learning, how the student is learning, the conditions under which the student is learning, whether the student is retaining and applying the learning, and how current learning positions the student for future learning. This shifts the balance of power in the classroom closer to but not totally in the direction of the student, as it would in student-directed learning.

In a student-centered online classroom the function of the content changes. Weimer notes that the content is not to be "covered" but becomes instead a vehicle for the development of learning skills and strategies as they relate to the content. Just as we discussed the transformative learning process involved in learning through the use of technology, learner-centered online teaching assists students in better understanding who they are as learners and how they learn. In other words, a learner focus through the use of technology assists in the development of a meta-cognitive process wherein learners become aware of their strengths and weaknesses, as well as ways to use their strengths to assist them in developing areas that might be weaker, thus learning how to learn.

The responsibility for learning falls to the learners in a learner-centered approach and the focus is on learning, not on grades. To some degree, this means that learner-direction is a part of the process. When a collaborative activity is used, for example, the learners should be empowered to take on the means by which they accomplish the task. Similarly, if learning contracts are used, whereby learners set goals for themselves and contract with the instructor for deliverables, the learners direct their own learning process. However, with both of these approaches, the instructor still retains overall responsibility for setting the stage for the course, creating a climate for learning, and monitoring progress to the desired outcome, which is learning.

The use of collaborative practices, which we discuss more fully in Chapter Eight, as well as other forms of learner-focused instruction, such as problem-based learning, active learning, and cooperative learning, are forms of instruction that work extremely well online. Weimer notes that many learners are not necessarily ready for this form of instruction. Fink (2003) describes the necessity to teach learners how to learn. He describes three aspects to this task: teaching students to become better learners, to inquire and construct knowledge, and to become self-directed.

The outcome of this endeavor, according to Fink, is that students are enabled to continue to learn and to do so with greater effectiveness. Derrick (2003) concurs and states, "Once learners are able to understand their own capacities for learning—any learning—they are fundamentally changed with regard to their personal view of their capabilities and competence. The learning reinforces beliefs and efficacious behaviors for lifelong and sustained learning" (p. 16). This is not a process that will occur overnight. Many students resist and will make comments such as, "I enrolled in this course to learn from *you*, not my peers!" Consequently, the implementation of learner-focused teaching online takes patience and attention to the changed roles and functions of both the instructor and learner in this environment. We now elaborate on these changes and how they emerge online.

ROLES AND FUNCTIONS OF THE INSTRUCTOR IN THE ONLINE CLASSROOM

Several authors who have written about online learning and the online learning community have noted the roles and functions that emerge for both instructor and learners in the online class. In the first part of this book, we discussed the concept of social presence and its importance in the development of a learning community. We also mentioned that negotiation of roles is a part of establishing a learning community. In order for the people within the community to act on the roles needed to make it function, there must be a sense of who everyone is as real people. Garrison, Anderson, and Archer (2000), in their model of online communities of inquiry, assert that two additional forms of presence—cognitive presence and teaching presence—can be found in online communities of inquiry (online classroom communities being one form) and are also necessary elements for teaching and learning. They propose that the three forms of presence overlap to create the educational experience. They describe cognitive presence as the element most often associated with success in education, and define it as "the extent to which the participants in any particular configuration of a community of inquiry are able to construct meaning through sustained communication . . . [it] is a vital element in critical thinking, a process and outcome that is frequently presented as the ostensible goal of all higher education" (p. 4). They note that teaching presence is generally the role and function of the instructor, although this role may be shared among the participants. Teaching presence is further divided into two major functions: first, the selection, organization, and design of content, activities, and assessment; and second, the facilitation of the course.

Collins and Berge (1996) offered an earlier and different, somewhat more detailed, categorization of the various tasks and functions demanded of the online instructor. They describe four general areas of function: *pedagogical, social, managerial,* and *technical.* The pedagogical function is one that revolves around educational facilitation. The social function, which we have described in relationship to the development of social presence and the online learning community, is the promotion of the friendly social environment essential to online learning. The managerial function involves norms in agenda setting, pacing, objective setting, rule making, and decision making. The technical function depends on the instructor first becoming comfortable and proficient with the technology used and then being able to transfer that level of comfort to the learners.

If we compare the functions of Berge and Collins to the model of Garrison and Anderson, as well as our own thinking regarding online learning communities, we begin to see overlaps. Exhibit 6.1 illustrates that comparison.

Our model, which we have been using to illustrate the various aspects and elements of the online learning community, takes into account (a) the *people* involved (social presence) and the social function, (b) the policies and processes involved (which we call *purpose,* which overlaps with the teaching presence function and the managerial function), (c) the *process,* which includes the interaction and communication that support cognitive presence, and (d) the teaching and learning environment, which supports the pedagogical function and creates the educational experience. We include the need to pay attention to the technology in the process area, for without it, no communication can take place online.

In our certification program for online instructors entitled Teaching in the Virtual Classroom, one of the participants provided the following list of competencies, which address each of the functions just discussed, for online instructors after reviewing much of the literature in this area:

- Create a learning community that is intellectually exciting and challenging
- Encourage learners to perform to the best of their abilities in all aspects

Exhibit 6.1.
Relationship of Three Models of Instructor Functions.

Palloff and Pratt (2007)	Garrison, Anderson, and Archer (2000)	Collins and Berge (1996)
People:	**Social Presence:**	**Social function:**
Students and instructional team	Emotional expression	Promotion of a friendly social environment
Social presence	Open communication	
Interaction and communication	Group cohesion	**Managerial function:**
Purpose:	**Teaching Presence:**	Norms
Establishing guidelines	Course design	Agenda setting
Shared goals	Activities and assessment	Pacing
Practical considerations (time and group size)	Facilitation	Objective setting
	Direct Instruction	Rule-making
Process:	**Cognitive**	**Pedagogical function:**
Interaction and communication	Construction of meaning through sustained communication	Educational facilitation
Collaboration		Model effective teaching
Reflection/transformative learning	**Outcomes:**	**Technical function:**
Teamwork	Co-constructed meaning	Transfer of comfort in using technology from instructor to students
Social constructivist context	Critical thinking	
	Creation of a community of inquiry	**Outcomes:**
Outcomes:		Empowered learners
Co-created knowledge and meaning		Decision making
Reflection		Guided discussion
Transformation		Increased level of student-to-student discussion
Increased self-direction		
Reinforcement of presence		

- Consistently use process-oriented instructional methods and keep the learning community centered

- Demonstrate effective use of group dynamics and dialogue techniques

- Use a variety of learning activities and demonstrate instructional methods other than lecturing

- Stress the interrelatedness of the complete curriculum and the value

- Know workplace trends and perspectives related to the subject matter being taught

- Establish objectives and [inspire] learners to achieve them

- Draw out creativity, innovativeness, and ideas in a collaborative manner

- Integrate curriculum designed to provide learners with a learning environment that is experientially based and in a learning style that is collaborative and supportive

- Evaluate learning outcomes

- Attend professional development workshops that will review learning theories and continually develop facilitator skills (Davidson, 2006)

In view of the competencies described, let us now take a further look at each of the functions Collins and Berge (1996) describe in relation to the concepts of presence, purpose, and process, based on the experience of our classes to further illustrate their importance in the establishment of the learning community.

Educational Facilitation

The role of the instructor, either in a traditional face-to-face or online setting, is to establish his or her teaching presence by ensuring that some type of educational process occurs among the learners involved. As we have discussed, in the face-to-face classroom that role is generally of the expert imparting knowledge to willing learners. In the online environment, the role of the instructor becomes that of an educational facilitator. As a facilitator, the instructor provides gentle guidance and a framework as a "container" for the course, thus allowing students to explore the course material, as well as related materials, without restriction. This is not done through the traditional use of lectures followed by some form of discussion. Instead, the instructor may provide general topics within the body of knowledge about which students together might read and make comment. Or the instructor may ask open-ended questions designed to stimulate critical thinking about the topics being discussed. Lectures may, in fact, play a role in the online classroom depending on how they are delivered. We discourage the use of posted lectures or lecture notes, as they become only one more article for students to read. We often encourage the use of "mini-lectures," however, that emphasize a point or stimulate discussion. Brookfield and Preskill (2005) suggest that lectures begin and end with questions; the beginning questions help frame the lecture as a way of trying to make sense of a topic, and the ending questions encourage the students to continue the inquiry. Online, the instructor might present some material and then use the unanswered questions from that presentation as a link to the discussion board and the assignments for the week. The instructor may also encourage the development of teaching presence among the learners by asking them to take charge of facilitating a topic of interest or a week of discussion. In so doing, the students can develop the mini-lecture for the week and develop the discussion questions for the week.

Regardless, it is important for the instructor to make thoughtful comments on student posts, designed again to stimulate further discussion. As a part of this function, the instructor acts as a cheerleader and guide, attempting to motivate students to go deeper and further with the material than they might in a face-to-face classroom. The following pieces of dialogue from one of our classes on organizational behavior demonstrate this function. The discussion was occurring around the reading of one of the books required for the course. A student comments on a number of other students' posts:

> When you speak of common ground and getting as many constituents involved as possible I can't help but think of the appreciative inquiry model I am learning about now, it is very similar. [The author] comments on the power of getting folks involved. . . . Also the idea that the external environment helps shape the organization-everyone we have been reading as well as the appreciative inquiry model works with this concept. . . . In order to survive in this quickly changing market place now one must work with the external environment/forces. [The author] also speaks to this when she talks about designing the organization through the customers eye-and when she talks about the interdependence of competitors. *Cindy*

One of us, an instructor for the course, responds as follows:

> I've done my review of [this book] and although I continue to be very impressed with her systems orientation, I'm going to do a little of my devil's advocate thing regarding her work. Quite honestly, it comes up a little short for me!! Does anyone else see her model as a little simplistic??

Although she asks great, wonderfully expansive questions on pages 60–64, the frameworks she presents on page 69 feel just as limiting to me as [some of the others we've discussed]. . . . The other concern I have is that I pick up a bit of Cartesian thinking throughout the book. The continuum model that she presents throughout the book. . . . seems to contain a value judgment that fixed and adaptive organizations are not functional while only the inventive organization is. If this is the case, how then do fixed and adaptive organizations survive?? Additionally, I think it's a little naive to assume that adaptive organizations are political but that fixed and inventive organizations are not. Lastly, I have some difficulty with her definitions of power. [The author] seems to be indicating that Power With [or relational power] is the only acceptable source in an organization.

Another participant responds:

What great questions, reflections, and analysis. I mentioned once, I think, that I find myself easily seduced by structural—categorical—thinking and theory. It is so nice and easy to put things in boxes. And I find that I am just now able to let go of this comfort. So, personally, Cindy, I think that I am an example of what you are wisely suggesting—which is that we need to have a bridge to the new paradigm. . . . (And, by the way, it occurred to me that [this author's] simplicity may serve as an easy introduction, a bridge, to change . . .). We live in a sound-bit, speedy society where I think that it is easy to forget this and instead to hope that we will be able to facilitate a paradigmatic—or even an incremental change—in short order. Instead, I think that we have to develop strategic vision and be comfortable with short-term goals. *Judie*

As these excerpts of dialogue illustrate, the instructor as educational facilitator gently guides the discussion by asking pointed, expansive, and sometimes difficult questions and then follows the discussion wherever it might lead.

Community Building

As we have discussed in previous chapters, the instructor in an online class is responsible for facilitating and making room for the personal and social aspects of an online community so social presence can emerge and to make the class a successful learning experience. Collins and Berge (1996) refer to this function as "promoting human relationships, affirming and recognizing students' input; providing opportunities for students to develop a sense of group cohesiveness, maintaining the group as a unit, and in other ways helping members to work together in a mutual cause" (p. 7). These elements are the essence of the principles needed to build and maintain a virtual community that were noted in earlier chapters. How, then, does an instructor go about building this sense of group or community? Most online instructors begin their classes with student introductions as a way for the class to begin to know one another as people. Simply jumping into the course material without this creates an atmosphere that is dry and sterile, devoid of any sense that there are real people engaged here. Many instructors make use of designed group activities, simulations, and group projects as another means of facilitating a sense of being a group.

What we like to do in every one of our courses is to create a space in the course site where everyone, instructors and students alike, can let their hair down and be comfortable with one another—a community space, if you will. We may give it a title to begin with but are open to changing that title as the course progresses and students have input into what it should be called. We have called it Keith's Koffee Kafe, Rena's Roadhouse, the Lounge, or simply Important Community Stuff. The following demonstrates how we might invite students to use this space in the course:

RENA'S ROADHOUSE

Picture a country inn along a beautiful rural road just outside a small town where the entire community gathers from time to time throughout the day. The food is good and the coffee is great and always flowing. There are also weekly specials to tempt you! This is the place we can go to partake of some casual conversation about any number of things—personal news, group problems or frustrations, or even tangents of interest started in the formal course discussion but left behind as the course moved on. This is also the place that we'll use to inform each other of special events, travel, and absences from the course and, of course, tell a joke or two. Hope to see you here and, by the way, the coffee is on me!

Certainly, some of the personal material will become mixed with the discussion of course material. However, we try to keep that space separate and sacred. The following was posted in the Roadhouse of a course after the completion of an intense term of highly collaborative work and a group project. It illustrates the degree to which a learning community was formed and celebrates the group's success:

BARRETT PROPOSES A TOAST!

To all my faithful colleagues in 643, cheerful collaborators in our exploration of resistance and diligent contributors to our handbook project, I propose a toast. May the resistance we encounter make us wiser and stronger, and may we always be learners, compassionate, honest, and fully present. And so, from where my postings come when I am at home, a dining table filled with the detritus of my studies and interests, slightly after midnight, I raise a glass of home-made Cabernet Sauvignon to us all! Well done and blessed holidays to everyone.

Everyone in the group joined in the celebration by "toasting" with virtual cups of coffee, glasses of wine and champagne, or simply by adding their thoughts of good cheer. This toast and photo ended a course in which students had felt comfortable sharing photos of their homes, vacations, and children, as well as providing information about their lives to one another—all within reasonable boundaries and all in the service of forming a learning community.

In Chapter Three, we focused on all of the issues and elements embedded in this kind of interchange and the need to address them in some way in the creation of an online community. These human elements inevitably emerge when people connect online. The sharing of our lives, including our travels, our observations, our emotions, and who we are as people is deliberately brought into the classroom in an effort to promote group cohesion and connection. The dialogue presented definitely helped this group to begin to know each other, thereby increasing their level of comfort in working together. Just as a face-to-face group about to embark on a group assignment needs to get to know one another as a part of the process of developing trust in order to begin their work together, so must an online group develop this same sense of trust. The sharing of who we are as people begins to build that container of trust. It bears repeating that this effort is critical to the development of a learning community in the online classroom.

Administration

The instructor in an online course is also the course administrator, who posts a syllabus for the course, including assignments and some initial guidelines for the group to discuss and adopt or adapt. The instructor then gently facilitates the flow of the course and evaluates the outcomes.

We generally post a syllabus, guidelines, and the accepted rules of "netiquette" at the beginning of a course. We then ask the participants to comment on all of this and to discuss their hopes for the course. What do they see as desired learning outcomes? What do they hope to gain by participating? Some of this is open to negotiation, within limits. For example, we generally set a minimum expectation of two substantive posts per week per participant. We would be unwilling to negotiate fewer than that number, but we certainly are open to negotiating more participation if the group wants that, as many have. In some cases, we have been willing—and we have done so—to renegotiate assignments if it becomes clear through interaction with the group that those assignments are not contributing to a positive learning outcome. (In Chapter Seven, we provide further illustrations of course outlines, guidelines, and assignments.) We also are willing to renegotiate due dates if conflicts emerge. How learners are assessed, however, is not open to negotiation.

Evaluating outcomes, both in terms of assessing the learning process and evaluating learner satisfaction with the course, is a more complex process in an online classroom. It is further complicated by the orientation or requirements of the host institution for particular outcomes. (Some of these are discussed further in Chapter Ten.) Although some instructors continue to use examinations in this setting, and many software applications for online education allow for that, we lean toward the use of papers that may be individually generated or generated by a small group and posted online or of authentic assessments whereby students are asked to apply what they have learned to a case or situation that they generate or that is generated by the instructor. Feedback on papers is provided by all participants, thus promoting the development of skills in providing good feedback as well. In addition, we assess the quality of posts throughout the course by using rubrics that outline evidence of critical thinking ability and learners' ability to generate knowledge and make meaning of the course material. Assessment of student learning becomes a more qualitative process as a result. Also, at the end of the course, we ask students to assess the outcomes through self-reflection based on their initial expectations. The following two excerpts are final reflections on course content for a class on teaching and learning online:

> The two things I have learned in this program that have had the greatest impact on me are (1) *who* my online students are and (2) the importance of community and how to implement it in a course that seemingly has no room for academically meaningful social activity. As we worked through the characteristics of successful online learners, the continuum of pedagogy to heutagogy and its impact on the role of the online instructor, and the needs of our students, I began to see my own online students in a new light. Although I have always wanted to improve my online course, I felt more strongly motivated to make changes for these "new" students I was discovering. Our experiences with community in the TVC program, the research we did on building community, the activities we participated in, and the input from my colleagues showed me firsthand the impact that social interaction can have on students and provided me with a wealth of ideas for how to build community in my course without simply creating busywork for my students or without distracting them from the course objectives or watering down the course content. . . . I am in the process of creating a developmental algebra course online for the summer, and although the focus of the course is pretty hard-core algebra tools, I am adding discussion and community-building activities to the course to give students the sense that they are not struggling through the material alone—that they have a support system and that they can learn from each other. I will also incorporate group work where students can tackle some of the most challenging problems (especially the word

problems!) together. I'm really excited to see how this works out!
Stephanie

This example indicates the evidence of critical thinking skills, as well as an attempt on the part of the learner to "bring it all home" by articulating the meaning that has been derived from the exploration. It indicates a positive learning outcome and successful completion of this learning experience. The next excerpt illustrates how this successful outcome comes to pass in an online course:

I also cannot express how valuable it was having everyone comment on my work. Engaging in dialogue with others who have such varying perspectives enhances the course work and has allowed me to see so many other sides to a situation. What I hope to take away from that particular experience is an ability to analyze a situation from multiple perspectives.
Robert

It is the ability to hear multiple voices on a topic that promotes the development of critical thinking skills as students evaluate what they hear and potentially rethink the ideas they initially presented.

Technical Facilitation

Collins and Berge (1996) discuss the technical-facilitation function in terms of the instructor first becoming proficient and comfortable with the technology so as to ensure the comfort of the participants and to make the technology as transparent as possible. We find that this function goes well beyond this, as we described in Chapter Five. Certainly, faculty need to be competent enough with the technology to facilitate the course. However, we would hope that there is sufficient support available to them so that even a less proficient instructor could successfully run a course online.

Another more important function here is the ability of the instructor to create a double-loop in the learning process, thus creating a transformative learning experience. In other words, because we know that instructors need to teach differently online and that learners function differently, it is important to acknowledge that stream of learning in the overall learning process. The following questions arise related to this stream of learning: How does learning and knowledge generation differ when we learn online? How does technology contribute to that difference? What do we learn about technology when we engage in learning in this way? How does the use of online learning affect the learning process?

Just as we create a separate space for community in our courses, we also create a separate space to track our responses to these questions in the form of reflections on the course. We may title it, as we did in one course, something like Online Learning and Other Friendly Stuff, or simply Reflections. What is important is that this stream becomes acknowledged and tracked. It is a place where participants can discuss their discomfort in interacting with technology, as well as celebrate their successes in mastering it. Take the following examples of reflections on on-line learning:

> Well hum, thought, thought, thought, hum. . . . (That is my brain in action.) This on-line component has been a big change for me. Although it isn't my style I see the great importance of the medium. The way I am dealing with this change is just making myself do it, and I must say I enjoy it more and more. I can just see it now, I will probably be one of those people who ends up loving on-line learning! Stranger things have happened. *Cindy*

> In my case you are right about the curriculum and the learning being of interest. The online program was also exciting because it was a new challenge for me, and would help me to have the tools [I need]. I am, however, having difficulty getting accustomed to learning this way. I don't seem to learn as solidly through this type of free discussion as I do from a more direct outline format. I tend to get lost trying to sort out what is important when there is so much discussed. The reading online is very interesting, but deciding what to respond to seems to take more of my energy than actually learning and applying my learning. *Julie*

Learning through the use of technology takes more than mastery of a software program or comfort with the hardware being used. It takes an awareness of the impact that this form of learning has on the learning process itself. In addition, as this last bit of dialogue reveals, some students believe that online learning is not "real" learning. Another responsibility of the instructor, therefore, is to help contextualize this form of learning and facilitate a needed paradigm shift for the learner in order to allow the learning to have its greatest impact. (We discuss concrete suggestions for facilitating this shift in Chapter Nine.)

THE ROLE OF THE LEARNER IN THE LEARNING PROCESS

What are the roles of the learner in the learning process? We have already stated that the successful learner in an online environment is active and engaged in knowledge generation. We agree with Garrison, Anderson, and Archer (2000) that learners in an online learning community can and do take on part of the teaching function.(Many of our students have commented at the end of an online course about how much they learned from one another, and one student once complimented her peers about what wonderful teachers they had been.) Just as we explored the roles of the online instructor from the vantage of certain categories, the roles of the learner can best be understood as they relate to *knowledge generation, collaboration,* and *process management.* Students often gravitate naturally to these roles, and we see knowledge managers, collaborators, and process managers emerge as the discussion unfolds. Some instructors choose to assign or ask students to deliberately take on those roles, particularly as part of collaborative activities and assignments. Often the roles are rotated so as to give students the broader experience of functioning in each. In our classes, we tend to allow these roles to emerge naturally from the group and work with students to support their development. As we did with the roles of the instructor, we will now examine individually each of these roles of the learner in the learning process.

Knowledge Generation

When we discussed the educational facilitation role, or the teaching presence, of the instructor, we stated that the instructor serves as a gentle guide in the educational process. What this implies is that the recipient of that guidance—the learner—is responsible for using the guidance in a meaningful way. In the online classroom, this means that learners are responsible for actively seeking solutions to problems contained within the broad confines of the knowledge area being studied and raising the level of those solutions to one of more complexity. They are expected to view problems and questions from a number of perspectives, including the perspectives of the other learners involved in the process. They are expected to question the assumptions presented by the instructor and those of the other students, as well their own assumptions and ideas. In so doing, learners in the online classroom are generating the preferred learning outcome for this type of course: the construction of new forms of knowledge and meaning, or cognitive presence. By engaging in the learning process in this way, learners are learning about learning as well as gaining research and critical-thinking skills.

Some learners gravitate easily to knowledge generation and will often share many resources with other students as the term progresses, along with critical reflection on their work. One of us had a student in an online class who was clearly a knowledge generator. As her peers were posting drafts of their final papers for review, she responded not only with substantive feedback for them around their ideas and their writing but also with a list of additional articles they might want to review in completing their papers.

As we have seen in some of the course dialogue, learners should be able to critically evaluate their own learning style in addition to learning something about the area under study. Simultaneously, students should gather additional resources that are pertinent to the area under study and that go beyond the materials assigned, thus developing their skills and their confidence as researchers. This development is considered to be a successful learning outcome, and the knowledge managers in an online class are often helpful in bringing it about.

Collaboration

Students in the online learning environment are not expected to undertake this process alone. The failing of many online distance learning programs has been the inability or unwillingness to facilitate a collaborative learning process. In this environment, students should be expected to work together to generate deeper levels of understanding and critical evaluation of the material under study. In the process of seeking out additional materials for this purpose, students should be expected to share the resources they are finding with the other members of the group. Frequently, students will find an interesting website, article, or book that they become excited about sharing with others. In fact, this type of search and the reporting back to the group on the results can be an effective assignment leading to the expected learning outcomes of the course. We frequently expect students to generate a bibliography of readings. We get them started with a few suggestions, but it is up to the group to seek and post other materials of interest in order to enrich the learning process for all group members.

The online classroom is perfect for the facilitation of collaborative learning, and those students who gravitate to the collaborator role help make it happen. In addition to meeting together at the course site, students with similar interests should be encouraged to "meet" in other ways and work together. Often this is initiated by the collaborator who may suggest a study session or a chat session to discuss a topic. Students might also be encouraged to collaboratively prepare a report or paper to share with the others in the group. In addition, students should be guided and encouraged in their ability to give each other meaningful feedback on their work—that is, feedback that goes beyond giving one another pats on the back for good work and that comments substantively on the ideas presented. All of these activities assist in the development of the critical-thinking skills necessary to effectively engage in the knowledge-generation role described previously. A collaborator assists the group by ensuring that all voices are heard and that all members are participating. A collaborator often will not allow the group to move forward until consensus is achieved and may create tools such as Web surveys to make sure that each group member's opinion has been included.

Another means by which collaboration can happen is by facilitating dialogue *between* learning communities. By this we mean that instructors who are teaching similar courses, either in the same or different universities, can encourage and even facilitate discussion among participants in those classes. One group might research and prepare a presentation for another group, the outcome being the enhanced learning of both groups. This type of collaboration also increases the resources available to the participants as they explore areas of interest within the loosely defined boundaries of the knowledge area under study. Just the ability to study online can stimulate interest in collaborative work. As students discover that they are able to connect, via the Internet, with other universities and learning communities, their interest in doing so while working in other course areas also increases. Instructors can promote this type of activity through creative assignments that promote communication with other groups. We have experienced students in the collaborator role who have suggested and facilitated this type of collaboration. (Further discussion of collaborative learning can be found in Chapter Eight.)

Process Management

The role of process manager is the one that most significantly sets online teaching and learning apart from the face-to-face classroom. Often, this is a role that emerges organically from the group. We welcome its occurrence, because students who take on this role will ask clarifying questions that others in the group may have been too shy to ask. As an active learner, students are expected to participate within minimal guidelines, interact and engage with one another, speak up if the course or discussion is moving in a direction that is uncomfortable for them in any way, and take responsibility for the formation of the online learning community. Process managers often accept these responsibilities without hesitation. Process managers will also point out any inconsistencies in instructions given, seek to clarify assignments, and generally take responsibility for ensuring that the course moves along smoothly. Some instructors may find this process managing intrusive, but we welcome it, as it illustrates the responsibility that learners will take in the development and maintenance of the learning community.

Consider the following example of a series of student posts that followed some reflections by the instructor. The students were struggling with process issues, and posting their anxieties in response is an illustration of the process management role:

> In terms of the course, I am feeling grounded and I am starting to enjoy myself. I am finding this course challenging in terms of process and that is a good thing – it means I'm learning new things! The content is also perfect from a timing perspective because of 2 groups I am involved in with very high level needs. I appreciate your validation that we are on track. That's reassuring.
>
> Reflecting back on last week, I think a number of things happened that, in combination, led to anxiety for me and I suspect would be similar for others.
>
> Group – we struggled to get started, not wanting to be too pushy and also wanting to be the leaders that we are. We swirled a bit. Anxiety resulted. Mid week, three people dropped out and others went missing. This triggered an even higher level of anxiety. With Candi's intervention and our own skills, we started to reach out to each other and sort things out. Anxiety was reduced!
>
> Course lead – Rena, a couple of times during orientation and just before you left, you made the comment that the syllabus was clear. I got the impression that you were a bit impatient and couldn't see that it wasn't clear in some areas. This opened the door for the impression that you weren't open to more questions on the syllabus. I personally chose to not worry about that because you've given lots of evidence that you want us to be successful. I can see though, how this would add to anxiety for some people.

So, as you say, flexibility and tolerance for ambiguity are the key. We hit a bump in the road but the bus is still heading in the right direction, and a few passengers realized they were on the wrong bus. We were just getting to know them so we miss them but hope they find the right bus. Thanks for letting us clear the air—*Cheryl*

Thanks, Cheryl! I really appreciate your comments and the gentle and authentic way in which they were delivered. You have captured a lot of what I have felt over the last week and wasn't quite sure how to say myself. Thank you! *Linda*

First, let me reiterate that you're all exactly where you should be!! Whether you believe it or not, you began to take control of your course last week and I'm thrilled with what I see. What groups do when they're anxious—they go for and to structure. So, sure, I admit that there are typos in the syllabus (inadvertent) and some openness of and even some lack of structure (purposeful). This is to allow you to take charge of the process. So, let's talk about what's making you anxious at this point and not whether there's a booboo on page 8 (or wherever!!) and what's due when—because I'11 tell you again and again, your process and what you're learning from your process is paramount to me. OK, I'm going to shut up now and let you talk!! What are your anxieties and how are you doing this week?? *Rena*

This example clearly shows the willingness of students in a process manager role to speak out when they are offended, uncomfortable, or simply have an opinion on something. The instructor's response to such an interchange shows the necessary willingness to leave behind the traditional power boundaries between instructor and student to resolve the conflict and move the learning process forward. This medium has been described as the great equalizer, essentially eliminating the boundaries that exist between cultures, genders, and ages, and also eliminating power differences. Faculty must be able to relinquish their role of power within and over the educational process in order to allow learners to take on a process management role. In fact, we frequently find that we learn as much from our students in an online course as our students learn from us. One author's response to a student post is an example of the ways in which this might occur:

Interesting thoughts, Cindy. You've made me look at Morgan's work from another angle! Frequently, I use his concept of metaphor and image to look at what already exists in the organization as a part of my assessment of it. And, in fact, Morgan in his application chapter suggests the same (ordering sort of hierarchically the metaphors in existence). I've not considered planful use of his metaphors in the creation of an organization, but I do think it has merit. Our discussion with [our guest speaker] on Sunday to some degree touched on this (I do hope you're able to get the tapes!). [He] talked about essentially doing a monthly "report card" in staff meetings where staff would each comment on how well the mission and vision of the organization are playing out in day-to-day operation. He felt that all "votes" would be equal in terms of looking at how well the organization is functioning, or not. If one area continuously shows up deficient, then they would need to strategize ways to improve it. When we discussed the need for consciousness in organizations. . . ., I think this is what we may have had in mind as an example of at least attempting to be conscious about the business at hand. [His] is a small organization and can probably accommodate this kind of conscious evaluation process easily. In a larger organization it would be lots more difficult, I agree. *Rena*

The ability to remain flexible and open and to relinquish control are characteristics that make not only for successful instructors in this medium but for successful learners as well. We must all maintain an attitude of being in this together and a willingness to adapt and adjust as we move along in the process. Students must be able to speak out in this regard, without fear of repercussion. Faculty must be able to communicate that this is not only acceptable but necessary in order for students to be able to assume the roles necessary to facilitate educational success in the online classroom. Teaching and learning through the vehicle of the online learning community requires giving attention to community development at the start, handing over the reins to the learners as the community develops and as the roles begin to emerge, and then monitoring and facilitating the process. In so doing, social presence, teaching presence, and cognitive presence, as well as to some degree the pedagogical, social, managerial, technical, and administrative functions, are shared between instructor and learners.

THE HYBRID COURSE AND ONLINE COMMUNITY

Hybrid courses, also known as blended courses, offer institutions, instructors, and learners a great deal of flexibility. Conducted both face-to-face and online, hybrid courses allow flexibility and the ability to move course components to either the online or face-to-face arena as deemed appropriate. Some instructors post "static" material, such as the course syllabus and guidelines, on the course website for easy access and review while predominantly conducting the class face-to-face; others use the online medium to extend class discussion or to reduce the number of times the class meets face-to-face; still others use class time for active learning and the online component for other collaborative work. The combinations are seemingly endless, and both students and faculty seem to appreciate this form of learning.

The question emerges, however: How does the notion of an online learning community fit with hybrid delivery? A study conducted by Rovai and Jordan (2004) addressed this very question. Their findings indicate that the sense of community in a hybrid course can actually be stronger because of a reduced sense of isolation created by even occasional face-to-face contact. They also note that this type of course appeals to more "dependent" learners who rely on direct instructor contact to support their learning process. The conclusions of Rovai and Jordan (2004) were, however, that although the hybrid course allows yet another means of delivering education, and one that is rather flexible in nature, it is still the skill of the instructor as facilitator that drives the effective development of the learning community and promotes satisfactory learning outcomes for the class.

MOVING TO SPECIFICS

Now that we have explored the roles and functions of instructors and learners that emerge in an effective online course, it is important to understand how these roles and functions are operationalized. During our presentations at conferences and workshops regarding teaching online, we have found that instructors are always most concerned with the following issues:

- How do I effectively move a course to the online environment?
- How do I create a different type of syllabus for my online class?

- How do I learn to feel comfortable online, and how do I help my students feel comfortable with their role in the learning process?

- How do I make this all happen and happen quickly?

In the next section, we focus on course creation and maintenance in the online environment. We include several examples of our own, as well as those created by other instructors who are successfully teaching online. In addition, we include questions for consideration that can help turn all of these details into action. We hope this will help readers understand the concept we call *electronic pedagogy* and begin to recognize that it is not course conversion that needs to occur but rather a paradigm shift regarding how we view ourselves as educators, how we view our students, and how we view education itself.

PART TWO

Teaching and Learning in the Virtual Learning Community

Building Foundations

Up to this point, we have described the issues and elements that make up the context of online learning. For this and the next several chapters, we focus on the details of the learning process online and how to create a successful course. In this chapter, we examine what is involved in the creation of an effective course: creating an appropriate syllabus for online teaching, setting objectives, negotiating guidelines, setting up the course site online, encouraging participation and student buy-in, and accounting for presence in the online classroom.

As we present each topic, we include concrete examples from our courses as well as those of other instructors who have had positive outcomes in their online teaching experiences. To delineate each piece of the process of building a good course foundation, the course syllabi have been divided into the components that correspond with the topic under discussion. We present a variety of examples from a number of disciplines. At the time of this writing, instructors from all disciplines teach a wide variety of courses online, including but not limited to English composition, humanities, hard sciences such as physics and engineering, computer science, mathematics, and even dance and fine arts. (Samples of complete syllabi are presented in Resource A.)

CREATING AN EFFECTIVE COURSE DESIGN

Many instructors have mistakenly assumed that teaching online involves what is termed *curriculum conversion,* which basically means taking a course taught face-to-face and simply putting that course online without making many adjustments.

We argue that it is not the curriculum we are converting but our teaching methodology; when our pedagogy changes, so must the course. The creation of an effective online course involves a paradigm shift regarding the mode of delivery of the course material. Four basic steps are involved in creating an effective syllabus for an online course. They are likely to be the same four steps involved in creating a course syllabus for face-to-face delivery. However, the important point here is that to design a course for effective online delivery, it is important to start these steps over again rather than simply move the course from one medium to another. The four steps for creating a syllabus for an online course are (1) defining outcomes and objectives, (2) choosing appropriate reading material, assignments, and tasks (3) establishing a topic-driven course outline, and (4) developing and aligning assessment of activities with outcomes and objectives. We now review the first three of these steps concurrently and provide examples of each task. We discuss the fourth step, assessment, in detail in Chapter Ten.

Defining Outcomes and Objectives

As with any good course, an instructor needs to begin with the end in mind. What do we want our students to learn as they interact with the course material? What skills and abilities should they be able to take with them at the end of the course? In an online course, the syllabus is deliberately left more open to allow students to develop new ideas, exercise critical-thinking skills, and develop research skills. Objectives may be more broadly defined so that participants can take a course in unanticipated directions, based on their own interests and needs. However, in planning an online course, it is still important to consider expected outcomes as the course is being developed. In addition, with the more recent emphasis on competency-based learning, it is important to establish the competencies the instructor hopes to see the learners achieve in completing the course. In other words, what do we want students to walk away with when the course ends? What do we actually want them to be able to *do* as the result of this course? Some examples of competencies might include the ability to design and deliver a training program, write a potentially publishable article, or debug a computer program, as seen in the "Programming Concepts" example in the exhibit that follows. Exhibit 7.1 shows examples of course objectives from three classes to illustrate this concept.

As is evident in these examples, the development of course objectives for an online course does not differ much from the development of objectives for a face-to-face course. In fact, those presented would work as well in a face-to-face class as

Exhibit 7.1.
Sample Learning Objectives for Online Courses.

Management and Organizational Theory (graduate level class):
Summary of Educational Purpose:
The purpose of this course is to introduce learners to post-modern philosophy as applied to management and organizations, to provide examples of new paradigm thinking in business, and to introduce one or more methodologies for applying new paradigm theories in the everyday, real world operation of businesses, non-profits, and government agencies. The course also provides a grounding in the history and theory of management and organizations in America. Finally, the course is intended to encourage learners to increase their exposure to and application of emergent management practices and organization designs that are humane, socially responsible, and ecologically sound.

Learning Objectives:
After completing this course, learners will be able to:
1. Understand the historical and cultural foundations of mainstream American management;
2. Articulate the strengths and weaknesses of the old paradigm;
3. Understand the historical and cultural reasons for a new paradigm;
4. Build awareness of what the new paradigm looks like and might include;
5. Appreciate when and how elements of the old paradigm need to be applied, and
6. Apply elements of new paradigm theory and practice.

Personality and Psychotherapy (undergraduate-level class):
Course Description:
This online course approaches the study of personality in a slightly different manner. The author of our text, Lawrence Pervin, notes that the typical approach to the study of personality takes the form of the "grand theories" of personality. This approach, however, does not address current approaches to personality, nor does it necessarily assist us in knowing how to apply the theories in a therapeutic context. In addition, being a more traditional approach, it does not account for issues of gender, culture, or politics in the study of personality, all of which play a significant role. Consequently, our approach will be two-pronged. We will read about the ways in which personality is studied, both through our text and also through articles assigned by me and articles you may find in your research. In addition, you will form presentation groups, allowing you to explore and present the "grand theories" to one another. In this way, we will have the best of both approaches and will learn from one another.

(continued)

Exhibit 7.1.
Sample Learning Objectives for Online Courses. *(continued)*

Learning Objectives:
1. Become knowledgeable about the major theories and approaches to the study of personality and their relationship to psychotherapy
2. Evaluate the similarities and differences of the various approaches and theories
3. Become familiar with changes and current developments in the field
4. Critically and creatively evaluate the strengths and limitations of the theories and practices
5. Examine assumptions about human nature and therapeutic relationships, with particular attention paid to multicultural approaches
6. Apply the material studied to personal experience and case examples

Programming Concepts and Applications (community college level course)
Course Description:
Students will learn the components of the programming cycle including problem analysis, algorithm development, design implementation, debugging, and acceptable documentation standards. Students will implement their algorithms using an object orientated language such as Java.

Students who successfully complete this course will:
1. Understand the programming development life cycle.
2. Display the ability to write algorithms, flowcharts, and pseudocode.
3. Have an understanding of the basic syntax of a programming language so that they can use that language to solve problems.
4. Have an understanding of object-orientated program design using an object oriented language.
5. Display the ability to design, write and debug structured programs.

Quantitative Methods (graduate-level class)
Course Description:
An examination of the formulation, use and interpretation of mathematical models for making sound business decisions. Models include linear programming, PERT/CPM, decision trees, inventory, queuing, and Markovian processes.

Course Objectives:
    To help students formulate, use, and interpret mathematical models commonly used in business.
    To see and use computerized models demonstrated in the text, software and others.

they do online; differentiation appears in how the course is structured and presented through the course syllabus.

Choosing Appropriate Reading Material, Assignments, and Tasks

Once the objectives and competencies have been determined, the next step is to create an effective syllabus, including assignments, topics for discussion, expectations for participation, and ways the class activities will be assessed (discussed in Chapter Ten); a detailed outline describing the topics to be presented or discussed in each class is unnecessary. Instead, broad topic headings give students a general idea of what will be considered and discussed in the course, along with some questions for consideration as they think about each topic. The syllabus in an online classroom should be more open, allowing students greater leeway for exploration. We have found that the most successful classes are guided by a syllabus that is topic-driven. In other words, the weekly "schedule" for the class includes a discussion topic for the week, with readings and assignments geared to spark discussion of that topic. Another successful format is to structure the course around the required readings, allowing the material in the readings to create the discussion. Examples of both types of course outlines are presented in Exhibit 7.2.

Establishing a Topic-Driven Course

Courses such as science, math, art, or music, which do not lend themselves to the reading and discussion format, may look very different. The computer science class we presented, for example, may have a written "mini-lecture" by the instructor to explain a procedure or theory. Students may be expected to complete problems on their own or in groups and submit the results to the instructor for evaluation. Discussion may take the form of questions about the material directed to the instructor or to other students to promote collaboration. Many science classes requiring labs make arrangements with remote facilities so that students can do their laboratory work. One instructor at Johns Hopkins University created a "virtual lab," where students could conduct simulated experiments on the World Wide Web (Kiernan, 1997). Lab kits are available so that students can conduct science experiments safely in their homes. Some of these kits contain digital cameras so that students can record their results and e-mail the photos to their instructors.

(continued on page 138)

Exhibit 7.2.
Sample Course Outlines for Online Courses.

Syllabus for Programming Concepts and Applications:
This is a community college level online class. This course outline illustrates organization of the course using the readings as an organizational tool.

Course Schedule:

Learning Module Topics	Topic Start Date	Topic End Date	Assignment Due Date (all assignments are due by 11:59PM on the due date)
Module 0: **Orientation and** **Ice Breaker**	**1/10**	**1/22**	**Ice Breaker Assignment (1/22)** **Ice Breaker Quiz (1/22)**
Module 1: **Problem Solving** **Read Lecture Notes** **Read Chapter 1**	**1/17**	**1/29**	**Reading Quiz 1 (1/22)** **Assignment 1 (1/29)** **Discussion 1 (1/29)**
Module 2: **Algorithms** **Read Lecture Notes**	**1/30**	**2/12**	**Reading Quiz 2 (2/5)** **Assignment 2 (2/5)** **Assignment 2 (2/5)** **Team Activity, part 1 (2/5)** **Team Activity, part 2 (2/12)** **Discussion 2 (2/12)**
Module 3: **Basic Java** **Programs** **Read Chapter 2**	**2/13**	**2/26**	**Reading Quiz 3 (2/19)** **Assignment 3 (2/19)** **Team Activity 2 (2/26)** **Lab 1 (2/26)** **Discussion 3 (2/26)**
Module 4: **Program Input and** **Output** **Read Chapter 3**	**2/27**	**3/12**	**Reading Quiz 4 (3/5)** **Assignment 4 (3/5)** **Lab 2 (3/12)** **Team Activity 3 (3/12)** **Discussion 4 (3/12)**
Module 5: **Control Structures** **Read Chapters** **4 and 5**	**3/13**	**3/29**	**Reading Quiz 5 (3/19)** **Assignment 5 (3/19)** **Lab 3 (3/29)** **Lab 4 (3/29)** **Team Activity 4 (3/29)** **Discussion 5(3/29)**

Syllabus for Topics in Business Administration:
The Search for Soul and Spirit in the Workplace. This is a graduate level online class. The course is organized around topics for discussion.

SCHEDULE OF DISCUSSIONS:

[NOTE: Reading is for the week of discussion. I will be checking all URL's to make sure that they are current. If a URL change is necessary, I will post the change in the course. I may also add or substitute articles from the BizSpirit site as new material becomes available. Feel free to seek out additional soul and spirit resources from the Internet or library to support your facilitation of the discussion as well.]

Discussions for this course will primarily focus on topics which are organized into 2-week blocks. You will be asked to facilitate the discussion for one week by posting a thoughtful question for all of us to consider and respond to, based on the readings and your responses to them. As the facilitator for the week, you will also post a summary of the discussion for that week. All of you are encouraged to bring your own experiences into the discussions as we go.

In addition, I will create a folder in which I'd like you to post your reflections for the week in journal fashion (also known as "blogging" or keeping a web log) and an idea or two that the reading and discussion triggered for you regarding interventions in the workplace related to soul and spirit.

The following is a beginning outline of the discussion topics and the reading assignments. This may be modified as we go dependent upon your interests and needs.

WEEK 1:
Post an introduction and begin a discussion regarding the definition of soul and spirit.

Read article by Rutte, "Spirituality in the Workplace," [http://www.soulful living.com/spiritualityinworkplace.htm]

WEEKS 2 and 3:
Defining the search for soul and spirit organizationally – What are the problems being surfaced? What are the organizational issues related to soul and spirit? Confronting the shadow organizationally.

Read Briskin, *The Stirring of Soul in the Workplace* (entire book) and articles by Johnson and Lewin:

Johnson, "How to Do Well and Do Good in Business," [http://www.bizspirit. com/bsj/archives/cedric1.html]

Lewin, "The Reality of Complexity,"
[http://www.bizspirit.com/bsj/archives/lewin1.html]

Lewin, "The Soul at Work," [http://www.bizspirit.com/bsj/archives/lewin2.html]

(continued)

Exhibit 7.2.
Sample Course Outlines for Online Courses. *(continued)*

WEEKS 4 and 5:
How do we define meaningful work? What are the roles of values and ethics in determining meaningful work?

Read Peppers and Briskin (entire book) and article by Levoy, "The Power of Work as a Calling," [http://www.bizspirit.com/bsj/archives/levoy2.html]

WEEK 6:
Discussion of the organizational assessments. Your assessment should be posted by midnight Pacific Time on Monday.

WEEKS 7 and 8:
Leadership and motivation as they relate to soul and spirit.

Read Bolman and Deal (entire book) and articles by Madigan and Dreaver:

Madigan, "Consciousness: A Principle-Based Paradigm for Leadership," [http://www.bizspirit.com/bsj/archives/madigan1.html]

Dreaver, "Fearless Leadership," [http://www.bizspirit.com/bsj/archives/dreaver1.html]

WEEKS 9 and 10:
Organizational transformation, soul, and spirit.

Read articles by Barrett, Renesch, Marcic, and in HR Magazine:

Barrett, "Organizational Transformation," [http://www.bizspirit.com/bsj/archives/barrett1.html]

Renesch, "The Conscious Organization," [http://www.bizspirit.com/bsj/archives/renesch1.html]

Marcic, Table 2 from *Managing with the Wisdom of Love,* [http://www.marcic. com/books/virtues.htm]

WEEK 11:
Discussion of final papers in dyads.

WEEK 12:
Report out from dyads.

Submit self-evaluation.

Syllabus for Quantitative Methods:
This is a required graduate level course which is taught completely online. The course is organized around the teaching of models and skills in addition to the assigned text.

Course Outline:

DATE	TOPIC(S)	READING ASSIGNMENT(S)
Week of Jan. 12	Introduction to course and probability concepts	Chapters 1, 2
Week of Jan. 19	Probability distributions, decision theory	Chapters 3, 5
Week of Jan. 26	Decision trees, utility theory, quality control	Chapters 6, 7
Week of Feb. 2	Inventory models	Chapters 8, 9
Week of Feb. 9	Linear programming and applications	Chapters 10, 11
Week of Feb. 16	Linear programming continued	Chapters 12 (skim), 13
Week of Feb. 23	Transportation models and assignment problems	Chapter 14 (sects 1-3, 7,10,12–15) and 15
Week of Mar. 2	Queuing theory, waiting lines, simulation	Chapters 16, 17
Week of Mar. 9	Continuation of simulation, Network models	Chapter 18
Week of Mar. 16	Markov analysis; wrap-up	Chapter 19
Week of Mar. 23	Case studies due	

Some instructors provide supplementary material on video or CD-ROM, to which students can then respond online. We recently met a dance instructor who was soliciting press packets from dance troupes across the country and including examples of their work on a CD-ROM to illustrate various techniques being discussed in the class. Some instructors use companion websites that accompany the texts they have adopted and that contain Web-based activities that supplement the course. Many art instructors scan artwork so students can view and discuss it online or create a virtual slide show that replicates, to some degree, the way in which art classes are traditionally taught face-to-face. Similarly, students can scan and upload their own artwork to complete assignments. Generally speaking, however, most online courses contain areas for presenting material to students, for asynchronous or synchronous discussion, for posting assignments, sending e-mail, and sometimes for taking exams. Some course management systems also allow the instructor to create areas for small-group work, which can occur between two or more students, that include a private discussion board for the group, the ability to share documents, and potentially a synchronous chat function.

Course Activities As already stated, what sets an online course apart from its face-to-face counterpart is not necessarily how the syllabus looks but how the course is delivered. Consequently, the activities contained within the course that address course objectives and competencies are a critical component to be considered. Carr-Chellman and Duchastel (2001) discuss the importance of the activities in an online course and further note that a good online course does not "teach," but instead makes resources and activities available that allow students to explore the content together in an effective manner. Often, it is the math and science instructors we talk to who have difficulty conceiving of activities for online courses. The following is the reflection of a statistics instructor who decided to try a "fishbowl" activity in her online class that successfully achieved the goal that Carr-Chellman and Duchastel describe. Based on techniques often used in face-to-face settings for counselor training, fishbowls allow a small group of students to practice a skill while being observed by the instructor and others in the class. Generally set up on the discussion board of a course management system, fishbowls can be used in a number of ways. A small group might interact with the instructor while the remainder of the class observes. Or the group may simply interact with one another around a topic or facilitate the discussion of the rest of the class from within the fishbowl. In this particular situation, the instructor chose to divide the larger group into smaller groups for discussion. Each group was to participate in their own discussion while observing one other group in action. The teams were to design a survey or an experiment while in the fishbowl.

My stat class just finished the fishbowl activity that I designed. A few of you on campus have already heard my jubilation about my student interaction over the past week, but I wanted to give a "final report" now that the activity is over.

I did have about 6 of my 18 students who either never showed up for class [or] left very few tracks, but the remaining 12 were brainstorming like crazy about their team's survey or experiment design – and (shockingly) appeared to be having *fun.* They came up with the most magnificent ideas, although I literally had to sit on my hands to keep from butting in as I wanted to give advice or set them on a different path at times. I did, however, drop notes into their discussion areas to let them know how pleased I was with their progress. For one panicky group, I had to leave several notes to let them know that everything was OK and that they were doing an impressive job.:)

If you recall, I had two follow-up activities. One was a survey about what went well and what needed to be improved. I was shocked by the overwhelmingly positive – almost glowing – responses to the survey. I thought that at least one student would say they didn't like the fishbowl or working with groups, but many of them even used words like <gasp> *fun*. In particular, I have a few nurses who were thrilled to be able to apply their expertise in the course and to see how statistics related to their discipline.

The other follow-up activity was a self-assessment with three main questions—the most important thing the student learned about surveys, the most important thing the student learned about experiments, and what they thought about working in groups. The quality of work I received for these assignments was unparalleled – and again, glowing reports about the activity. I wanted to share a few quotes . . .

- "I like the project we were assigned to. This gets everyone to know each other more, which is good. Now, if I were about to design a survey for my research paper, or any assignments that require designing a survey, I would be able to. Thanks!"

- "I thought that working in a group within an online environment was pretty useful and worked out pretty well. I also realized that when you are working in an online group on a project that you have to check in almost everyday in order to respond and [actively] participate."

- "After monitoring the Survey Design team's discussion this week and then reading over their final post, I realized just how time consuming it is to create a decent survey. Filling out a survey takes minutes maybe even seconds, but it seems to take days to hash out all the details necessary to make one."

- "I thought surveys were easy to construct and the data collected, easily compiled. I now know you must thoughtfully contemplate what you really want to glean from the data you collect."

- "I think the anonymity of the internet allows for more honest responses and people tend to be more like themselves, not putting on appearances. After all, we will probably never meet. Conversely, it is nice to put a face and a name together. I personally think it odd that you can post something and have a response very quickly. Here you are, sitting alone in your 'whatever' room, thinking you are doing this on your own and one of your teammates returns your post. That means they are sitting in their 'whatever' room alone also, struggling just like you. Together separately."

- "I see statistics now as a big process, not just [a] bunch [of] tables and graphs."

I could keep going, but I have probably bored you by now.:) I just want to say, to Drs. P&P and to my esteemed classmates, thank you so much for what you have taught me over the past few months. *Stephanie*

Another element to consider in designing activities for online courses is building in some form of choice. This helps address the various learning styles of students and adds variety to the course. For example, students might be given two choices in preparing an integrative paper that illustrates their understanding of course concepts such as the following example from an undergraduate psychology course, Personality and Psychotherapy:

Choose one of the following options for your final paper:

1. Theory and personal application – Take one theory or approach to personality and present yourself in reference to this theory or approach. Use at least 3 outside references not read for class. You also have the option of taking a personality inventory, such as the MBTI, and using that as the theoretical basis for your analysis. If you do so, make sure to also discuss the theory to which the inventory relates. Your content should be 60% theoretical and 40% personal process.

2. Watch the film, "Don Juan de Marco" and write a paper that applies the theoretical material we have discussed this term as well as the therapeutic approach used with Don Juan. What theories in action do you see in the film? Support your paper with at least 3 outside references not read for class.

This collaborative small group project is from a graduate-level course in group process and team building and also involves a significant degree of choice:

Please construct a 3000–4000 word paper analyzing the group dynamics of one of two films. The film choices are: Twelve Angry Men (1957) or Calendar Girls (2004). The paper should integrate theory and practice and the following are some directions you might take in your analysis. These options are suggested ways to approach the paper, however, if your group has a different way you would like to approach the paper, that is fine. I'm available for a consultation about approach if you like.

Assume that the movie needs little description in terms of plot and characters.

Option 1:
• Of the major topics we have discussed through our readings and postings, please pick 4—5 which seem to be most applicable to the movie your group has chosen. Discuss how these are illustrated in

the movie and what implications there are for the group and its functioning (1–2 pages per topic/concept).

- Considering yourselves a consultants to the group, what exercises or interventions might you use, given the forces at play (which you have just discussed)? What are the potential pitfalls? Any points of leverage or strength?
- Summarize your analysis and proposed interventions by noting the major points of insight into this group and if your intervention(s) were successful, what would be visible evidence of this?

Option 2:

- System features can be a structural way to observe group dynamics. Do the following features help you understand how various theories play out in the movie?
  - Boundaries – how are the boundaries of the group established?
  - What, if any, sub-systems exist?
  - What is an example of:
    - The influence of the group on an individual?
    - The influence of an individual on the group?
    - The influence of a sub-group on an individual?
    - The influence of a sub-group on the group?
    - The influence of an individual on a sub-group?
    - The influence of the group on a sub group?
  - Do specific roles become visible?
  - What are the group norms and how are they established?
  - What are the communication patterns?
  - How are decisions made?
  - Are there power differentials in the group?
  - How is conflict handled?
  - Is more time and energy devoted to content or process?
  - What is the level of emotionality present? Trust?

Remember that this is a group paper and should be completed with one posting from the group. You are responsible for developing the process that you will use to write this paper.

Stein and Wanstreet (2003) conducted a study in which students were given the choice of participating in small groups face-to-face or online in the same class.

Twenty-two students chose to work online for their collaborative small group work and eleven chose to be in face-to-face groups. What Stein and Wanstreet found was that the element of choice seemed to enhance the learning process and the sense of social presence, hence community, that developed among the learners. There was essentially no difference in the sense of social presence between the two groups, and satisfaction levels with the class were high. Stein and Wanstreet concluded that the element of choice is critical to adult learners and that this element fosters learning; the ability to choose becomes a matter of learning style and individual preference.

One final consideration for course activities is that of alignment. We have already stated that course activities should relate to the learning objectives of the course. The objectives and activities should also align with the ways in which they are assessed, a topic we return to in Chapter Ten. In looking at the assessment of student performance and its relationship to the activities performed, Morgan and O'Reilly (1999) note that it is important to design courses that contain a clear rationale and consistent pedagogical approach. In other words, courses should be designed with objectives, activities, and assessments that are in alignment and the delivery of those activities should be consistent throughout. For example, an instructor might want to assess the success of a collaborative small group activity. Using a test or quiz is not likely to assess that activity well, whereas the use of a rubric that students can measure their performance against and then complete a self-assessment might. Tests and quizzes might not measure skill acquisition and application well, whereas a simulation or case application of the concepts might. Instructors, then, need to think out of the box when developing assessments rather than relying only on the use of tests and quizzes to measure student performance. Mixing up assessment techniques has the added benefit of minimizing the ability to cheat, a topic we discuss further in Chapter Ten.

Course Guidelines It is extremely important to begin the class with clear guidelines for acceptable participation. These guidelines are generally presented along with the syllabus and course outline as a means of creating some structure around the course. In addition, the guidelines can be used as a first discussion item. We have learned the hard way that if clear participation guidelines are not established, the course does not go well. What we assume is understood may not be as clear to our participants. For example, simply stating that participants must log on twice a week says nothing about what they are expected to do during that online session.

One of our students who was not posting to the discussion felt that she was fulfilling the guideline of logging on twice weekly because she checked the site and read what others had posted. We were able to track her presence on the site through the software being used and were able to verify that, in fact, she had been doing what she said. However, without making some sort of contribution to the discussion, it was difficult to give her a grade for participation in the course. Having learned from this experience, we now are explicit about what an online session consists of and what is expected of students when they post to the discussion. A post involves more than visiting the course site to check in and say hello. A post is considered to be a substantive contribution to the discussion, wherein a student either comments on other posts or begins a new topic. Exhibit 7.3 gives examples of guidelines from online classes.

In addition to providing guidelines of what is expected of students, it is also good practice to be explicit in terms of what students can expect from the instructor. Exhibit 7.4 provides examples of two sets of faculty expectations.

A final thought regarding guidelines is the need to take the educational level and setting into account, as we have illustrated with our examples. Undergraduates may need tighter guidelines than do graduate students. A course that is being taught with an option of online or face-to-face delivery may create an opportunity to move students to either option, depending on need and ability to work in one or the other setting. Regardless, the guidelines should act as an initial structure for the course and provide information to participants regarding expectations for participation and conduct in the course; feedback from participants regarding the guidelines should be solicited. This, along with the posting of participant introductions, should constitute the first week of discussion in an online class. We return to this topic as we discuss what it takes to gain student buy-in.

CONSTRUCTING THE ONLINE COURSE SITE

Although the guidelines provide a framework from which to operate, the online course site provides the organizational structure through which participants can engage with the course material being investigated and with one another. It is therefore a critical contributing factor to an effective outcome. To some degree, the software used to deliver the course, and sometimes institutional policy, determines the ability to construct the site. Some software applications allow for flexibility and

Exhibit 7.3.
Online Course Guidelines.

Sample Course Guidelines for Graduate Level Courses:

Guidelines for online participation in *The Search for Soul and Spirit in the Workplace*

Co-Instructors: Rena M. Palloff, Ph.D., and Keith Pratt, Ph.D.

"Attendance" and presence are required for this class. Students are expected to log on at a minimum of twice per week and are expected to post a substantive contribution to the discussion at that time. Simply saying "hello" or "I agree" is not considered a substantive contribution. Students must support their position or begin a new topic or add somehow to the discussion when logging on.

Students cannot pass this class without participation in the online discussion.

Assignments, including case studies and papers, will be posted online. Students will be asked to comment on and provide feedback to one another on their work.

Although we strongly suggest that all issues, questions, and problems be dealt with online, students can feel free to call the instructors regarding these issues at any time.

Use good "netiquette" such as:

a. Check the discussion frequently and respond appropriately and on subject.

b. Focus on one subject per message and use pertinent subject titles.

c. Capitalize words only to highlight a point or for titles—Capitalizing otherwise is generally viewed as SHOUTING!

d. Be professional and careful with your online interaction.

e. Cite all quotes, references, and sources.

f. When posting a long message, it is generally considered courteous to warn readers at the beginning of the message that it is a lengthy post.

g. It is considered extremely rude to forward someone else's messages without their permission.

h. It is fine to use humor, but use it carefully. The absence of face-to-face cues can cause humor to be misinterpreted as criticism or flaming (angry, antagonistic criticism). Feel free to use emoticons such as :) or ;) to let others know that you're being humorous.

(continued)

Sample Guidelines for Undergraduate Level Course:
My expectations are quite simple. You have enrolled in a college course. The purpose of the course is to expand your knowledge of computer programming. The course will require you to spend time seeking information, evaluating that information and sharing it with your professor and fellow students. I make the following suggestions for completion of the course:

1. Log on to the course and read the assigned textbook reading for the current module.
2. Complete all course work on time.
3. Log onto the course at least 3 times each week. The purpose is to get any messages and participate in Discussion Topics.
4. Participate as much as possible in class discussion. No offensive terminology (racist, sexist or ethnic slurs) are permitted or tolerated.
5. Each learning module of the course is preceded by a date. You should begin this module by this date at the latest.
6. Ask for help when you have difficulty. Do not wait until you fall behind.
8. Submit ALL work prior to the deadlines.
9. Keep up to date on reading assignments.
10. Let me know when you have a problem. I can give you an extension if you notify me ahead of time.

creativity on the part of the instructor; others are more limiting. As we discussed in Chapter Five when we looked at technology, the amount of flexibility desired in course construction should be one of many determining factors in choosing course software.

Regardless of the software application used or the type of course taught, we routinely build the following elements into the course site:

- A welcome area, which includes a place for important announcements or additional guidelines that emerge as the course progresses

- A social area or forum on the discussion board where group members can interact on a personal level, apart from course material

- Course content areas, organized according to the way the syllabus was constructed (meaning either by week, topic, or readings)

Exhibit 7.4.
Sample Instructor Expectations.

The following are two sets of sample instructor expectations:

WHAT YOU CAN EXPECT OF ME AS YOUR INSTRUCTOR:

1. I highly value instructor-learner communication. We can communicate via my personal e-mail and telephone if you need to speak to me. To prevent telephone tag, you may want to e-mail me for telephone appointments. Generally, I can be reached by telephone most days. If I am away from the phone, please leave a message and I will return your call as quickly as possible.

2. If at anytime you are dissatisfied, confused, or unclear about how the discussion is being facilitated, please contact me via e-mail. I will respond to your inquiry within 48 hours, and we will work together to resolve the identified issue. We will use the course discussion area as our primary place of communication. In the event a private conversation is required, we will utilize e-mail. I'll get back to you usually within 24 – 48 hours; and if necessary we can arrange a time to talk/chat/exchange ideas.

3. I do give myself one day off every weekend. So, if you post a message or try to reach me on a Saturday, it is likely that I will not respond. I will respond, however, within my 24–48 hour timeframe.

4. I will share my travel schedule with you all and will post any away times in the Café area, which I call Rena's Roadhouse. I do travel frequently as I consult as well as teach, but I always travel with a laptop. There are rare times where I have been unable to connect for a couple of days (i.e, very slow dial-ups and travel outside of the US). When those occur, at the very least I will post a message in the Roadhouse letting you know.

5. I do my utmost best to respond to assignments with feedback within a week of receipt. Again, sometimes life and other work intervene in that, but if it does, I'll let you know.

6. I will treat all of you with collegial respect! I believe that you have as much to contribute to this learning process as I do and I look forward to our exchange as colleagues.

7. I will provide a warm, fun course environment where we can have fun and learn together!

(continued)

- An area or forum on the discussion board devoted to reflections on learning and the course evaluation

- An area or forum for student questions

- A separate area for assignments and exams or for posting assignments as discussion items, depending on the course structure

We have found in working with faculty new to online learning, or who are experimenting with the inclusion of discussion or collaborative activity online, that the organization of the discussion board can be something of a mystery that is difficult to comprehend. Given that the discussion board is the heart and soul of the online course, constructing it in a well-organized fashion is critical. The following example illustrates the concept of a well-constructed discussion board.

This example illustrates a course organized around weekly discussion topics, following the organization of the readings for the course. In more structured courses, such as courses in mathematic and scientific methods, the course might be structured around the specific skill set to be learned in a given period. The syllabus example provided in Exhibit 7.2, taken from Computer Programming and

Exhibit 7.5.
Sample Discussion Board.

FIELDING Graduate University FELIX
OM373 Soul & Spirit in the Workplace w/Palloff Term Ending 4/21/06   SiteScape :: Forum

Rena Palloff   Site map | Bookmarks | Search all | Help | Log out

Workspace | My summary | Discussions ▾ | Calendars ▾ | Tasks | Chat rooms
Add ▾ | Modify/delete ▾ | Tools ▾ | Next unseen | List unseen | Search
Show folder map ▸
OM373 Soul & Spirit in the Workplace w/Palloff Term Ending 4/21/06 Discussions and Documents
   Blogs   Syllabus and Housekeeping
   Dyads for final paper
User filters   None
Add/modify/delete filters

Unseen	Number ▾	Type	Task	Title	Replies	Author	Activity date
	19.			Course Evaluation		Terri Cruz OMD Course Administrator	17 April 2006 02:26 PM
	18.			Thoughts and musings on New Orleans...	(3)	Rena Palloff	10 April 2006 05:15 PM
	16.			Beth to All - emergency trip to Florida...	(6)	bethb	13 February 2006 09:49 AM
	14.			Rena's Roadhouse	(76)	Rena Palloff	21 April 2006 11:21 AM
	13.			Questions for Dr. P	(26)	Rena Palloff	16 April 2006 12:43 PM
	12.			Week 12 – Report out from dyads and final reflections (April 17)	(25)	Rena Palloff	23 April 2006 05:54 AM
	11.			Week 11 – Discussion of final papers (April 10)	(3)	Rena Palloff	14 April 2006 05:36 PM
	10.			Week 10 – Organizational transformation, soul and spirit (continued) – (April 3)	(12)	Rena Palloff	14 April 2006 02:56 PM
	9.			Week 9 – Organizational transformation, soul, and spirit (March 27)	(63)	Rena Palloff	14 April 2006 10:05 AM
	8.			Week 8 – Leadership, motivation, soul and spirit (continued) – (March 20)	(36)	Rena Palloff	08 April 2006 03:11 PM
	7.			Week 7 – Leadership, motivation, soul and spirit (March 13)	(13)	Rena Palloff	02 April 2006 10:45 AM
	6.			Week 6 – Organizational Assessments (March 6)	(66)	Rena Palloff	07 April 2006 08:05 PM
	5.			Week 5 – Meaningful work (continued) – (Feb 27)	(50)	Rena Palloff	26 March 2006 06:51 PM
	4.			Week 4 – Meaningful work (Feb 20)	(10)	Rena Palloff	04 March 2006 11:55 AM
	3.			Week 3 – Organizational soul and spirit (continued) – (Feb 13)	(55)	Rena Palloff	27 February 2006 03:44 PM
	2.			Week 2 – Organizational soul and spirit (Feb 6)	(6)	Rena Palloff	12 February 2006 02:53 PM
	1.			Week 1 – Introductions (Jan 30)	(58)	Rena Palloff	12 February 2006 08:22 AM

View entry number: [   ] OK   Top of page

Applications, illustrates this type of organization, and the discussion board should parallel the organization of the course (Exhibit 7.5).

Regardless of the type of organization used, participants should be able to easily navigate the course based on the layout of the course site, which should reflect the structure presented in the course syllabus. The course site and the ability to navigate it with little or no difficulty should ease the burden of the participant who is learning to use the technology while participating in the course. Consequently, whatever limitations are present in the software must be taken into account in course organization. The better the organization of the course site, the more easily participants will be able to use the technology. The less the participants worry about how to use the technology, the more likely they are to participate actively in the course. In simpler terms, the fewer mouse clicks required of students to complete a task, the more likely the task will be completed and completed well. We now turn to more specific means of gaining student buy-in and participation.

IF YOU BUILD IT, WILL THEY COME?

Many instructors have expressed frustration because they cannot stimulate participation in an online course. Some instructors have described courses in which students communicated with the instructor but not with each other. Others have described a complete absence of participation. We have discussed several strategies for securing student buy-in (willingness to participate in an online course) and then for securing ongoing participation as the course progresses. To summarize:

- Establish clear participation guidelines that the participants discuss and agree to.

- Be clear about how participation will be assessed and how it figures into the grading scheme for the class.

- Create a clear syllabus and course structure that is easy to follow but allows for flexibility.

- Be clear about how much time is involved in participation in an online course so there are no misunderstandings about what it means to work in this medium.

- Create a course site that is welcoming, easy to navigate, and to which there is little difficulty posting messages.

- Be a good role model of online participation by being visible on a daily basis, or at a minimum as much as is expected of learners.

- Be willing to step in and set limits if participation is waning or is heading in the wrong direction.

- Be willing to make phone calls to people who are not participating to ask why and to draw them back in.

- Most important, strive to *create community* through inclusion of the human elements involved in the course.

A good place to start in implementing any of these techniques is to begin the course with what we call "Week Zero." Instead of jumping into course content at the very start of the course, we start with ice breaker activities and introductions, and ask learners to post their own learning objectives for the course. Even if learners are taking the course because it is required, we ask them to discuss what they hope to get from it beyond the credit for taking it. We also post our own expectations for the course, as well as what students can expect from us as their instructors. We find that spending the time during the first week to set the stage for the course helps create the foundation of the learning community by encouraging learners to connect with one another and with us as their instructors.

When working to draw participants in and keep them connected, it is important to remember that real people are attached to those posted messages—people who have lives as well as human needs and expectations. Be prepared to use humor and inject fun into the process. We tell jokes and get students to laugh in a face-to-face classroom; humor is just as valuable in an online setting. Take, for example, the introduction to the online class, Human Behavior in the Management of Organizations, taught by Arlene Hiss:

WELCOME TO ORGANIZATIONAL BEHAVIOR

I hope that this will not only be a learning experience for you but will be FUN in the process. If you need to talk to me, you will find me at my desk during the day (Pacific Time). I'm usually teaching on-ground at night so it is a bit harder to catch me in during the evening. However, I have an answering machine and I will get back to you if I'm not in.

This course is going to cover such subject areas in organizational behavior as Theories of Motivation; Job Design; Group Behavior; Power, Politics, and Conflict; Leadership; Decision Making; Communication; Performance Appraisal and Evaluation; Rewards; Organizational Design; and Organizational Change, Employee Development, and Legal Issues and Current Trends.

Now for the SECOND week. . . . Just kidding. How's that for an action packed six weeks? So, hang on to your hats, grab your PC's and jump right in.

Arlene's welcome message is designed to draw students into the process and make it appealing; it also conveys who she is. It helps develop interest in the class while indicating the level of work that will be involved. Here are Arlene's expectations for participation, drawn from her course syllabus, also delivered clearly and with humor and tact:

> The student is expected to attend the virtual classroom at least 5 out of 7 days of each week. The standard is that an average participant should "attend" class 5 of 7 days per week. This is measured by recording the date of each entry you make to the system—whether it be a response to one of the assignments, a comment on the work of another, or a question to the group or to your faculty. An absence does not excuse the student from the responsibility of participation, assigned work, and/or testing. Students may be dropped for poor attendance after two consecutive weeks of absences are accumulated.
>
> It is extremely important to generate and participate in class discussion. The understanding and application of concepts is best reinforced by "lessons learned" of others. You should strive to participate in the meeting rooms and branches at least five out of every seven days. I would like to see you comment on your classmates' discussion questions, reports, and lessons learned. Besides commenting on other students' work, you will be given a final overall participation grade of 10 points. All discussion questions, comments to each other, or just plain 'ole rapping will be done in the Virtual Classroom. The Virtual Classroom is your "student lounge" so you should keep your "chatting" there. You may comment on each other's Reports, and Lessons Learned right in the same "Branch Meeting" where it was sent and this should all be topic related. I will be the observer/facilitator of this process and will be assessing your contributions to the topic related discussions. From time to time I will interject comments but for the most part, the discussions will be left to you. I will also be throwing out some "goodies" that you can hash over. I send handouts every day and you may comment on any of those. There will be plenty to talk about so you don't have to fear that you will run out of things to say. I would also like to mention that it is our online policy that you log on and *participate* 5 of the 7 days in the week minimum. Of course, since you will be so excited about this class, more than likely you will be logging on 7 of the 7 days;-). Remember that just logging on is not the same as logging on and *participating*.

This example also raises the issue of attendance. How does one account for attendance in the online classroom? Many software applications allow an instructor to track when and how often students log on. However, when that is not possible, the only means of tracking attendance is by monitoring the number and frequency of student posts on the course site. If a student logs on but posts nothing, his or her presence is not accounted for. Consequently, it is extremely important that this be clear to students from the outset. Some institutions are now requiring faculty to submit attendance reports along with grade reports at the end of a term. Creating those reports for an online classroom can be difficult when participation is low. When students are logging on and posting, however, accounting for attendance becomes a much easier task.

FINAL THOUGHTS

This chapter has focused on the organization and development of an effective online course. What follows are some guiding questions to allow you, the reader, to consider the elements presented and apply them to the creation of a course of your choosing. We also include what we look for as we evaluate effective online courses. In the next chapter, we turn to another important element of participation: How does an instructor facilitate the collaborative learning process that is so critical to effective learning outcomes in this environment?

GUIDING QUESTIONS TO ASSIST IN BUILDING AN EFFECTIVE COURSE SYLLABUS

The following questions are designed to assist with the development of an effective online course. Remember that we are not talking about course or curriculum conversion per se. Instead, this is an opportunity to reflect on teaching methods and how those might need to change as a course is being designed for online delivery.

- What are the desired learning outcomes for this course? What do I want to accomplish?

- What criteria must be included, as dictated by the institution (for example, disclaimers and office hours)?

- Are there any unique requirements that my students need to be aware of, such as methods to assess progress, desired outcomes, guidelines for participation, content, and context, or the need to be aware of good grammar and punctuation?

- What guidelines, rules, roles, and norms do I want to establish up front and stand firm on? Which can I be flexible about and negotiate? What do I let the participants decide?

- How do I want to organize the course site? What are my options? How much flexibility will I have based on the software available?

- How do I plan to assess the students? Are traditional means such as exams and quizzes adequate and appropriate? Or do I need to consider collaborative assignments, case studies, essays, and online exercises?

- How do I address attendance requirements? Will I rely on the quantity, quality, and frequency of postings, or simply the number of log-ons and postings?

- Do I want to establish "office hours" online? What times can I make myself available and be able to respond quickly to student concerns, questions, and ideas?

- Do I want to offer face-to-face tutoring sessions, meetings, focus groups, and so forth? If so, what are the logistics of those?

EVALUATING AN EFFECTIVE ONLINE COURSE

In evaluating an effective course, we look for evidence of the following:

- Course fits with the curriculum
- Course is learner focused
- Accessibility
- Relevant content
- Collaborative activities, including case studies, small-group work, jigsaw activities, simulations, and rotated facilitation to stimulate critical thinking
- Interactivity
- Cohesiveness

- Learning styles and culture are addressed by varied course activities and approach to the topic
- Clear instructions about course expectations and for completing assignments
- A reasonable load in terms of the amount of reading, posting, and e-mails required
- Use of technology that serves the learning objectives
- Web pages designed with one screen of text and graphics
- Limited use of audio and video and judicious use of synchronous media
- Use of introductions, profiles, and bios
- Use of ice breaker activities at the beginning of the course
- Use of experience-based exercises and activities
- Use of a social area in the course
- Clear guidelines for communication, including netiquette
- Clear expectations about posting requirements, timelines, and assignments
- Open-ended questions to stimulate discussion and encourage reflection
- Assessment and evaluation that is in alignment with learning objectives and course content

Promoting Collaborative Learning

Throughout this book, we have discussed the importance of collaboration in facilitating the development of a learning community and in achieving the desired learning outcomes for the course. Harasim (2005) notes that from the earliest explorations in online educational theory and practice, collaborative learning has been the most powerful principle of online course design and delivery. Collaborative effort helps learners achieve a deeper level of knowledge generation while moving from independence to interdependence, thus strengthening the foundation of the online learning community. We believe that a cyclical relationship exists in online classes wherein collaborative activity supports the creation of community, and the presence of community supports the ability for collaborative activity to occur successfully. Johnson and Johnson (2005), in their seminal work, *Joining Together,* talk about positive group interdependence, an element in both collaboration and community, which they state exists "when one perceives that one is linked with others in a way so that one cannot succeed unless they do (and vice versa) and/or that one must coordinate one's efforts with the efforts of others to complete a task" (p. 115). In other words, group members "sink or swim together" (p. 115). Through this definition, Johnson and Johnson aptly describe the very foundation of collaboration: when I succeed, we succeed.

In their article, "Making Distance Learning Collaborative," Christiansen and Dirckinck-Holmfeld (1995) postulate that the development of collaborative skills requires a means of study and an environment for study that "(a) lets a group of students formulate a shared goal for their learning process, (b) allows the students to use personal motivating problems/interests/experiences as springboards, (c) takes dialogue as the fundamental way of inquiry" (p. 1). Jonassen and others (1995) note that the collaboration in a constructivist classroom results not only in personal meaning-making on the part of the individual student, but also creates a container wherein social construction of knowledge and meaning can occur. Brookfield (1996) contends that collaborative processes promote initiative on the part of the learners, as well as creativity, critical thinking skills, and dialogue.

The online environment can be a lonely place. Students and faculty alike report feelings of isolation when working online. The benefits of taking or teaching an online class—the ability to connect any time and any place, from one's bedroom in pajamas and bunny slippers or from a library or computer lab—also can be a detriment of sorts because, for the most part, the people with whom one interacts are represented only by words on a screen. Collaborative activity can help alleviate those feelings of isolation by purposefully connecting learners with one another through various learning activities and promoting interdependence.

By learning together in a learning community, students have the opportunity to extend and deepen their learning experience, test out new ideas by sharing them with a supportive group, and receive critical and constructive feedback. The likelihood of successful achievement of learning objectives and achieving course competencies increases through collaborative engagement. Conrad and Donaldson (2004) state, "[The] collaborative acquisition of knowledge is one key to the success of creating an online learning environment. Activities that require student interaction and encourage a sharing of ideas promote a deeper level of thought" (p. 5).

In this chapter, we further explore the concept of collaboration by suggesting ways to promote it. The skills necessary to promote collaboration are not necessarily imparted to us during our academic preparation, which takes place for the most part in classrooms promoting independent work. The skills of interdependence must be developed and taught through a process of active learning. Let us now explore the applications of these skills to the distance learning arena.

FORMULATING A SHARED GOAL FOR LEARNING

An important element of community, whether it is face-to-face or online, is the development of shared goals. Clearly, in the online classroom, those goals should relate to the learning process. An instructor can use a number of techniques to move students in the direction of embracing a shared goal, beginning with the negotiation of guidelines early in the course and continuing through an end-of-course evaluation of how well those goals were met. Beginning an online course with a discussion of learning objectives and working toward a common goal creates not only the foundation of that learning community, but also is the first step toward collaboration. If students are clear from the beginning of the course that "we're all in this together," then incorporating collaborative activity into the course happens much more easily. The following is a discussion of techniques that can be used, along with specific examples.

Negotiating Guidelines

We cannot assume, as instructors, that our students will simply understand why collaboration is important or how it fits into their online course. Often, students express resistance to participating in collaborative exercises because of past negative experiences wherein other students did not share the load, it was difficult to connect with one another across time zones, or because of the amount of work collaborative activity entails. Consequently, in setting the stage for collaborative work, the instructor can ease the degree of resistance in the group by simply explaining why the activity is occurring and how it contributes to learning objectives for the course. In addition, including expectations for collaboration in the guidelines for the course can assist students in understanding how the course will proceed. We have discussed the importance of engaging the group in discussion of the guidelines posted by the instructor at the beginning of the course. Through the negotiation process with one another, the group members form a contract for their learning. Should a team member not fulfill that agreement, it then becomes the responsibility of the instructor to follow up with that learner and remind him or her of the agreed-upon responsibilities and tasks.

But what form does that negotiation take? What does it look like? The following is an example of what we have been describing as the negotiation of guidelines.

This online discussion took place in a graduate-level course in management and organizational behavior. It related to the discussion forums that had been created for the course and whether to separate our reflections on online learning into a separate discussion. One of us began the discussion by stating:

> Maybe what would be a good adjunct to our learning would be to create a separate discussion item to process the learning experience as it happens—not the discussion of the books, but how we're experiencing this online component of the course. Is anyone game for this?? If so, I'll gladly create the item. But I'll wait to see if people think this is worthwhile. *Rena*

A student replied as follows:

> I think that you are right on target, Rena, suggesting that we share our experience, feelings, and process. How we do that is up to everyone. Last quarter people complained that there were too many folders and they wanted to limit them. Perhaps now—as experienced cyberspace journeyers—that is different . . . ? I can go either way with it. If we don't do that, I would encourage everyone to feel free to add bits of their process and their selves to our content discussion. Or, perhaps you could delegate some time at each monthly session to process. Again, you are getting a sense of me, I try to interelate things all of the time. I think that you are raising issues that arise in business. How do we create an environment that invites our staff to have a space to discuss their process, feelings, and issues? We get so immersed in task management that this (important) piece is often not tended to. *Judie*

> Judie, Strange that you bring up the subject of "task management" vs "people/process management", that is the basis for Fiedler's theory of leadership and also part of a discussion that is continuing in my OB class now. How often we forget that there may be a time, place and situation that warrants one style or another. We often try to reach such a balance, but is it needed all the time?? *Keith*

> As far as another place to chat, Rena runs a very tight ship and I think there would be room for one more section for that purpose. My only concern is that fatigue will get the best of us and the chat section will fall by

the way side. Possibly making timely communication a bit uncertain. *Tonia*

I'm amazed that every time I join this conversation, more wonderful insights have been shared and there's more to think about. I agree with both Judie and Keith that there's time for balance and there are times when balance be damned contingent on the situation–thank you, Fiedler!! I also hear Tonia's concern that if I create an additional item, will people feel like they have the time to use it?? Or. . . . we could just continue the conversation about process here along with task whenever that's appropriate. Obviously, I'm open to whatever!!! *Rena*

I think it would be interesting to have a special item to discuss online learning, although I see Tonia's point that it could be a bit too much. Maybe we could give it a shot and if it doesn't fly we will let it land where it will??? *Cindy*

Well let's try one more section. It seems this is a lively group. Will the addition be for online comments or other random friendly stuff? *Tonia*

How about an item for both reflections on our online learning as well as other friendly stuff. I'll create the item just like that and we'll see where it goes. We can also take time out of both of our next two f–2–f meetings to process our online learning. *Rena*

It is difficult to imagine a conversation like this one—about how to organize and contain the learning process—occurring in a face-to-face classroom. Although some may find this type of discussion tedious, it does not detract from the learning process; it contributes to it positively. The discussion allows participants to take responsibility for how they will engage with the course and come to shared agreement about how they will interact with each other. This creates the first step in moving toward greater collaboration in learning.

Posting Introductions and Learning Expectations

As we discussed in the previous chapter, it is important to begin the course with introductions. Students should be able to introduce themselves and get to know each other. Barkley, Cross, and Major (2005) suggest that an effective way to promote student introductions is through ice-breaker activities. Structured activities designed to help students greet and get to know one another, ice breakers are fun and a good way to ease the tension and anxiety that often accompany the start of a class. However, to achieve collaborative learning, an important addition to the process of getting to know each other is the sharing of expectations for the course. This is the one time in the course in which it is appropriate for the instructor to comment on every student post. The purpose of this is to encourage interaction among the learners and to welcome each learner as they "enter" the class. The following are the expectations shared by the same group studying management and organizational behavior. The discussion begins with the instructor modeling the process.

> My hopes and expectations for this course are that we will engage in lively discussion about the topics of management and organizational behavior. I have chosen readings that I hope will spark this discussion and broaden our perspectives on these topics. My role in this, as I see it, is to act as a facilitator but not a director. I hope to see each of you taking a great deal of responsibility for making this course work. I am happy to share from my personal experience as appropriate, but I clearly don't want to impose that on all of you. Hopefully, you will all share your personal experiences in this area as well. —*Rena*

> My expectations and hopes for this class are that I would like to get more understanding of the theory and skills and knowledge through the discussion about the topics regarding Organization and Management. Also I'm interested in business organization consulting, so I'd like to share some information relating this with classmates. And one of my problems, it's my responsibility, English is not my native language so I'm still struggling with learning English. I'll try hard but everyone's consideration will be appreciate regarding this matters in advance. —*Soomo*

> I am very interested in learning about various models of organizational management. I plan to eventually start my own company and would like it to be a sustainable organization and I therefore feel that this class will be very useful for me. I am very pleased to have met you all and I am looking forward to spending the next quarter with you. —*Cindy*

> I'm hoping to learn about Management in this course. For me it has been one of those oft bandied big words I've heard about a lot but never really known what it meant. —*Jennifer*

I am really excited about expanding my understanding of management styles and theories so I can act in a meaningful way in the future. Thanks to all for your interesting personal info. I love biographies. *Tonia*

Asking participants to comment on expectations gives the instructor a process check, a means by which to determine whether or not everyone is beginning this journey from approximately the same starting point. If congruence in expectations does not exist, this does not necessarily signify a problem. Instead, it allows the instructor an additional opportunity for negotiation. Given that we are creating and facilitating a learner-focused process, it may be the instructor whose expectations need to shift to correspond more closely to the needs of the learners. If conflict results from these negotiations, again this is not a problem. The handling and working through of that conflict can move the group closer to congruence in its expectations. The more closely we can achieve congruence in the area of expectations, the more likely it is that a collaborative learning process will be the result. What is being created at this juncture is a contract for learning; the process of contracting includes negotiation.

Another means by which expectations can be negotiated is through the use of team charters. The use of team charters or agreements has been noted to be of significant importance in promoting learner satisfaction with collaborative learning experiences online (Doran, 2001). A team charter serves as an agreement or contract between members, outlining how they will interact together, determining the roles each member will play in the collaborative activity, and creating benchmarks and deadlines for the completion and submission of collaborative work. Generally speaking, it is a good idea to assign the completion of a team charter early in a course in which collaborative group work will be used, or at least as soon as groups are formed, so that it can serve to guide the activities of the group.

Encouraging Comment on Introductions

Frequently, students post their introductions and simply move on with the course. We have had the experience, however, of students feeling unrecognized when that happens. Our first encounter with this confused and surprised us. We were facilitating our first online course. Initially, ten participants posted introductions to the group, but one participant disappeared immediately thereafter. She rejoined the group later in the course, explaining that her absence had been due to the lack of comment on her introduction. She felt that she had shared quite a bit of herself and was hurt that none of the other group members had commented on any aspect of what she had written. We have learned from that experience and have since begun to model a way to respond to student introductions, which encourages other participants to do the same.

Not only does this practice enable students to begin opening up to each other but it also begins creating a safe space in which they can interact. We have discussed the importance of social presence, and in Chapter Five we discussed the relationships that develop between the students and the instructor and among participants, as well as with the machine. The posting of an introduction is the first step in developing social presence by revealing who one is to the remainder of the group. Because participants feel more comfortable revealing parts of themselves online that they might not reveal elsewhere, it is critical that they feel acknowledged so they can continue to do that safely throughout the duration of the course. This is the first point of connection—the point at which these important relationships begin to develop.

The following are a few brief examples of the type of acknowledgment that can be helpful. They are taken out of context and are not meant to represent the threads of a conversation.

> As I suspected, I'm learning more about all of you than we had time for in our face-to-face meeting. I'm impressed with the scope of your previous experiences and look forward to seeing you apply them as we discuss the readings in this class! *Rena*

> Welcome Keith! I don't know Jim from Florence, but we will have to talk sometime to see if we have any acquaintances in common. I actually didn't grow up in Florence, (it was just Home Base) since my father was a career Army Officer. As you probably guessed, being from Columbus, he was stationed at Fort Benning several times during his career. I went to the 4th grade in Columbus! *Julie*

> That was deep! I'm so glad you're joining us, Joyce! *Jennifer*

All of us need acknowledgment and to feel welcomed into a new situation. The promotion of human connection allows students to begin forming the relationships that are the basis for collaborative learning. The excerpts of dialogue presented illustrate attempts to reach out to one another and connect. They indicate that this group is at the formative stage—a fragile stage where acknowledgment of contributions is particularly crucial.

Forming Teams and Posting Guidelines for Their Performance

Another means by which to deliberately promote collaboration in the online classroom is to create teams for the purpose of small-group discussion, completion of group assignments, and engagement in small-group activities and simulations. This can be particularly useful when working with a large group or when a group needs an extra push in working collaboratively. Teams can be formed by the instructor or through a directive to the group to form teams of their choosing. The latter option can be time consuming and may result in teams that lack heterogeneity. Therefore, it is advisable to provide some guidance to students in team formation and to establish a deadline by which the group must form itself into teams or lose the element of choice. If students have the option of meeting face-to-face, the formation of teams may optimally occur in that setting. We have found that team formation can be difficult in the asynchronous online environment because potential team members are logging on at their convenience and may not receive or respond to a request to join a team immediately. Enough time, along with encouragement and reminders from the instructor, can help students move beyond this barrier.

When teams are formed, it is important to post guidelines and expectations for the performance of that team; it is also important to encourage the teams to negotiate their own set of expectations, thus creating their team charter.

In order to make group work successful, all group members must agree to abide by norms established by the group. In our book *Collaborating Online* (2005), we shared a few simple guidelines for the creation of team charters that work well to get students started:

> As your group is forming, please reach consensus on the following items and post your group's charter to the main discussion board:
>
> - How will your group identify itself? (Your group may choose a name under which to function.)
> - How will the group communicate? (For example, through the discussion board, e-mail, virtual classroom, phone, or a combination of methods?)

- What day during the week will the discussion begin?

- How quickly should group members be expected to respond to emails or discussion board postings? (For example, within 12 hours, within 1 day, etc.)

- What role or duties will each person in the group perform? (Possible roles include: initiator, secretary, liaison to the instructor, motivator, organizer, etc.)

- Who is responsible for posting group responses to the main discussion board?

- How will the group handle a member that is not participating?

- Discuss any other topics that are unique to your group.

The team's response to these questions can form the beginning of their first collaborative assignment and guide how they work together in the future. How that team should connect and relate to the overall learning goals of the class should also be posted. The following is an example of guidelines that were posted by one of us in an undergraduate class in organizational behavior.

1. Each team will designate/elect/appoint a team coordinator/leader.

2. The leader will remain the same throughout the course unless replaced by a majority vote of the team or by the professor.

3. The team leader may make a decision unless overruled by a majority.

4. Any project assigned to the team will receive a grade that applies to every member of that group.

5. The team leader will have the final authority to modify any team member's grade up or down (except for his/her own).

6. The instructor will have the final say in all cases where the team cannot reach a decision.

Embedded in these guidelines is an expectation that team members will evaluate each other's work, participation, and contribution to the collaborative product that ensues from their work together. Some writers in the area of collaborative education have argued that this practice instills a sense of competition in the group rather than cooperation (Felder and Brent, 1994). However, we have found that in the online environment, when students may not be in contact except through that course, this can serve as an incentive to promote collaboration as well as to equalize the workload involved. Team self-evaluation may also promote the desire to become part of an actively working team.

PROBLEMS, INTERESTS, AND EXPERIENCES AS SPRINGBOARDS FOR LEARNING

To actively engage learners in the online learning process and facilitate the meaning-making that is a part of the constructivist approach through which this learning occurs, the content of the course should be embedded in everyday life. The more that participants can relate their life experience and what they already know to the context of the online classroom, the deeper their understanding will be of what they learn. The process of connecting the learning gained from everyday life to the learning of the course not only creates a deeper sense of meaning for the participants but it validates them as people who possess knowledge and who can apply what they know in other contexts.

As we consider collaborative approaches, it makes sense for participants to connect around shared problems, interests, and experiences. The instructor can use group exercises and simulations to encourage connections; using questions that relate to the lives of the participants outside the classroom is useful. Connection can also occur naturally as the discussion evolves. In the next section, we examine approaches through which collaboration can be facilitated in online learning.

Encouraging a Search for Real-Life Examples

The types of questions asked to kick off the discussion of a topic within a course can encourage students to bring their life experiences into the classroom. Also, we often ask students to reflect on what they see happening in the online classroom. When we ask students to process the work of the online group as they see it occurring, the same purpose can be served. Here are some examples of questions:

- As we consider the topic of leadership, think of someone who you feel displays good leadership qualities. Describe those qualities, and tell us why you think this person is a good leader.

- What phase of group development would you say our group is displaying? How would that be different (or would it?) if we were meeting face-to-face?

- Based on this experience, what do you feel are the issues involved with the development of distributed teams (that is, teams in which the members are physically separated and do their work using e-mail, teleconferencing, computer chat sessions, and so forth)?

- Describe an organization with which you have had experience where you feel that power and politics played a significant role. How were you affected by those issues?

- How have you been affected psychologically, socially, physically, and spiritually by your participation in this course? What changes have you noticed?

- What do you see as the organizational structure of our university? How would you recommend its restructuring?

Asking such questions helps create an environment in which participants feel safe in bringing material of a more personal nature. We find that by modeling the use of real situations or by asking students to comment on a situation they share in common outside the classroom, they begin to work collaboratively on the solutions to other problems and situations they face throughout the course.

Developing Assignments Related to Real-Life Situations

Creating small-group assignments that deal with real-life situations is another means to achieve the same goal. These assignments can take the form of a problem the group is asked to solve together, the preparation and writing of a collaborative paper, or the completion of a simulation that can be processed with the larger group. The following are a few group assignments that we have used to promote collaborative work in our online classes:

ASSIGNMENT FOR GRADUATE LEVEL CLASS IN MANAGEMENT AND ORGANIZATIONAL BEHAVIOR

You have all been asked to read the case study entitled, "Sunnyvale Youth Center," which was distributed in our face-to-face session. Once you have read it, begin an e-mail discussion with the partner you chose in class regarding the case. Your task is to come to consensus on the issues involved in the case and to present your thoughts and suggestions regarding the case to the large group during next week's discussion. Your team's position should take the form of a one to two page position paper which you will post to the course site. Each dyad should then comment on at least one other team's post.

ASSIGNMENT FOR UNDERGRADUATE LEVEL CLASS IN ORGANIZATIONAL BEHAVIOR

Doing Business in the GOOD OLE USA!!!!

Utilizing any resources you can (preferably the Internet) find a company from a country outside the U.S. that has a branch or subsidiary in the U.S. and do a one-page report/paper on the significance of that company. This is your first team project, so remember it will be graded. Guidelines for team grading will be posted tonight.

SIMULATION FOR GRADUATE LEVEL COURSE IN ADDICTION STUDIES

You have been formed into treatment teams consisting of 5 people. Each team will be given two actual cases, one adult and one adolescent, to work with. The material you will receive is an intake assessment completed at the time of admission to a treatment program. I will be posting your case material to your team on the course site. Once you have completed the work outlined below, submit the forms to me in the area for that purpose on the discussion board. We will discuss the outcome next week. Feel free to contact me with any questions.

Your team is expected to do the following with the case material provided within one week:

a) Come to consensus about the level of care at which you are working (outpatient or inpatient).

b) Complete a collaborative problem list outlining the issues this client is facing in treatment. The form to use is included in the case material you have received. Please submit only one form per team.

c) Complete an initial treatment plan based on the problem list you have generated. Please refer to your previous reading material on formulating goals, objectives, and action plans to assist you with this portion of the assignment. Again, you have received the form to use with your materials. Please submit only one form per team.

It is assumed that as groups work through collaborative assignments, they are likely to encounter conflict as they form a subgroup of the larger class group. Once again, working through this conflict assists with the learning process. If a group becomes stalled as the result of the conflict, the instructor needs to act as mediator to assist the group in moving through the problem and reaching a solution. In addition, as the results of collaborative assignments are fed back to the larger group, a discussion of the process each of the smaller groups went through can be helpful to the rest of the group in learning about how to work collaboratively.

DIALOGUE AS INQUIRY

When students engage in discussions with each other rather than with the instructor, the possibilities for collaboration grow significantly. Brookfield and Preskill (2005) state:

> If the conditions for democratic, critical discussion are carefully created and respected, students can end up learning collaborative habits. They learn to listen respectfully and attentively to each person's contributions to the group. Through valuing devil's advocacy and critical analysis, they learn to reduce the tendency toward groupthink whereby certain ideas come to be regarded as off limits, sacred, unchallengeable. They learn to create spaces in which everyone's efforts are recognized. They learn that being a productive group member is not the same as directing everybody else or speaking all the time. . . . Learning to do these things is crucial if students are to work well in collaboration. [p. 33]

It is important for the instructor to be able to facilitate this dialogue without dominating it, so as to allow for a "volley of views." This can be done in several ways. First, instructors, as well as participants, must learn and develop the art of asking expansive questions. Next, the responsibility for the facilitation of discussion can be shared among the participants. And last, students should be encouraged—even required—to provide constructive feedback to one another throughout the course. The sharing of this responsibility among the participants is one way instructors learn to stretch their facilitative skills and increase their learner-centered focus. Rather than being at the forefront of the discussion, the instructor is an equal player, acting only as a gentle guide. This is a new skill for many instructors. Therefore, as we develop our abilities in this area, we grow as instructors, just as our students grow as learners. Brookfield and Preskill (2005) state that collaboration can become addictive: the more successful students are at collaborating, the more they will seek it out. Therefore, promoting good, collaborative discussion can assist them in developing an appreciation for other forms of collaborative work.

ENCOURAGING EXPANSIVE QUESTIONING

Questions posed in the online environment need to be the jumping-off point of a discussion promoting deep exploration of a topic and the development of critical-thinking skills. There are no right or wrong answers to these questions. They serve only to stimulate thinking and are a means by which to tackle what may be a large body of knowledge. The instructor in an online course needs to model this form of questioning so that students can learn to ask them of each other. A measure of whether a question has achieved these goals is the level of discussion and participation it creates. For example, if an instructor asks, "List three critical factors involved in team-building," what students will post are lists of three things but probably not much more, whereas asking, "Based on your reading and research, what do you see as the critical elements in team building? Please defend your position based on the reading," is much more likely to promote substantive responses from students.

Poor or minimal response to a question indicates that it has not done the job of stimulating a level of thinking that excites the learners and compels them to respond. An instructor who is closely monitoring a discussion can jump in with another question when this occurs, thereby expanding the level of thinking on the original question. What is important is to provide a kernel or a nugget of a question that serves to begin a dialogue and empowers students to pursue the issue at hand.

When students become excited by the learning that expansive questions create, they can become adept at asking the same types of questions themselves. This serves to propel the learning of all involved to much higher levels. The following excerpts of dialogue are examples of where students can take a discussion by asking questions of the other participants. This first one was posted to a discussion about leadership:

> It seems that mass media is quick to pounce on any story that could sell newspaper, magazines, or raise television ratings. My question is, if there was mass media in the early years of the country (Washington's term for instance), do you think today we would have a different view of our founding fathers? Also do you think it would be better for the American people to not know every aspect of the president's personal life? Somehow I bet that the first presidents did some questionable things in their lives. What do you think? *Jason*

The following was the first post to a discussion of "The Search for Soul and Spirit in the Workplace" in a course of the same name:

> I had occasion to watch "Jerry Maguire" with Tom Cruise last nite on Showtime with some of my family members. Did anyone else see it then or previously? I couldn't help but think of how the protagonist tried to infuse meaning into his job and the result was that he was fired. Like Bolman and Deal [2001] portrayed in "Leading with Soul", – leading means giving – and when you give, you run the risk of your gift getting rejected, and unfortunately sometimes, "you" along with it. I thought the movie provided food for thought and some interesting discussion related to soul and spirit issues in the work place. Has anyone else experienced this in their work? *Sandra*

These posts not only illustrate good thinking and questioning but also they bring the outside world into the online classroom. As we previously mentioned, the more we can do that, the more likely we are to stimulate the kind of interest in the course material that will expand the level of thinking and exploration occurring. Additionally, the posts illustrate the means by which one student can encourage others to work with him or her by opening themselves to possible challenge as well as support. This is the essence of collaborative work.

SHARING RESPONSIBILITY FOR FACILITATION

Because an active learning process is a desired outcome of distance learning, one way to ensure active participation is to share the responsibility for facilitation with the participants. Usually this is accomplished by assigning students responsibility for leading a portion of the discussion. The assignment can be made on the basis of a student having expressed interest in a particular topic or a rotation of presentations to the group by individual members, or roles can be rotated throughout the duration of the course. For example, participants may be assigned dates by which to post a paper. The other members of the group would have the responsibility for reading that paper and posting feedback and a response. Or one participant might be asked to lead the discussion while another acts as an observer and commentator on the process; yet another may record and summarize the process. If teams are assigned within the context of the larger group, these roles can be established and remain fixed throughout the duration of the course, or they may be rotated. The roles that students might take in an online course include:

- Facilitator of the discussion
- Process observer, commenting on group dynamics
- Content commentator, summarizing the group's learning over the previous week
- Team leader, with or without the additional responsibility of evaluating the work of the other members
- Presenter on a particular topic, book, or area of interest

In addition, all students are responsible for providing feedback to each other—a topic we explore in more detail in the next section of this chapter.

The following are examples of the ways students kicked off discussion in a graduate-level class on management and organizational behavior. The facilitation assignments were based on students' expressed interest in the books assigned for reading and discussion. Julie begins the discussion on Bolman and Deal's

Reframing Organizations (2003):

> For those of you who were able to get the book, I hope you have gained as much from the reading as I have. I would like to start the discussion with some feedback on what you are learning, what impact your reading has had on you, and which areas seem to resonate with you the most. I was particularly interested in the evolution of varied theories about how organizations work, and the authors' approach on consolidating these theories into the four frames. I agree, from my own experience, that a wise manager or leader will need to be able to pull from many theories or perspectives in order to be effective. Every management situation has a different twist to it and calls for a different combination of tools. The four frames discussed in the book offer a solid set of tools for understanding organizations. On page 19, the authors state that "an artist reframes the world to help us see new possibilities." They also say that "modern organizations rely too much on engineering and too little on art in their effort to foster such attributes as quality, commitment, and creativity." I agree wholeheartedly with these statements and cannot help but respond with a great big WHY?? I watched, at my most recent place of employment, how employee morale and spirit was crushed under the "leadership" of the bright, young engineering type who was given total authority by upper management to "manage" half of the company. This engineer had no understanding of how people think, feel, or create, and upper management seemed to think he was doing a great job. I heard just last week that this plant is currently in the process of being shut down. I would have liked to have the opportunity to work as a consultant with this company to help them reframe, to see what was really going on within the company. I probably would have started with the Human Resource Frame, since this one especially resonates with my own thinking. I agree with Argyris and McGregor that when employees are unproductive, it is the direct result of the inability or unwillingness of management to provide an environment that nurtures the needs of the employees. What do you think everyone?

Tonia begins the discussion on Morgan's *Images of Organization* (2006):

I am pleased with this book. It is open minded, interesting and thought provoking. It is invaluable for me, as a student to be assigned a book like

Morgan's Images of Organization. This is so because the scope of discussion is broad and easy to read. Some of the books we've been assigned in the program have been a bit trying to say the least. Usually I'm glad to glean whatever I can, but in this case I give thanks to Rena for introducing this book because I think it's substantial and we'll be well off for reading it. Having found myself bogged down and confused in the past within my real estate organization. . . . Uncertain how to get a handle on the total chaos surrounding me, I am greatly comforted to finally see that the company was very mechanistic. There were two of us who were trying with all of our might, to figure out how to create an open system environment. Unfortunately, neither of us had the training to be able to recognize clearly what was happening . . . and what we were trying to do . . . anyone else been that confused? Luggage in hand with a ticket to quagmire? It is really empowering as Judie said in the last section, to know where WE are coming from first. That way we have a chance of getting past the filmy walls. I appreciated the discussion on contingency theory. This appeals to me personally as well as professionally because I think the need to control in a traditional sense is ultimately a dead end. Steel can be inflexible but humans?

Cindy begins the discussion on Janov's *The Inventive Organization* (1994):

I thought it would be interesting to begin our discussion of Janov's book around the subject of systems thinking. I thought this would be rich because it is one of our core program philosophies, it has been discussed in all of our books and many of us were in the Systems class last quarter. Janov states; "This increased turbulence [within organizations] will result in an increased need to think systematically about how our individual realities are mirrored in society and vice versa. We will be challenged to see the connection between individual actions and collective outcomes and, thereby, we will be challenged to create more interdependence rather than more independence-to find our common cause and not just recognize and respect our diversity. Janov p.367 Janov speaks about relationships as being key to inventive organizations, which again relates to interdependence/systems thinking. Her reflection that we need to "create more interdependence rather that more independence" is just so darn un-American. I have argued this point with many a person who tells me that at the core people are selfish and they care more about independence/the individual than they do about interdependence/the collective. Is it possible to create/inspire a systemic paradigm within a culture that has prided itself on its rugged individual paradigm? I wonder what all of your thoughts and reflections are on this in relation to your experiences and feelings, and Janov's thinking around this. How do we create a systemic paradigm? Is finding a common cause and respecting diversity enough to create interdependence? Have any of you worked with or for an Inventive Organization? If so what influence did it have on you as an individual and how did it inspire the culture of the organization? If you have not worked for an Inventive Organization, what was it about the organization/s you have worked for that related to one/some of the aspects of the Frameworks for Inventive Organizations (p.96 etc.)? We will start here and see where it goes-I hope to "see" you all soon. . . .

In order for the facilitative role to be successfully shared, an instructor must be willing to give up control of the direction—even the content of the discussion—and act as a participating member, allowing the students to take the discussion wherever it might go. Certainly, if the discussion is straying too far from course objectives, the instructor should step in to set gentle limits and redirect the flow. However, for the most part, the instructor must control the urge to lead and become more like a follower, thus engaging in the type of collaborative work we have been discussing.

PROMOTING FEEDBACK

An important element that should be built into an online course is the expectation that students will provide constructive and thoughtful feedback to each other. This may occur as part of an ongoing discussion or specifically related to the work submitted in fulfillment of the course requirements. The ability to give meaningful feedback, which helps others think about the work they have produced, is not a naturally acquired skill. It must be taught, modeled, and encouraged by the instructor. Students tend to give feedback that does not promote collaboration or enhanced learning. It is not uncommon to see students respond with "Good job" or "I agree with you" as their initial attempts at providing feedback. Therefore, the expectation of substantive feedback should be built into the course. Once again, this should be delineated in the guidelines posted at the beginning of the course and discussed and negotiated by all participants. If students "forget" about this responsibility, the instructor should gently remind them. In addition, providing examples of what substantive feedback looks like can assist the student who is new to online learning in meeting this expectation.

Because this is a new experience for many students, providing substantive feedback can be a source of conflict; the instructor may need to act as mediator and to reassure students that the feedback is on their ideas and presentation and is not to be taken personally. In one of our early online courses exploring systems theory, one student wrote a paper about family systems, which was posted to the course site for comment and discussion. Another student, who worked as a family therapist, took issue with some of the material in the paper. The writer became upset and felt as if a bond of friendship had been violated by the feedback she received. We stepped in and talked about good feedback and encouraged the students to work this out "in public," so to speak. The students were both able to expand on the points they were attempting to make, creating not only a broader understanding of the theories being studied for all participants but an understanding of how to resolve conflict online as well. Take the following exchange between two students as evidence of increasing competence with the art of giving good feedback:

Stephanie,

I don't know if this is really a problem of resistance. What/where do you think the resistance is? I think you lay out some pretty clear deficiencies in the operation.

"The people in charge of change must develop a clear vision of an altered and improved future" (Luecke, 2003, p. 36). Sounds like there is a vision "become profitable ahead of schedule" but the next step is to develop the requirements to achieve it.

Leadership and skill training would probably help the supervisors. The supervisors spend a lot of time fixing problems. A goal for the organization should be to eliminate the problems. A training program for the line workers would be helpful. Assuming the supervisors are technically competent they could fill the role of mentors for the line workers. One of their primary responsibilities as mentors should be to provide on the spot training. The supervisors should be subject matter experts for all aspects of the line work environment.

The supervisors could conduct a double-loop (Morgan, 2006, p. 84–87) learning session, or After Action Report to find out from the line workers what the problems are. The supervisors could facilitate brainstorming sessions for the line workers. The goal would be to identify solutions to the problems/inefficiencies and create an implementation plan. "The implementation plan is part of the solution, and shouldn't be imposed on the people asked to push it forward. If the implementers and the other people affected by the change are involved in making the plan, they'll be more enthusiastic in supporting the initiative" (Luecke, 2003, p. 54–55).

I'm assuming the line workers will identify a lack of training as one of the cause of quality control. An internal/external training program would be helpful. If portions of the training can be performed in a classroom setting that would be good. I'm assuming most of the training will happen on the job. Have the best most influential line workers design an on the job training program. The supervisors could help with the development of the program. Create a certified OJT Trainer/train-the-trainer program. That will give the line workers something to strive towards. Additionally, pay certified trainers a little more. Give them a financial reward for working harder and making the operation run better.

The mere mention of line production brings Deming's 14 points (Wikipedia, 2006) to mind. It may be prudent to institute a quality control program managed by the lead OJT. From the scenario it sounds like personnel problems, staffing and attendance issues will fade away as line workers take control of the line problems. *Robert*

References:
Luecke, M. (2003), *Managing change and transition.* Boston, MA: Harvard Business School Press.
Morgan, G (2006). *Images Of Organizations.* California: Sage Publications.
W. Edward Deming. Retrieved November 8, 2006, from Wikipedia: http://en.wikipedia.org/wiki/W._Edwards_Deming

Hi Robert:
Where I see resistance is in the first generation of managers. I was specif-

ically brought on board to educate and shape the leaders and to help create and manage change in order to grow the organization. At this point in time, I am the only manager who is not part of the founding group – I am second generation. However, within another month, 2 more managers will come on board to join me, both bringing additional technical expertise to the plant and who can also observe the organizational culture with a fresh perspective and make positive changes and work toward plant goals with me. The plant is in the middle of big changes (see my comments above to Kim) as well as in transition from the two founding leaders to a newly promoted direction of operations. These big changes will propel the pace of culture change, which has slowed under the founding managers. Issues concerning the hourly employee base are now coming out into the open (failure to continuously train, poor hiring decisions, failure to embed corporate values, supervisor neglect, worker injuries, etc.) and so I am working with the individual managers to help them see the gap between their beliefs and their practices and to critically look at the results they are getting.

You are correct that we need to lay out an action plan on how the plant is going to become profitable ahead of schedule as well as more explicitly set out the expectations for the supervisors. I am in the process of working with the supervisors to identify their non-value added work and to get other clerical resources to perform those administrative tasks. Your thoughts on mentoring requirements, small group learning and problem-solving are good suggestions. Having our best operators help design the continuous technical training and create certified trainers as well as a pay incentive is good advice, too. *Stephanie*

The feedback exchanged through this bit of dialogue goes much deeper than just saying, "Good job." It creates a point of connection between the two participants and allows them to look at their ideas in another light. Through the exploration of consensus as well as difference, the students are able to construct a collaborative view of the material being discussed that goes far beyond the ideas each held at the start. Stephen Covey (1989) talks about developing the ability to "seek first to understand, then be understood" as a means by which to promote interdependence. Without interdependence, there can be no collaboration and, ultimately, no community.

INTERGROUP AND OTHER FORMS OF COLLABORATION

The online environment is perfect for the development of collaborative skills. Students learn to work with and depend on each other to reach their learning objectives and enhance the outcome of the process. Other forms of collaboration, however, can be promoted in this environment—forms with the potential to expand the level of learning achieved. Some of those are intergroup collaboration, resource sharing, and collaborative writing.

Intergroup Collaboration

The vastness of the Internet allows us to connect with individuals and groups all over the world. Exposure to some of these individuals and groups can provide students with a deeper understanding of the subject they are studying, allow them to develop greater facility with online research, and create connections that can serve them long after a course ends. Instructors should include assignments in their courses that push students to explore the Internet as a resource. An example of this type of assignment would be to find a website that deals with a particular element or topic being discussed. In our class titled "The Search for Soul and Spirit in the Workplace," we asked students to find a website dealing with spiritual issues, write a paper about what they found, and post that paper to the course site. One student got so excited about what she found "out there" that she ended up visiting seven or eight websites to complete the assignment. In an undergraduate class on organizational behavior, students were asked to visit a site that was related to power and politics and post the address of that site with a brief description to the course site. As the result of being given that assignment, one student commented that he now uses the Internet as a resource for doing research for his other classes as well.

What we are doing by encouraging students to explore the Internet is promoting collaboration with other learning communities around the globe. Instructors can also facilitate that type of collaboration by creating connections among groups of students enrolled in different courses. In other words, if two sections of the same course are operating at the same time, or if an instructor is teaching two courses that are interrelated, students enrolled in both can be given opportunities to interact; this mimics the development of residential learning communities on college campuses. In these communities, instructors from two different disciplines may join together to offer a joint exploration of a topic from the perspective of those disciplines. In the case of online collaboration, one group could prepare and present to the other group on a topic of mutual interest and concern. Furthermore, instructors can promote collaboration with colleagues at other universities and the students in their classes. Some ways to facilitate this process include (1) providing a list of e-mail addresses of instructors or students in another university who are interested in receiving messages from members of the group, (2) creating a common discussion area that can be accessed by participants and visitors, (3) creating and posting a list of websites of interest, and (4) presenting "guest speakers" to the group online.

Glogoff (2005) describes a very creative approach to intergroup collaboration through the use of blogs. Blogs, or Web Logs, are an online journal of sorts. Blogs are websites where links are posted, commentary and opinions expressed, and any other material that the owner of the blog chooses to post. Glogoff created a blog for his course in Decision-Making for Information Professionals and created spaces for his students to develop their own blogs. He encouraged his students to publish their assignments to their blogs as well as commenting on his blog and those of others. He also invited guest speakers and experts in the field to engage with the students around their blogs. He notes that this learner-centered approach helped increase the level of discussion in the course as well as providing the opportunity for students to collaborate with professionals in the field.

Involving the participants in developing these possibilities helps make this type of collaboration more meaningful to them. The possibilities are limitless and can greatly enhance the educational experience.

Resource Sharing

The assignments we just described have the additional component of allowing students to share resources—Internet resources as well as readings. In this way, a greatly expanded bibliography of readings can be developed to allow students to explore far beyond the confines of the readings assigned for the course. A separate area of the course site can be created to house this growing list so that students can add to it and refer back to it whenever they choose. Expanding the resources in this way encourages students to take greater responsibility for their own learning and allows the instructor to act as an equal participant.

Collaborative Writing

Technology in its various forms makes the transmission of documents easy. Students can work together or with an instructor to complete course assignments, usually by sending documents between or among participants. E-mail, as well as the ability to attach documents to posts on a course site, has been extremely useful in composition courses conducted online, as well as in the completion of team learning assignments. In addition, whiteboarding software in a course allows for brainstorming sessions and for completing collaborative work by simulating what might occur in a face-to-face session. Requiring students to complete papers collaboratively and evaluating that work on a group basis also promotes interdependence.

Other Forms of Collaboration

It is clear at this point that there are numerous ways in which an instructor can create collaboration online, regardless of the content area being studied. Here are some of the suggestions we have discussed:

- Small-group assignments
- Research assignments asking students to seek out and present additional resource material to their peers
- Group work on case studies
- Simulations
- Shared facilitation
- Homework forums
- Asynchronous discussion of the reading and discussion questions
- Papers posted to the course site with mutual feedback provided

Newer forms of technology are allowing us to creatively add to this list and include the following:

- Blogs, or online journals or Web Logs, where students can reflect and invite comment on those reflections
- Wikis or collaboratively created Web pages
- Jigsaw activities where students are either assigned or choose a piece of a research puzzle and collaborate to bring the information together
- WebQuests, where teams of students are sent on an Internet-based scavenger hunt, the result being a comprehensive presentation or solution to a problem

- Learning cycles that allow students to progress through a series of activities resulting in increasing skill acquisition

Regardless of the way in which collaboration is used, it is critical for the instructor to set the stage for it through the formation of a solid learning community. Although collaboration helps shore up the foundation of that learning community, the presence of community certainly helps facilitate successful completion of collaborative work.

FINAL THOUGHTS

Collaboration and the ability to promote interdependence is a critical element in the formation of an online learning community. Consequently, it is important that the instructor in an online course pay close attention to ways collaboration can be incorporated and facilitated throughout the course. The inability to promote collaboration in this environment generally results in low levels of participation and in two-way interactions between the instructor and any given student. Collaborative work also forms the basis for the student's ability to engage in a transformative learning process—the topic of the next chapter. The questions that follow are designed to help instructors think about ways to incorporate collaboration into the planning for an online course.

GUIDING QUESTIONS TO PROMOTE COLLABORATIVE LEARNING

The following questions are designed to assist in the development of a collaborative learning approach in online courses. Just as with all other aspects of an online class, collaborative learning must be planned and purposefully facilitated. These questions should help create a planning process whereby these goals can be achieved. In addition, we are including questions for students to consider when engaging in collaborative activities.

Questions for Instructors

1. What is the content of this course? What aspects of the content lend themselves to collaborative group activities?

2. What are the goals of the small-group activities?

3. What size groups or teams should be formed in order to achieve those goals?

4. How should groups or teams be formed? By the instructor? By the students? Dependent on interests? Dependent on strengths?

5. Should the groups be homogeneous or heterogeneous?

6. Will the participants remain in the same groups throughout the course, or will new groups be formed for each activity?

7. How will activities be structured to ensure participation by all members of the group?

8. Should roles be assigned to various group members?

9. What rewards or motivations will be built into the process?

10. How will accountability be built into the process?

11. How will individual and group performance be evaluated? Who will evaluate this performance? The instructor? The participants themselves?

12. Is there an expectation that students will provide feedback to each other on their work? How will this be built into the course?

Questions for Students

1. How well did I participate in my group? Was I a team player?

2. Did I make a significant contribution?

3. Did I share my portion of the workload?

4. How comfortable do I feel with the group process?

5. Did I feel comfortable expressing any problems or concerns openly?

6. Did I provide substantive feedback to other group members?

7. How do I feel about the collaborative work produced by my group?

8. How well did the collaborative process contribute to my learning goals and objectives for this course?

Transformative Learning

Thus far, we have discussed the process of establishing connections among participants in an online course and with the instructor. We have also described ways a group can carry on a dialogue throughout the course. It is now time to turn our attention to the "real" learning that takes place as the result of participation in an online course. We call this form of learning *transformative learning* because it represents a self-reflective process that occurs on several levels.

Jack Mezirow (1990, 1991, 2000) coined the term *transformative learning* to refer to learning that is based on reflection and on the interpretation of the experiences, ideas, and assumptions gained through prior learning. This type of learning is rooted in the meaning-making process that is central to constructivism, which we have already established as a major feature of the online classroom. The goal of transformative learning is to understand why we see the world the way we do and to shake off the constraints of the limiting perspectives we have carried with us into the learning experience. Patricia Cranton (2006) adds that in order for the questioning of personal assumptions and self-reflection to occur, the environment must provide the support and the ability to dialogue and critically reflect on the material presented, as well as on the self.

Participants in an online course engage with and reflect on the course content. Parallel processes should also be put in place that allow participants to consider the learning that comes out of this engagement. Participants should explore not only how learning in this medium is different but also how engaging with the medium and the machine allows them to learn something about the technology itself (see Chapter Five). Another parallel process should be self-reflection. Participants should ask themselves, "How am I growing and changing as a learner and as a person through all of these interactions?" Often we build self-reflective questions such as this one into our online courses. We periodically ask our learners to reflect on their learning as they go. Brookfield and Preskill (2005) recommend regular use of tools such as the Critical Incident Questionnaire to promote such reflection. The Critical Incident Questionnaire asks five questions that prompt students to look at specific points during a week of discussion when they were most engaged in or distanced from the discussion. They also are asked to reflect on elements of the week's work or contributions by others that may have surprised them. It is these "aha" moments that help to promote transformative learning.

We have previously referred to this element of online learning as a *double loop* in the learning process, based on a term coined by Chris Argyris (1992). This loop provides a means of self-reflection that fuels further inquiry. However, transformative learning is actually a complex series of interactions that is multidimensional. It is what Robert Hargrove (1998) calls *triple loop learning,* which he describes as "learning [that] involves altering the particular perspective, underlying beliefs, and assumptions (or old rules) that shape *who we are* as a human being—what we identify with" (p. 62).

In this process, learners do not complete one set of reflections and then move on to the next. Instead, they may visit the next level while returning to previous levels to further reflect on the learning contained there. It is a vibrant, dynamic process that is typically not completed when a course ends. Ideally, the first experience with this process creates a hunger for more and sets the stage for participants to become lifelong, reflective learners. This is very much in keeping with learner-centered instruction and is a process that needs nurturing along the way in order for it to continue. We have seen many students become frustrated when their attempts to continue their learning in this manner were thwarted by an instructor who preferred to teach using fairly traditional methods, either online or in the face-to-face classroom.

To tackle this complex topic and demonstrate its implementation in an online course, we first examine the process by which it occurs. We then explore each of the parallel processes previously mentioned: learning about new forms of learning by using technology, learning about technology by using it, and encouraging the self-reflective process.

THE PROCESS OF TRANSFORMATIVE LEARNING IN THE ONLINE CLASSROOM

Transformative learning is, to many participants, an unanticipated result of the online learning process. If students were informed in advance that a process of transformation would be the outcome of their participation in an academic course, is it likely that they would enroll? Intellectual growth is anticipated, but personal growth is not necessarily a reason students engage in a process of online learning, nor is engagement in a learning community. Consequently, we do not inform learners up front in our course outcomes or expectations that they are engaging in a learning community and that transformation will be the result of the course. In fact, we rarely use the "c" word, meaning community, at the start of a course. Instead, we support and reflect on its emergence as we see it happening and ask for reflection on it as we go.

Mezirow (1990) states that perspectives are transformed when learners encounter what he terms *disorienting dilemmas*—dilemmas that cause the learner to critically assess distortions in the areas of the nature and use of knowledge, belief systems related to power and social relationships, and *psychic distortions*—or presuppositions that cause anxiety and inaction. By simply getting involved in an online class for the first time or even on an ongoing basis, a learner immediately encounters a disorienting dilemma. This is a new medium in which participants interact differently and in which students are expected to engage with material, each other, and the instructor in a completely different way. Thus the online classroom is fertile territory for transformative learning.

Because this process is an unconscious one for the most part, it is important for an instructor to make space for transformative learning and to surface it as the course progresses. In so doing, an awareness of increasing competence and independence as a learner begins to emerge for the participants—an outcome they can carry with them to subsequent learning experiences. Thus personal growth becomes a companion to intellectual growth as the student assumes greater responsibility for the learning process, competence, authority, self-confidence, and an overall sense of mastery and power. We now review this process in more detail and provide examples of its emergence in online courses.

Reviewing the Process

The transformative learning process is one that moves a participant from student to reflective practitioner. It begins with the practice of acquiring knowledge. Students, by enrolling in an online course, commit to that process. They enter the online environment and begin to form new relationships, which deepen as students post material to the course site and are acknowledged for their ideas and their participation. As the result of acknowledgment and feedback, students perceive that value has been added to their contribution. Their contribution has been recognized and appreciated by the group. Consequently, their ideas may be supported and expanded, or they may begin to branch off in another direction of inquiry. They then begin to question why this has happened. Why should I begin to look at this idea in a new way? Do I need to? Why are my assumptions being questioned by others, forcing me to look deeper? As a result, they begin to develop new ways of explaining their ideas and the material with which they are interacting. This creates a network of learning through which new ideas and means of reflection provide a feedback mechanism regarding the ideas being studied and the learning process itself. Exhibit 9.1 illustrates this process.

The excerpt of dialogue that follows is an example of the effect of this process. A student posts material and receives feedback, an action that stimulates the process of questioning and reflecting on ideas and self. The result is movement to the next level of reflection. That next level is illustrated here.

> At this point I'd like to approach this from a more personal inquiry. Joyce has done an impressive synthesis and an outstanding analysis of the book. I apologise for the less academic and the simplistic approach I'm capable of.
>
> This is my favourite of the books so far, in that it has the most personal connection for me. Around about 3 months ago, before this class and before coming across this book, when people asked me what I was studying/doing at graduate school, I began to say "new paradigm business" instead of just "business". I did so to find a way, to find some way to convey that I wasn't studying business in the common definition of the term but something different. Always I would be asked what that was or I would take the initiative to elaborate. "It's not the typical business program" I would add. "It's about learning to do socially and environmentally responsible business, sustainable economics, spirituality in the

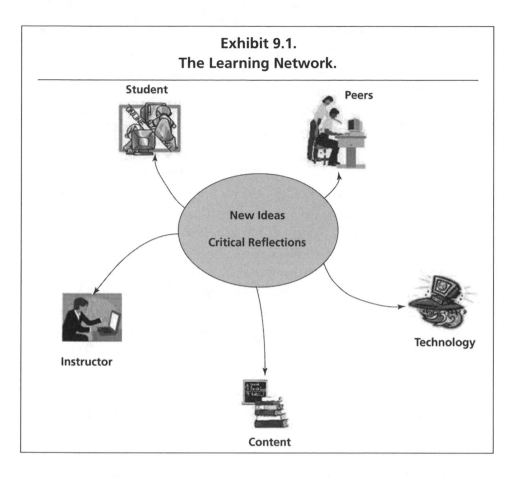

Exhibit 9.1.
The Learning Network.

Student

Peers

New Ideas

Critical Reflections

Technology

Instructor

Content

workplace-as different from religion" would be my standard intro, for that's the longest I find one can push it to in the typical standard one minute intro time. So it was very reassuring and validating to come across the concepts and points put forward [in this book].

The chapter on new-paradigm thinking immediately drew me. Overall I think [the authors] put forward something valuable, and I tend to agree with a lot of their points. However I did think they were overly concerned with style, and their chapter was a lot of stylish writing, and what they're actually saying can be condensed into half the size. I found myself going through the list on p6 of ch1 of the attributes of the New Paradigm Manager and assessing how many I make. Out of the 7 I would say I fit 4 (though I disagree with #4 in putting people ahead of the environment, the same way I get irritated when people say save the planet for our grandchildren kind of thing-the world does not belong to the human species, though we act like it does). I don't know that I "have the scope, range and power to manage the entire staircase of your own, of others', of your organisation's and of society's history," nor if I am "skilled at recognising and dealing with different levels of development, each in the process of change." And realised that though I do believe/know "that everything connects to everything else," I should always remind myself to remember that and be mindful of it all the time. So how about you? Do you agree with this definition and list of attributes of what a New-paradigm Manager is?

One thing that really struck me was a sentence in Ch 18: "Doing business in the new paradigm starts with managing yourself" (p347). I thought, well, how do I manage myself ?, and I thought, well, not very well, right?! No I don't manage myself very well at the moment; and I thought this simple statement has a lot of significance for me and is something I should be continually aware of and direct the changes I need to make in my life. *Jennifer*

While engaging with the course material being read, this student began a process of self-reflection. Not only does she explore the meaning the material has for her academically but she reflects on the meaning it has in her own life. The questions she asks throughout are, "Where do I fit? What does this mean to me personally and professionally? What changes do I need to make in my life to accommodate this new learning?" In addition, she questions the way the material is written and presented. Her inquiry is more than just a review of the book; it involves questioning where the ideas came from and where those ideas fit in her reality. The level of reflection in which this student is engaged goes well beyond trying to make sense of the book she just read for class, as it expands the relevance of the material for her, as well as for the others in the group. Because of its importance, this process needs to be initiated by the instructor and guided if it is not occurring spontaneously.

The expected outcome of the transformative process in the online environment, then, is significantly different from that which might be experienced in a face-to-face class. To frame it simply, the results of the transformative learning process are the student's ability to stay focused on a position or idea or to achieve a shift in paradigm, thereby adopting a new view of the same idea. Students may be able to develop new ways of explaining their ideas, or they may be able to enhance or expand upon those ideas; they may also be able to reflect on how the process itself has affected them. The example just presented illustrates this desired end result. Jennifer begins her post by stating that she now has a better way of explaining her idea of what *new-paradigm business* is by having engaged with the reading material for the course. She has not necessarily shifted that idea but has found new ways to explicate it. The process does not end there, however. She goes on to reflect on herself by seeing herself in the material and sharing that with the group.

Although it is certainly possible to see this type of reflection occurring in a traditional classroom, it is not necessarily encouraged. Students in a traditional setting are asked to reflect on the meaning and importance of the course material but are not always expected to apply it to their own lives or to reflect on its potential impact on present or future behavior, attitudes, and actions. By encouraging students to engage in self-reflection related to the learning process, however, their ability to make meaning is greatly enhanced and the learning outcomes become deeper and more permanent. Previously, we discussed the importance of bringing real-life into the classroom or asking students to apply their learning through the use of real-life examples. As we can see now, this not only helps make online learning more relevant but it also assists in the transformative learning process.

Making Room for the Process in the Online Classroom

In order to encourage this level of inquiry, a space needs to be created in the learning process in which it can occur. As we have described, we deliberately create two streams in the course site for that purpose. One is the area for online reflection, which we discuss in the next section of this chapter. The other is a place for self-reflection. These streams can be joined in one section of the course site to minimize the number of items to which participants need to pay attention, as long as the instructor is clear about how to use that area of discussion. For example, one of us, while teaching an online course, created an area titled "Reflections on the Class." The explanation for using that area was, "This is a forum for discussing the impact, issues, problems and concerns or any other idea relevant to how this type of class is affecting you in any way."

Another means by which to create space for this type of reflection is to ask questions that promote it as a part of the ongoing discussion. Questions that relate the course material to the interaction occurring in the online classroom will achieve the same result. The author, in the same course mentioned earlier, also asked questions that facilitated this type of thinking. To kick off a discussion on teamwork, he asked the following:

> As you should well know this week's chapter is about "Group Behavior and Team Work." The material in the book mostly relates to things that happen in Face-to-Face (F2F) situations. Are any of these concepts, ideas, theories and viewpoints relevant in groups in "Cyberspace." If so tell me why? If not tell me what are the concepts, ideas, theories, viewpoints and issues that are important to look at when dealing with groups and this medium. (HINT) You may want to think about some of the issues that we have dealt with here.

The creation of this space opens the door to reflection. It conveys a message to the participants that says that this type of inquiry is expected and completely acceptable. Furthermore, by setting it apart from the discussion of content, participants are more likely to visit that section of the course site on a regular basis. This allows them to develop their skills in the area of self-reflection as the course progresses, and does not limit their involvement with this process to the points during the course that call for self-evaluation. It is important, however, when students are being asked to assess their work or participation, to include a self-reflective piece in that assessment. (We discuss this concept further in Chapter Ten.)

LEARNING ABOUT LEARNING
THROUGH THE USE OF TECHNOLOGY

As students engage in the self-reflective process that is a part of transformative learning, it is important for the instructor to remind them that the medium they are working in allows this process to occur. In so doing, the instructor opens a new area of inquiry: What are we learning about learning by using technology? We have discussed the fact that the learning process occurring online is a learner-centered process. It is essentially directed by learners from the time the instructor posts guidelines that are open to negotiation and allows the process to go where it will, with only guidance and facilitation by the instructor. As the learners begin to feel and acknowledge an increasing sense of empowerment, they will begin to make comments about how this type of learning differs from that of the face-to-face classroom. For some this is uncomfortable. For others it opens new vistas. Learning about the ways we learn is an important outcome of the online process that needs encouragement and support. It provides the participants with a foundation for future learning experiences. The following post illustrates this concept.

> I have had several courses online. [I have noticed that] the students take a little time before becoming comfortable with the online courses. Of course the professors are challenged by the new style of teaching their course. Also, the computer software package can impact the transition for learning at a distance. Ideally, the learning would be nice if everything ran smoothly.
>
> All the professors who I have had for distance learning have found a way to convey their passion [to] the students. Each professor has his or her unique style for ensuring that students are learning the course material. I am learning about distance learning and we are all learning about distance learning.
>
> I was working with another student on a paper on distance learning and read a website about the subject. Harvard University's entire business school is connected on line. At Harvard the business students can talk with each other from their dorms and I believe they retrieve lecture notes too.
>
> Yes, we have suffered through some days in our class. However, in the end what I am hearing is that the students haven't lost their Soul and Spirit. I've got to go now. With Courage. With Compassion. *Greg*

As this post indicates, the ability to differentiate the type of learning that occurs online is important in the meaning-making process. Greg noted the differences in both learning and teaching that occur in this environment and became interested enough in those differences to pursue research with another student about it. Transformative learning is not easy; in fact, it may be somewhat painful for some. Just recognizing that it is different and that "I function differently here" is important to the learning process, allowing students to proceed with courage and compassion, even though the going may be difficult.

CREATING OPPORTUNITIES TO ENCOURAGE REFLECTION ON THE DIFFERENCES

Once again, it is important to make space for this type of reflection in the learning process. Instructors should ask, "How is this different for you? How are you different as a learner online? How are you experiencing this process?" Acknowledging the fact that the process is different and may be difficult can relieve anxiety on the part of learners that they are not "doing it right." In addition, institutions should include questions about the technology in their course evaluations, as the technology can and does influence the outcomes of the course and student satisfaction with it. This response to one of our questions presented earlier illustrates that when the opportunity to reflect on these differences is created, participants will go to that level of reflection.

> Okay, don't you think that everyone has a hard time accepting disagreement f2f. Only a few people have the confidence to stick with their opinions without going back to the book and looking. I know that we have all had some life experiences that can be transferred to this medium but you still have to squirm a little when you are not real sure. Cyberspace lets you squirm in peace. You are able to rethink without having people questioning you. . . . Is this making sense? Maybe we all need that time to realize that we are full of ideas that we sometimes have to let grow. . . . Maybe some good ideas too. *Rob*

We discuss this element further when we talk about assessment and evaluation in Chapter Ten, as reflection on the differences in this type of learning frequently becomes a part of the evaluation process that is so critical to an online course. The following are final posts from an online course that demonstrate the reflection on new ways of learning as a result of learning electronically.

> As I write this, my final note, I do so with a real sadness. The last few months have been personally transformative, in large part because of this seminar. The sharing, collaboration, and learning we have all experienced is boundless. Most interestingly, I note how many of us have experienced major life changes during this brief period. . . . And yet, the continuity of [this course] acted to provide stability and support during those difficult times. Not only have I suffered loss and pain, I have changed both my dis-

sertation interests and knowledge area focus. Currently, I am investigating the proliferation of online learning programs globally as well as why, despite our illusory discomfort with telecommunications, we like it so much. *Cyd*

Thank you to each of you for what you have given me over the past several months. My view of the world has been expanded and challenged. You have shared your courage, sadness, frustration, support, and caring. You have asked dozens of hard questions and raised the important issues of the electronic transformations surrounding us. You have given me hope and some courage of my own – to keep asking the questions; to get more involved as our government, communities, and institutions grapple with the changes; and to focus my dissertation work in the area of Information Technology and Society. I wouldn't be here without your help. *Claudia*

We frequently have students who become so intrigued with the process of online learning that they choose to engage in further study about it or determine that they would like to teach online at some point. Noting the transformations that have occurred for them in the process, they seek to understand why. This is the essence of transformative learning.

LEARNING ABOUT TECHNOLOGY BY USING IT

In Chapter Five we discussed the importance of the technology being used for online courses and the fact that learning through the use of technology allows participants to explore its use in more general terms. Students participating regularly in an online course cannot help but improve their ability to use technology. As they engage with the machine, they learn more about word processing, logging on to the Internet, using some of the newer synchronous tools, and using a browser. By the end of an online course, a complete novice is likely to have gained enough skill to continue to engage with technology with some degree of confidence. He or she may feel less threatened and intimidated by using more advanced forms of technology as well. One of us was approached by a student who wanted to take an online course but had absolutely no technical experience. She referred to herself as technologically challenged and stated that she knew that learning about technology was something she needed to do as well as taking the course in question. She enrolled, her son helped her with the technological aspects, and she did extremely well in the course. Her final reflections included a sense of accomplishment and pride that she had mastered something she considered daunting and felt competent to do more work using technology.

Often, students who are new to online learning will begin to ask about having chat sessions and about how to use technology to collaborate on documents. As previously mentioned, however, in order for this to occur, the technology must be easily mastered and transparent within the course. In addition, the instructor and the institution must be available to provide answers to questions regarding the technology, as well as technical support. An instructor should not be put off by students posting questions to the course site that relate to the technology. This is not a distraction from dealing with course material but rather a way for students to begin to learn about technology by using it.

ENCOURAGING QUESTIONS AND COMMENTS ABOUT THE TECHNOLOGY

As instructors allow students to ask questions about software use and other technical questions, we find that some of the best responses, encouragement, and advice are frequently supplied by students themselves. As students support each other with their growing technical expertise, this promotes a feeling that everyone is in this thing together. In addition, we have found that more advanced students are patient with their less knowledgeable colleagues and are willing to provide instruction and support that is appropriate and easily understood. We once taught an online course using software in which an "edit" button appeared in each post, allowing students to change a post once it appeared if they were dissatisfied with it. However, some of the students found it confusing and began asking about it online. What is it? Can we get rid of it? Has anyone tried using it? Before we had a chance to respond, we found that they had supported each other in figuring out the button's use. As the less experienced students began to discover the button, the more advanced students very patiently explained again and again what it was for.

In another case, a virus warning appeared every time a student posted an attached document to the course site. A couple of students became nervous when they saw this and were reluctant to download the attached documents. They stated online: "I want to read your paper, but I get a virus warning every time I try to access it." In this case, we had to intervene to reassure students that this was simply a routine warning generated by the software and could, in fact, be turned off.

In a more recent, and unfortunate, situation, a student complained because she had posted a response to another student that had been inadvertently deleted when the first student deleted his initial post. Although students had been cautioned by us that this was a feature of the software and were encouraged to modify rather than delete posts, this incident occurred. It allowed us, however, to open an area of discussion around the impact of technology on the learning process from which all of the students benefited.

When a student has ongoing concerns that seem unresolvable online, it is important for the instructor to encourage phone or e-mail contact to resolve these concerns. The instructor must be familiar with the software or be willing to do what it takes to get the issue resolved. If the student is having difficulty obtaining satisfactory technical support from the source designated by the institution, the instructor may need to act as an intermediary in order to maintain the flow of the class and instruct the students around technical issues. Face-to-face sessions may need to be set up to ensure that students can use the technology. In one situation, we were geographically distant from a student who was struggling with the technology used in a course, so we paired that student with another student in his geographic area to help him get connected and functioning online.

Once the process of learning about technology has begun in whatever way necessary, students will begin to feel comfortable about acquiring additional knowledge about technology. If there are numerous issues and concerns about the use of the technology, or if students are interested in further exploring the use of technology as part of their involvement with the course, the instructor may want to consider setting up a separate discussion forum to deal with those issues. If a separate item is created, it is then important to direct students to use it. Often we use the questions forum for these issues and encourage students to use it to ask questions about either the content or the technology. A gentle reminder about where to post what helps keep this material separate from the discussion of course content.

Comfort in starting is the key, however. If early attempts are frustrating, students may become reluctant to further explore their abilities in this area, thus thwarting further involvement with online learning. Consequently, learning about technology by using it becomes one of the desired learning outcomes for an online course.

SELF-REFLECTION

Self-reflection is distinctly different from the types of reflection we have been discussing. Cranton (2006) and Mezirow (2003) believe that critical self-reflection is a crucial component of transformative learning and that, in fact, transformative learning cannot occur without it. It is not about how I learn or what I am learning about technology; it is instead about who I am as a person. Has that perception of myself changed as I have participated in an online course? Have I revealed a part of myself that has not been revealed in other settings? Again, it is a process that participants may or may not be conscious of. When an opening is created through which students can reflect on change, however, students are likely to note the changes.

> Okay, I am going to jump right in this conflict. It seems to me that if we were to go back to f2f classroom situation we would have some conflict. It could be the type that helps or betters the group. We have become an organization. We have decided in a way that there are a lot of good things that come out of this bunch. We have some ideas that do help us all understand a little better what we are talking about and to also help jar our thoughts to think a bit farther. We have become so dependent on the ability to do this at our time and our own rate of thinking that the creative thinking is beginning to develop. I am afraid that the openness and the ease of typing would out weigh the f2f tension. We each one sit back and think over each posting before we join in. *Mason*

The changes in self being reflected here are the ability to connect to others, the ability to take time to think and thus think more deeply, and the emergence of creativity. This occurs through a constant process of looking back and taking stock. As the course progresses, participants cannot help but remember what things were like for them as they entered this new, perhaps previously unexplored realm, and to comment on the differences. This process, then, is historical; it takes stock of our shared history and records it as we progress through the course. But the reflective process does not end with history taking. It also looks ahead as to how this process will affect the learner in the future. Mezirow (1991) refers to this component of learning as a process of using a prior interpretation to revise or create a new interpretation of one's experience as a means by which to guide future action. Encouraging students to keep a journal of reflections during the course can assist them in participating in this reflective process. Journals can be kept privately or can be posted to the course in the form of a blog. Regardless of how the journal is kept, Cranton (2006) notes that it should not be graded for content or grammar, but instead, students should be given credit simply for doing it.

The Reflective Process

Cranton suggests that students be given some suggestions for keeping their reflections, but that the reflective process through the use of a journal or blog is highly individual—students should reflect in whatever way seems comfortable to them. When we incorporate this historical process into the online classroom, we find it is important to ask such questions as, "How were you as a learner before you came into this course? How have you changed? How do you anticipate this will affect your learning in the future?" As previously mentioned, this is an important component of the evaluation of a course, as it helps us know whether we have achieved our learning objectives. However, in order to promote the process of transformative learning, we must ask these questions throughout the course. The answers help us stay on target and provide additional support for the process of transformative learning as it occurs. The following final post illustrates the historical nature of transformative learning.

> Uniqueness? Boy that is not the only word for it. This class was the first class that I have taken on a computer. This has allowed me to expand my paradigms of learning. I have used many different ways of studying from the Internet to just thinking in an unusual manner about what was said on-line. I have always been a listener and not much of a face to face interaction person or at least the interaction may not have a great deal of thought. But with this communication resource we have developed a method of feedback that has seemed very effective for a better learning base. . . . . The openness gave us a chance to follow up on the postings,

research the subject, develop empathy, trust in everyone's thoughts, simplify the language, and use our time effectively. Although we did not have the nonverbal traditional communication, we did have the personalities and the quirks of some come through the postings. I really feel that we have had a good group of people to work with and we have all come a long way. . . . I really feel that this medium of an online class has given me the best opportunity to learn in the method that meets my learning style. . . . This class has been an opening into the confidence of tackling a business organization. On a scale of learning material from a class that will be useful in the business world——this class would receive a 9 to 9.5 (10 being the best). . . . But I have found myself asking other people in the business world for input. That's new for me . . . I think you could say I have grown up some. I would love to see more classes like this. . . . I know that I have not done well in the traditional classroom on several occasions but in this class I feel pretty good about my work. . . . It really got to the point that we (the participants) were all the teachers. *Rob*

This post illustrates that, as instructors, we were successful in initiating a process of transformative learning. Rob is able to reflect on how he has been as a learner, what he has gained, how he has reframed and reinterpreted his learning as the result of this learning experience. He has already begun to apply his new views of himself and of knowledge in the world outside the university. Rob will take this new view of himself into future learning experiences and will probably experience greater success as a learner, even in a traditional setting, because his sense of empowerment and confidence have grown.

Encouraging Conscious Reflection and Acknowledging the Unconscious

In Chapter Two, we discussed the concept of the *electronic personality* (Pratt, 1996), meaning that what is going on inside the learner inevitably shows up on the screen. As we encourage conscious, critical reflection of the material and self, this is far more likely to occur. As a course progresses and participants become more comfortable with the environment, as well as feel the increasing support from their colleagues, they may feel more comfortable with letting elements of their personalities, previously unrevealed, emerge on the screen. The following are examples of posts by an undergraduate student in a class on organizational behavior. At the beginning of the term, his posts typically looked like the one that follows (it appears exactly as it did in the online classroom):

> I THINK ONE OF THE DRAWBACKS IS A TIME FACTOR WE DONT HAVE AS QUICK OF A DISCUSSION, WE AREN'T ALL ON AT THE SAME TIME AND THAT CAN MAKE THINGS A LITTLE DELAYED. ALSO IF YOU WANT TO SAY SOMETHING SOMETIMES YOUR FACIAL EXPRESSIONS AREN'T INVOLVED AND THERE COULD BE A BARRIER TO CROSS AND THIRD SOME PEOPLE CANT WRITE AND THIS COULD AFFECT THEM THE MOST CAUSE THEY Can't put their thoughts into words, but for the most part i am happy with this class overall! *Mike*

Mike was immediately given feedback about posting all in capital letters. In the online world, posting in capital letters generally means that one is screaming. He continued to experiment with the way he posted, and by the middle of the term he had discovered a way of posting that was comfortable for him. The following two posts illustrate the method he chose.

> i think there are many issues which we have dealt with in our little cyberspace world and each person has had a different way of dealing with them. most of the people on here have went to dr. pratt when they have experienced some sort of problem, f2f that is. not many have emailed or tried to get in touch with dr. pratt on here though. i think that is because of the newness of all of this. we still feel a little uncomfortable dealing with everything on here. also the people who do not want to talk f2f do not do anything on here to communicate they just wait for someone to get a hold of them. *Mike*

> to me conflict is a disagreement n beliefs or thought, it doesn't necessarily have 2 b verbalized, but it is known. if there is conflict btween 2 people n a group they each know it, but don't have 2 make it affect them. *Mike*

Although these posts might make a professor of composition shudder, we are thrilled to see posts like this. They are indications that students are attempting to express who they are textually. Mike is clearly expressing his uniqueness as a person while reflecting on the material being studied in the course. He switched from all capitals to all lowercase letters. Although this generally means that someone is diminishing their contribution in the online world, Mike is clearly not doing that. His posts are transformative in nature. He is looking at and commenting on the process of online learning as he is experiencing it, as well as how he sees the involvement of his student colleagues. In addition, he is clearly engaged with and reflecting on the course material. If Mike had submitted these posts as written material in a traditional classroom, he would probably have failed the assignment or been asked, at the very least, to revise it. In the online classroom, however, he is surfacing a part of him that others would not normally see—his online personality, also known as social presence.

FINAL THOUGHTS: WE ARE THE EXPERTS WHEN IT COMES TO OUR OWN LEARNING

Although it may seem daunting to an instructor in an online course to be far more than someone who imparts knowledge, there is no need to be fearful of the transformative process that this form of learning sets in motion. It is a process that will occur, whether or not an instructor purposefully facilitates it, when the course is designed to allow participants to explore beyond the confines of the course material. The subtitle of this section—We Are the Experts When It Comes to Our Own Learning—defines the transformative learning process.

When students are empowered to become experts at their own learning, they cannot help but be transformed as people. Their self-esteem rises, as does their confidence in their abilities. They learn about areas they never thought possible before, one of which may be technology. The main task of instructors as facilitators of this process is to bring forth their best instructional practices and then get out of the way. If an instructor is willing and able to give up control of the process, amazing things can happen. Students who may sit quietly and not do well in the traditional classroom may emerge as the leaders in the online classroom, presenting thoughtful and knowledgeable material for others to consider. Rather than something to be feared, the transformative learning process is one of the most exciting aspects of online learning. It can also be purposefully integrated into the assessment of individual performance within the course, as well as evaluation of the course itself—topics we discuss in the next chapter. The following are some questions to consider in order to welcome and facilitate the occurrence of transformative learning in an online course.

GUIDING QUESTIONS TO PROMOTE TRANSFORMATIVE LEARNING

The following questions are designed not only to allow for reflection on the transformative learning process as it occurs in an online course but also to reflect on an instructor's level of comfort with the process. Stephen Brookfield (1995) notes that "those of us who are trying to get colleagues to identify and question their assumptions, or to look at their practice through different lenses, must do the same" (p. 205). If an instructor is uncomfortable with this aspect of online teaching, it is likely to be missed or discouraged in the context of the course. Therefore, the questions that follow are self-reflective. We cannot encourage our students to engage in a transformative process if we are unwilling to do so ourselves.

- How do I view myself as an instructor? Do I see myself as an expert? Am I open to the views and opinions of others? How do I process those views when I encounter them?

- How much more do I feel I need to learn about teaching and about my subject matter?

- How do I generally run a class? Do I rely on lecture and discussion methods?

- In the traditional classroom setting, do I empower students to pursue knowledge on their own? Do I routinely incorporate collaborative exercises and assignments into my courses?

- How do discussions generally go in my courses? Are they dominated by a few? Are my classes truly interactive?

- How comfortable do I feel with the concept of promoting self-knowledge in learners? Do I honestly feel that this should be the work of someone other than a teacher, such as a counselor or therapist?

- How comfortable am I when students disagree with my point of view? How would I feel if a student suggested that I read material they have discovered in their learning process?

- Do I feel that I need to maintain control of the learning environment? How comfortable would I feel in giving over that control to the learners and being an equal participant?

- How comfortable am I with receiving material from students that is not grammatically correct and well written but is nevertheless an expression of self?

- How do I define learning? What do I hope to see as learning outcomes from an online class?

Student Assessment and Course Evaluation

In the previous chapter we discussed several places in an online course where the process of transformative learning logically connects to assessment and evaluation. When we refer to *assessment,* we are referring to assessment of student performance, including student critical self-evaluation. *Evaluation* refers to the course and the quality of instruction, as well as the technology being used, including its functionality and user-friendliness. Finally, the total online program should be evaluated in terms of its usefulness in the overall institutional context. All of these forms of assessment and evaluation should lead to an ongoing process of planning and review so that online courses and programs can be continuously improved.

ASSESSMENT AND EVALUATION BASICS

Course and student progress evaluation generally take two forms: *formative* and *summative* evaluation. Formative evaluation is an ongoing process that can occur at any point throughout the course; it can surface gaps in course material or in learners' ability to grasp that material. Formative evaluation gives instructors a way to shift focus if the course is not proceeding according to plan. Summative evaluation assesses the completed course and is most often the model of evaluation used in academic institutions. Stephen Brookfield (1995), in commenting on the reliance on summative evaluation, states that this form of evaluation is really a measure of student satisfaction with the course and the instructor and not a measure of the dynamics and rhythms of student learning. He advocates for another form of evaluation when he states: "Knowing something of how students experience learning helps us build convincing connections between what we want them to do and their own concerns and expectations" (p. 93).

Evaluating an online course using only summative methods ignores many of the important concepts we have been discussing that are related to this form of teaching and learning. If instructors are truly establishing a collaborative, transformative process, then formative as well as summative evaluation must be used. Formative evaluation helps determine to what extent instructors are successfully facilitating reflection on the course material under study, reflection on this means of learning, and reflection on self as a learner as the course progresses. Summative evaluation helps us know how well we have achieved the goals and learning outcomes we established going into the course. We now look at each of these forms of evaluation and discuss ways to accomplish them in an online course. In addition, we explore the areas in need of evaluation and suggest ways to do so.

STUDENT PERFORMANCE

Harasim and others (1996), in reflecting on the evaluation of online courses, state: "In keeping with a learner-centered approach, evaluation and assessment should be part of the learning-teaching process, embedded in class activities and in the interactions between learners and between learners and teachers" (p. 167). They are describing an ongoing formative evaluation process that is built into the class structure.

If instructors have done a good job of establishing learning guidelines and outcomes, as well as the criteria for evaluating student performance, then establishing a formative process of student assessment should be relatively easy. These assessments should take multiple sources of data into account, such as the quantity of posts and the quality of participation in the online discussion. Performance on course assignments and other class exercises should also be considered. Morgan and O'Reilly (1999) note that the purpose of student assessment is to provide support and feedback to enhance ongoing learning and to report on what students have already achieved. Angelo and Cross (1993) state that most instructors aspire to assess more than the skills and knowledge related to the content area being taught. The goal is to use the course content to teach students to think—in other words, to help them develop good critical thinking ability and to apply what they are learning in other contexts. How to do that effectively becomes the primary concern of the instructor.

As can be noted by the examples of student posts used to illustrate various points throughout this book, we continuously scan the online dialogue for spontaneous comments related to learning objectives and the quality of the learning experience. The dialogue generated in an online course can be a rich source of evaluation material if an instructor remains alert to its presence, seeking examples as they appear.

Using the Dialogue as a Source of Evaluative Material

In addition to scanning the dialogue for spontaneous posts of evaluative material, instructors can post questions for students to consider that relate the material under study to the process of the online group. This can provide yet another source of data for evaluation of course effectiveness and assessment of student performance. For example, in one author's undergraduate organizational behavior class, he related the material in the text on conflict in organizations to conflict in the group when he asked the following: "The book states that 'conflict between groups is inevitable' and that the conflict will be either positive or negative. Do you believe that if I put this group back into the face-to-face classroom that there would be conflict? If so what type of conflict? What could be done to prevent the conflict? What steps could I take to build a cohesive team if this happened?" By asking this type of question, we hope that, through their responses, group members will begin to look at and evaluate their own process, thus providing the instructor with important information. In this case, students were asked to compare their process online to what might occur if they were face-to-face. We were looking here for indicators of how well the group was coalescing online and whether or not the skills being learned in this medium were transferable to the traditional face-to-face classroom. The following responses to the question posed indicate how well this process was occurring.

> As a group I think the online students would have positive conflict with the traditional class. We would have different opinions, because we are different types of people. We had the choice to enter the online class. Like last week's discussion stated, we think that the advantages outweigh

the need to be in the classroom. The people who chose the traditional class obviously felt the classroom would be better for them. There is conflict, but we could learn from each other about our experiences. I think the first step in building a cohesive team is to recognize and understand each individual's strengths and weaknesses. Consider a group working on a project, composed of traditional and online students. The traditional students might be more comfortable around people. It would make sense for them be the presenters. The online students might be more comfortable putting the ideas down on paper. *Jason*

I agree with Jason. I think that we are sensitive to each others feelings in the online class because we like to keep the conversation going and respect that the other people are posting. For example, when Stacy and I discussed that one week about [another professor], I saw her at track practice and she asked if I was offended by anything that she said. We were honest and just said we were only stating our opinions, no hard feelings. In the normal classroom, sometimes things are taken the wrong way when there is disagreement and one person may have hurt feelings or hold a grudge. *Carmen*

These posts indicate that students are reflecting on the process of the online classroom and offering ideas and opinions about why they feel it is working well for them. We can also tell that the group has coalesced and that this coalescence is extending beyond the online realm. They are seeking each other out in other situations and checking with each other about the nature and impact of their work online. In addition, inferences are being made about how the participants might deal with issues in the face-to-face classroom differently, based on their experiences online. This material provides a part of the ongoing evaluation of the occurrence of collaborative and transformative learning—two desired learning outcomes for this course. Through asking this type of question, the instructor has contributed to the ongoing formative assessment of student performance in this course.

Assessing Student Assignments

One of the fears we frequently hear expressed by instructors as we present our workshops on teaching and learning online has to do with cheating. Instructors want to know how to monitor or eliminate cheating in the online environment.

Because the instructor is not in complete control of the learning process in online courses and is unable to physically see the learners, it has been assumed that the occurrence of plagiarism and cheating is greater online than in the face-to-face classroom. Some institutions have adopted surveillance methods such as desktop cameras and retina scanners to authenticate virtual student identity during exams. Others use plagiarism detection services to scan student papers for evidence of plagiarism. Unfortunately, this creates a sense that institutions and their instructors believe that students are inclined to cheat rather than do their own work. Recent studies, however, indicate that this is not the case: plagiarism and cheating occur as frequently online as they do in face-to-face classes (Kellogg, 2002). Although Morgan and O'Reilly (1999) believe that most distance learners are adults and therefore uninterested in taking the work of another, this may be a fairly optimistic view in that cheating and plagiarism do happen online and we cannot ignore their occurrence. Harris (2002) notes that most plagiarism and cheating in online courses occur because of lack of knowledge about copyright and fair use regulations. Proactive steps to avoid cheating and plagiarism are therefore far more effective than the various extreme reactions of denying their existence, overreacting to the possibility that they do occur, or alienating students through a lack of trust.

We hope we have conveyed that when a course is well constructed, is learner-centered, community-based, and promotes learner empowerment and self-reflection, the notion of cheating should not become a concern. Benson (2002) notes that a mistake instructors make is reliance on one assessment measure throughout the course, which can increase the incidence of cheating. If the assignments are varied, promote the use of critical thinking, and are designed to be shared with the remainder of the group, then participants gain a sense of responsibility for producing pieces of learning that will be useful for the others in the group and also take more care and pride in producing it. In addition, the inclusion of varied assignments that promote critical thinking skills and collaboration, rather than individualism and competition, will also help reduce the temptation to cheat. As one of our participants aptly put it, "We [the participants] were all the teachers for one another." Our experience has shown us that if we trust and empower our learners, they realize that they are the experts at their own learning. Cheating should become irrelevant in this process because the participant would be cheating only himself or herself.

Grading student assignments can be accomplished in a number of ways. First, we frequently ask students to submit a self-assessment as part of the closure process for the course. In it, we ask how well students feel they have met their learning goals for the course and how well they feel they performed overall. We often ask students in a graded course to determine what grade they think they have earned. Second, in a large class that has been divided up into work teams, the group may be asked to appoint a leader who can, if the instructor feels comfortable with this, suggest grades for team members based on their level of contribution to the group. The group itself can also negotiate a group grade on collaborative assignments. Finally, we frequently refer to the guidelines established at the beginning of the class to determine the relative weight placed on each course aspect. In a class that relies heavily on discussion, the quality and quantity of student posts become assessment material. Assignments or exams are reviewed separately; all are averaged, along with participation, at the end of the class.

We also use rubrics to assess student performance. Rubrics, when posted in the course, can assist students with their self-assessments by allowing them to compare their own performance against the performance standards established by the instructor. This is particularly useful in assessing participation in discussions—an area that is often more subjectively assessed than performance on a particular assignment. We use the following fairly simple standards to create a discussion rubric and then build a more substantive rubric from there:

A = Synthesis level work. The student is demonstrating the ability to evaluate course material and apply it, thus leading to the development of new knowledge.

B = Analytic level work. The student demonstrates the ability to critically analyze material, but application is lacking or inconsistent.

C = Summary level work. The student demonstrates that course material has been read, but little to no evidence of analysis or application exists.

Exhibit 10.1 is an example of a discussion rubric that incorporates these principles.

If an instructor wants to include examinations and quizzes in the assessment of student performance, additional planning must be made. Most course management systems allow for the creation of online tests and quizzes, with the added feature of allowing students to receive immediate feedback on correct answers. The results of these tests and quizzes are usually stored in an encrypted data file that is not accessible to students. Consequently, an instructor can be relatively assured

Exhibit 10.1.
Discussion Grading Rubric.

Criteria	Non-Performance	Basic	Proficient	Distinguished
Includes and applies relevant course concepts, theories, or materials correctly with citation of sources	Does not explain relevant course concepts, theories, or materials. Does not provide citation of sources.	Summarizes relevant course concepts, theories, or materials. Provides citation some of the time.	Applies and analyzes relevant course concepts, theories, or materials correctly. Provides citation most of the time.	Evaluates and synthesizes course concepts, theories, or materials correctly, using examples or supporting evidence. Consistently provides citation.
Responds to fellow learners, relating the discussion to relevant course concepts and providing substantive feedback.	Does not respond to fellow learners.	Responds to fellow learners without relating discussion to the relevant course concepts. Provides feedback, but it is not substantive.	Responds to fellow learners, relating the discussion to relevant course concepts. Feedback is substantive most of the time.	Responds to fellow learners, relating the discussion to relevant course concepts and consistently extends the dialogue through provision of substantive feedback.
Applies relevant professional, personal, or other real-world experiences.	Does not contribute professional, personal, or other real-world experiences.	Contributes some professional, personal, or other real-world experiences that may or may not relate to course content.	Applies relevant professional, personal, or other real-world experiences.	Applies relevant professional, personal, or other real-world experiences and extends the dialogue by responding to the examples of peers.
Supports position with applicable resources beyond assigned reading.	Does not establish relevant position.	Establishes relevant position but does minimal outside research.	Consistently supports position with additional resources.	Validates position with applicable resources and supports the learning of others through the contribution of additional resources.

that once students take an exam, they will be unable to alter the results. The instructor cannot be certain, however, that the student whose name appears on the exam is the person who actually took it. Consequently, some instructors have used proctored testing sites, either on campus or in remote locations, to gain some assurance that this form of cheating will not occur. In addition, instructors have made arrangements to use remote facilities in courses in which lab work is necessary. This allows for the online teaching of science courses, as well as courses that require face-to-face contact, such as courses in counseling techniques. Other techniques include laboratory exercises on videotapes or CD-ROMs that are sent to the participants, as well as computer-based simulations. Once again, however, we issue a caution: including such materials assumes that students can receive and work with them. Instructors must either make the use of these materials a condition of enrollment in the course or adapt them for those who, for whatever reason, cannot use them.

Using Collaborative Assessment

The assessment of student assignments in an online course should not be the job of the instructor alone. Students should be asked to assess their own performance and to receive feedback from each other throughout the course. Developing skills in giving effective feedback and in self-assessment can be useful in the promotion of collaborative and transformative learning. Wiggins (1998), in his book *Educative Assessment,* gives further credence to the use of ongoing feedback when he states: "The receipt and use of feedback must be an ongoing, routine part of assessment. The reason for making feedback concurrent with performing is that this is the only way students can learn to self-assess continually and then self-adjust their intellectual performance, just as musicians, artists, athletes, and other performers continually self-assess and self-adjust" (pp. 59–60).

We are describing a form of *360-degree feedback,* as it is termed in the business world (London and Beatty, 1993). In a business organization, an employee receiving such feedback compares anonymous feedback from a superior, subordinates, and peers with self-perception of performance. In the online course, self-perception is compared against feedback from the instructor and peers—feedback that may be private but not anonymous. This feedback can be delivered to a participant privately, through the use of e-mail or private postings on the discussion board, or it can be posted on the course site for the group to see and review. If the latter approach is used, the instructor needs to feel comfortable that adequate trust exists within the group, that feedback is professionally delivered, and that it will promote continuous quality improvement and enhancement of the learning process. Although feedback on performance can be shared in this way, grades, which are a private concern, should never be posted to a public discussion board.

Brookfield (1995) discusses the importance of taking into account the students' perception of their own progress. What seems like minimal progress to an instructor may be a major leap in a student's eyes. Consequently, students' self-assessment regarding the amount of learning gained and learning objectives achieved is often just as important, or more so, than the instructor's opinion of their work. The following is an example of the type of self-assessment we seek:

> I have learned—I have so much to learn!
> I have learned—Online communication gives a whole new meaning to "reading between the lines!"
> I have learned—Even if it feels bad, it might not be bad. Growing pains?:-)
> I have learned—How rich and wonderful are the perspectives of others!
> Thank you to all of you for being partners and teachers! *Judy*

And another example:

> My experience in this program has really been an exercise in trust. Trusting myself, trusting others and trusting in the process. I now have a clearer understanding of the "trust" concept thanks to Johnson & Johnson. It was a light-bulb moment for me when I read Johnson's & Johnson's assertion that, "Trust exists in relationships, not in someone's personality." (Johnson & Johnson, p. 132) This was significant for me because I was often confused about my ability to trust easily in certain situations, (e.g. this course, my women's empowerment group) and not others (e.g. with certain work colleagues). My experience in [this group] also reinforced another of Johnson's & Johnson's thoughts about trust, "Initial trusting and trustworthy actions within a group can create a self-fulfilling prophecy." (Johnson & Johnson, p. 132)
>
> At mid-term, [this group] was described as somewhat of an enigma – that our group development path didn't necessarily conform to a traditional model. I embrace the fact that we carved our own path and have

created some synergies. I know that both the text and the interaction with my fellow group members continue to be revealing to me (about me?!) and for that, I am grateful. *Linda*

Collaborative assignments should be assessed collaboratively. Often we ask our students to send a private e-mail with a self-assessment of their performance in the group along with an assessment of the performance of their teammates with a grade assigned. Generally, we will use those assessments in conjunction with a group grade for the final product of the collaboration.

Additional Assessment Considerations

Additional considerations in assessing student assignments in an online course are the needs and learning objectives students identified at the start of the course, their educational level, their familiarity with technology and online learning (and any problems that may have occurred as they adjusted to the use of technology), and issues related to writing. Finally, the assessment of participation is critical.

Because we use a learner-centered approach in the online classroom, assessment of student assignments must take into account how well the assignment met the learning needs of the participant. Requesting that students give us feedback on the utility of an assignment in their learning process assists us with ongoing evaluation of the course as well. We have received feedback such as, "This was a great case to work with. It stimulated my thinking." However, receiving feedback such as, "I didn't find the question of the week very interesting and I really had to push myself to say anything," also gives us a great deal of information about how well we are meeting the learning objectives of a particular student and what kinds of adjustments need to be made in order to make the class more challenging.

As feedback is provided to students, it is once again important to consider their level of experience educationally and in the online environment. Some students may take longer to become involved in the online discussion if they are experiencing technical difficulties or adjusting to the use of technology for the first time. These students should be encouraged through feedback about the progress they are making in this regard and not penalized in their assessments because they are not as technologically adept as others in the group.

Except in the submission of assignments, we usually do not comment on the mechanics of writing as they pertain to online posts. Because students frequently compose their posts while online, they are likely to make spelling and grammar errors. Students for whom English is not their primary language may have numerous writing errors in their posts. We have found that encouraging students to post without editing promotes spontaneity and liveliness in the discussion. When students are concerned about being corrected for the spelling and grammar in their posts, they may not post as often or may become uncomfortable and discouraged with the medium. However, if a student's writing is such that the student is unable to convey his or her thoughts well online, or if other students express concern about their ability to understand, then the instructor should make contact with the student privately and suggest ways in which the student can receive writing assistance. At the very least, the student should be encouraged to compose responses in a word processing program, where he or she can check spelling and grammar more easily prior to posting.

Significant weight must be placed on the level and quality of participation in an online course, which is not true in a traditional face-to-face course. We have discussed the importance of establishing participation guidelines at the onset. Having established guidelines, we have a responsibility to follow up and assess the quantity and quality of participation at the close of the course when we award grades, if letter grades are an institutional requirement. Many course management systems allow an instructor to request reports of how many times and when students have accessed the course site, whether they posted or not. If this is not built into the software, an instructor may choose to count the number of posts per student as a means of evaluating attendance and level of participation. These measures are particularly useful in academic institutions requiring attendance reports from instructors at the close of a term.

Good participation should be recognized and subsequently rewarded, and instructors must feel comfortable with the added weight that must be placed on this element of the course. A department chair, who had taught only one course online and whose responsibility was to review all course syllabi in his department, established a requirement for all instructors that the maximum weight permitted for the grading of class participation be 10 percent. Discussion with him revealed that he thought it was punitive to quieter students to demand more participation. He had a difficult time understanding that in the online classroom, posting to the course site represents the bulk of the course. He also admitted that his first online course had been a dismal failure due to lack of participation. The "quieter students" in an online course are simply not there. Following our conversation, he agreed to reconsider his decision and allow online instructors the leeway to establish participation guidelines that make sense for that medium.

Aligning Assessment with Course Design

One critical factor in assessment that is often overlooked is the need to link course design and assessment. In other words, assessment should fit the context of the course, align with learning objectives and the competencies that the instructor wants to see learners achieve, and fit with the types of activities in which the learners are engaged. For example, an instructor would not want to assess a collaborative small group project through the use of a test or quiz, but that might be useful in helping students see how much they had gotten from the reading for a course. The use of authentic assessments, or simulated real-life application of material, can help achieve alignment in that these types of assessments directly address outcomes and competencies for the course. Assessment should not be seen as a separate, cumbersome task but should flow from course activities (Morgan and O'Reilly, 1999). When assessment is in alignment with the course as a whole, learner satisfaction with the online learning experience increases significantly and instructor worries over potential cheating decreases due to the authenticity of the material produced by the learners.

COURSE EVALUATION

Many academic institutions require a course evaluation format that is standardized across the organization. These evaluation forms rarely address whether a class has supported students in achieving their learning objectives. Instead, they tend to evaluate whether the student liked the instructor or the course (Brookfield, 1995). Particularly in the case of adjunct instructors, these evaluations are used to determine whether the instructor will be retained to teach again and are more a measure of popularity than of learning achievement.

Given the nature of the online course and the myriad goals it is attempting to achieve, this type of course evaluation form is not very useful in determining whether the course was successful in achieving the course objectives. However, it will tell us whether students enjoyed learning in this fashion. In addition, the interpretation of the data received is at issue because of the technology being used to deliver the course. We now turn to the elements of a good course evaluation in the online environment, as well as the elements that need to be taken into account as that evaluation is interpreted.

Elements of Course Evaluations in the Online Classroom

At the beginning of this chapter, we discussed the importance of using formative evaluation in the online classroom. Questions need to be asked throughout to determine how students are experiencing the course, the mode of instruction, and the online environment. At a minimum, these types of questions need to be asked of students midway through the course and again at the end. Based on the answers, instructors need to be prepared to alter the direction of the course to make it more responsive to the needs of the learners.

Participants are often unwilling to be completely honest about their evaluation of a course or an instructor due to fear of repercussions (Brookfield, 1995). Consequently, the willingness of participants to be honest will relate to whether a trusting, cohesive community among the learners has been established—one that includes the instructor as an equal member. The following responses to questions evaluating an online course at its conclusion are indicative that trust has been developed and that students are willing, at least to some degree, to be honest about their experience in the course.

> I loved this class! It gave me the freedom to come to class when I wanted and not have to look at that ugly teacher for another class. I think that teaching a class through this medium forces people to learn to communicate through words, and gives them confidence in what they are saying. In a classroom some people are afraid to speak because of the thought of being wrong, but here they have no choice, saying nothing is wrong. For me this class allowed me to sleep when I wanted to and study when I wanted. At a university that is as controlling as [ours] is this class was the complete opposite. We all had the freedom that [our university] does not want us to have, to come and go as we please. *Mason*

> Another shortcoming I saw in the class was the actual work itself. It was difficult to discuss one question for a whole week. Sometimes an

expression of our views was all that was required. Once my thoughts were posted, there wasn't much more to say. With that, I would like to express my thanks to the instructors for trying to keep the ball rolling every week. More variety would have made for a more interesting class. I liked the group work. It was different to collaborate to achieve a common goal instead of expressing individual opinions. I realize that this medium has certain limitations but other group projects would have been fun. . . . I didn't like the confusion we experienced when choosing teams. I know that it was mostly the students' fault but that was one situation where it would have been easier to have everyone together in a room. . . . I was also disappointed with the user interface. I thought it was a bit outdated. That is a tedious complaint and should receive no real attention, but I thought I would share my view. *Jason*

When students are given the opportunity to provide course and instructor feedback anonymously in a face-to-face classroom, they sometimes feel comfortable being painfully honest about their experiences in the class. The difference here is that the feedback is being owned and shared by the participants. Clearly, these students felt that their opinions and feedback would be used in the spirit in which they were delivered—to work toward continuous improvement of the class and instructional methods they had just experienced. The honesty with which these thoughts are delivered indicates that trust has developed in the group and with the instructor. The comments demonstrate the achievement of the more important learning objectives for the class.

Interpretation of the Feedback

The difficulty with receiving feedback such as that presented in the previous section lies in its reception. The instructor and the institution should receive and interpret it without assuming that the course has been a failure. Stephen Brookfield (1995) comments on this phenomenon.

> Many teachers take an understandable pride in their craft wisdom and knowledge. They want to be good at what they do, and consequently, set great store by students' evaluations of their teaching. When these are less than perfect—as is almost inevitable—teachers assume the

worst. All those evaluations that are complimentary are forgotten, those that are negative assume disproportionate significance. Indeed, the inference is often made that bad evaluations must, by definition, be written by students with heightened powers of pedagogic discrimination. Conversely, good evaluations are thought to be produced by students who are half-asleep [p. 17].

As we think about the receipt of feedback, it is important to consider the additional constraints that the online classroom provides. In a face-to-face classroom, an instructor can fairly easily establish a sense of presence. Students can see them and interact with them. One instructor may be active and lively. Another may tell lots of stories and jokes; yet another may be more somber and serious. When students evaluate a course in which they see the instructor in action, they cannot help but take these factors into account. In an online classroom, however, the instructor is represented predominantly by text. Just as with their students, an instructor's engagement with the material and the course is demonstrated through the number, length, and quality of his or her posts. In many cases, the students and instructor may never meet. The physical manifestation of the instructor may be a photograph on a homepage. Although this creates a difficult evaluation process, it also serves, on some level, to make the feedback received from students more valuable, as it relates directly to their experience of the course and the material they have studied rather than reflecting the personality of the instructor. The degree to which the instructor can successfully establish his or her social, teaching, and cognitive presence (Garrison, Anderson, and Archer, 2000) should be part of what is being evaluated by students, and questions that address those elements should be included in a good course evaluation.

Brookfield (1995) recommends soliciting a letter to successors as a form of evaluation for a course. He asks his students to write letters to the next group of students who will take the course, offering advice and suggestions for preparation. We have used this technique online as well and find that even though students are either posting these letters to the course site or e-mailing them to us, the idea that they are communicating with another student, even fictitiously, frees them up to be more honest about their course experiences—sometimes painfully so! We have used these letters to help us rethink a course or course activities and find this technique to be extremely useful.

PROGRAM EVALUATION

The last but certainly not the least important area in need of evaluation is the online program itself. Ideally, good planning and thinking have gone into the creation of an online program. But even when this is not the case, it is important to receive feedback from participants on their overall experience of working online through the institution. It is important to determine how well the technology worked for them and whether they received the technical support they needed, as well as solicit any suggestions they might have for additional courses to be offered online. Not only do participants need to be involved in this level of evaluation but also faculty should also provide feedback on their experience of teaching in the online environment and offer what they feel is needed to improve it.

Program evaluation begins with the planning phase of an educational program and concludes with follow-up studies to determine the program's effectiveness. At its core is an attempt to determine the value of the educational program being offered (Caffarella, 2002). Given this, all constituents involved with the program need to be involved with its evaluation. In the case of the online program, the constituents include the participants, the faculty, and the institution through which the program was delivered. The three groups have different needs and concerns, however, that should be reviewed.

For participants, ease of access to the program, smooth, seamless delivery, instructor involvement, and availability of immediate support are generally of greatest concern. In addition, the breadth of the program, meaning the numbers and types of courses available, is important.

Faculty are also concerned with the ease of access and smooth delivery of the course. They, too, expect to receive support when needed. However, the greatest need for faculty in online learning is the availability of training to support their work online. The training they receive should not be limited to the technology used for course delivery but should include the pedagogy involved in online teaching. Institutions offering online distance learning programs need to ask faculty what their needs are in order to improve their work and offer courses that are of high quality. Which courses would faculty like to see offered online? Is there a need to assess student appropriateness for online courses? If so, how will this occur?

Currently, institutions tend to take all students who express an interest in or desire to participate in online work, as long as they meet internal academic requirements. Few institutions are assessing the appropriateness of a given student to participate in this medium. The following self-assessment appears on the website of De Anza College in Cupertino, California, but can be found on many sites on the Internet to help students determine whether they should participate in online learning. It has been adapted by a number of other institutions along the way, but thus far it is the only one we have encountered.

How well would Distance Learning courses fit your circumstances and lifestyle? Circle an answer for each question and score as directed below. Answer honestly—no one will see this but you! (Adapted from "Are Telecourses For Me?" and printed in the PBS-Adult Learning Service *The Agenda*, Spring, 1994, this questionnaire was developed by the Northern Virginia Community College Extended Learning Institute.)

1. My need to take this course now is:
   a. High—I need it immediately for a specific goal.
   b. Moderate—I could take it on campus later or substitute another course.
   c. Low—it could be postponed.
2. Feeling that I am part of a class is:
   a. Not particularly necessary to me.
   b. Somewhat important to me.
   c. Very important to me.
3. I would classify myself as someone who:
   a. Often get things done ahead of time.
   b. Needs reminding to get things done on time.
   c. Puts things off until the last minute or doesn't complete them.
   4. Classroom discussion is:
   a. Rarely helpful to me.
   b. Sometimes helpful to me.
   c. Almost always helpful to me.
   5. When an instructor hands out directions for an assignment, I prefer:
   a. Figuring out the instructions myself.
   b. Trying to follow the directions on my own, then asking for help as needed.
   c. Having the instructions explained to me.
6. I need faculty comments on my assignments:
   a. Within a few weeks, so I can review what I did.

b. Within a few days, or I forget what I did.

c. Right away, or I get very frustrated.

7. Considering my professional and personal schedule, the amount of time I have to work on a Distance Learning course is:

a. More than enough for an on campus course.

b. The same as for a class on campus.

c. Less than for a class on campus.

8. Coming to campus on a regular schedule is:

a. Extremely difficult for me—I have commitments (work, family, or personal) during times when classes are offered.

b. A little difficult, but I can rearrange my priorities to allow for regular attendance on campus.

c. Easy for me.

9. As a reader, I would classify myself as:

a. Good—I usually understand the text without help.

b. Average—I sometimes need help to understand the text.

c. Slower than average.

10. When I need help understanding the subject:

a. I am comfortable approaching an instructor to ask for clarification.

b. I am uncomfortable approaching an instructor, but do it anyway.

c. I never approach an instructor to admit I don't understand something.

Scoring

Add 3 points for each "a" that you circled, 2 for each "b," and 1 for each "c." If you scored 20 or over, a distance learning course is a real possibility for you. If you scored between 11 and 20, distance learning courses may work for you, but you may need to make a few adjustments in your schedule and study habits to succeed. If you scored 10 or less, distance learning may not currently be the best alternative for you; talk to your counselor.

Explanations

1. Distance Learning students sometimes neglect their courses because of personal or professional circumstances. Having a com-

pelling reason for taking the course helps motivate the student to stick with the course.

2. Some students prefer the independence of Distance Learning; others find the independence uncomfortable and miss being part of the classroom experience.

3. Distance Learning courses give students greater freedom of scheduling, but they can require more self-discipline than on-campus classes.

4. Some people learn best by interacting with other students and instructors. Others learn better by listening, reading and reviewing on their own. Some Distance Learning courses provide less opportunity for group interaction than most on-campus courses.

5. Distance Learning requires you to work from written directions.

6. It may take as long as two to three weeks to get comments back from your instructor in Distance Learning classes.

7. Distance Learning requires at least as much time as on-campus courses. Students surveyed say that Distance Learning courses are as hard or harder than on campus courses.

8. Most people who are successful with Distance Learning find it difficult to come to campus on a regular basis because of their work/family/personal schedules.

9. Print materials are the primary source of directions and information in Distance Learning courses.

10. Students who do well in Distance Learning courses are usually comfortable contacting the instructor as soon as they need help with the course.

Not all students will be successful in online learning. This self-assessment is one attempt at helping students decide whether this form of learning is appropriate for them. As mentioned earlier in the case of the student with no technical experience, however, even students with minimal technical expertise or who have not done particularly well in a face-to-face classroom may do well online. Another way, then, to establish appropriateness is to empower faculty to make that decision early in the course and enable them to move the student to a face-to-face situation should that be in the student's best interest. Furthermore, as students apply for admission to an online program or course, someone should discuss with them the rigors involved with this form of study, as well as the orientation to the demands of online learning. The use of well-developed online orientation courses can provide another screening device for students. A student who cannot successfully complete an online orientation course is not likely to be successful in the remainder of the program online.

It should not be assumed that all students can succeed in an online course; not all students succeed in a face-to-face environment. Institutional investment in this type of screening and orientation will provide benefits down the line. A continuous lack of success in an online program can reflect on the institution, resulting in lower enrollments and a perception that the online program is of poor quality. Therefore, these types of considerations are critical to the institutional planning of online coursework, as well as the evaluation of the effectiveness of the program.

Finally, institutions may want to consider the use of focus groups and strategic thinking with the students and the facilitators of online classes; focus groups should be conducted by someone outside the participating group. The use of this type of evaluative technique can provide the institution with valuable information from all sectors that can be used for the purpose of continuous quality improvement.

FINAL THOUGHTS

We cannot place enough emphasis on the importance of evaluating all aspects of the online course, from the performance of individual students to the effectiveness of the course and instructor to the effectiveness of the overall program. The ongoing use of good evaluation assists in expanding online programs and course offerings in a more deliberate way and helps attract students to this medium. Evaluation is an important component of good planning. It provides a feedback loop in the planning process that enables us to "walk our talk." As we ask our participants to reflect on the ways they have changed through their involvement in an online course, so should we ask ourselves how we might transform and improve our teaching and delivery of online classes and programs. This medium does not allow us to become complacent. It is developing much too rapidly for instructors and institutions to become too comfortable with their existing online programs.

Therefore, we owe it to our students and ourselves to keep abreast of the changes as they occur, be prepared to accept feedback, both positive and negative, and adapt our approaches and programs to the needs of our learners. In this learner-centered environment, this is the only approach that makes sense.

QUESTIONS TO CONSIDER IN STUDENT, COURSE, AND PROGRAM EVALUATION

The following is a sample of evaluation questions that might be used both midway and at the end of an online course to evaluate course effectiveness, the experience of online learning for the participants, and self-evaluation of the participants' perceptions of how well they achieved their learning objectives. This is not meant to be an exhaustive list but rather to stimulate thinking regarding the types of questions that might be asked in order to move beyond the traditional forms of evaluation. Many authors have written on the topics of course, student, and program evaluation. Three have, in part, inspired this list of questions: Stephen Brookfield (1995), Rosemary Caffarella (2002), and Grant Wiggins (1998). We encourage readers interested in moving in new directions with evaluation to review their work.

Student Evaluation

What was most useful to me in my learning process? What was least useful?

Did I achieve my learning objectives in this course? If yes, what did I achieve? If no, what got in the way of achieving those objectives?

What did I learn about my own learning process by taking this course? How did I change as a learner through my involvement with this course?

Do I feel that what I learned in and through this course will have application in other areas of my life? If so, where will I apply this knowledge?

How well did I participate in this course? Am I satisfied with my level and quality of participation?

Did I see myself as an active member of the group? Did I contribute adequately to collaborative assignments?

How would I evaluate my performance in this class overall?

Course and Instructor Evaluation

How well did the class meet your needs as a student?

How did you feel about the mode of instruction?

Did you feel that the instructor was responsive to you and the rest of the group?

How do you feel overall about online learning?

What did you see as the strengths of this class?

What recommendations would you make to the instructor of this course to improve it?

What advice would you give to future students who will take this course online?

Program Evaluation

How easy was it to access the course site?

How easy was it to navigate the course site once it was accessed?

Did you have any concerns about the software used?

Were you able to receive technical support when needed? How would you evaluate the quality of that support?

Do you feel that the online program should be expanded? Reduced? Kept about the same?

If you think the program should be expanded, what additional courses would you like to see offered?

Are you enrolled in an online degree program? How well is that program meeting your learning needs? What suggestions would you make to improve the quality of the program?

Lessons Learned and a Look Ahead

Online learning continues to be a growing phenomenon. When we wrote the first edition of this book, some people were dismayed by this fact; they believed this signaled the end of traditional classroom education as we know it. Others feared that as more and more courses appeared online the need for faculty would disappear. We have attempted to dispel some of those fears through the presentation of the form of pedagogy required for this mode of instruction—electronic pedagogy.

Distance learning will not replace the traditional classroom. However, it continues to appeal to growing numbers of nontraditional, and now traditional, students for a number of reasons, the main one being that the structure and confines of the traditional classroom simply do not work for many.

Electronic pedagogy does not advocate the elimination of faculty in the delivery of online courses. In fact, just the opposite is true. We are promoting the development of new approaches and skills for faculty so that their teaching online might be more effective. Electronic pedagogy is not about fancy software packages or simple course conversion. It is about developing the skills involved with community building among a group of learners so as to maximize the benefits and potential that this medium holds in the educational arena. In this final chapter, we summarize and review the important lessons we have learned through our experience of teaching online. We highlight the unanswered questions with which institutions continue to struggle as this phenomenon grows. Finally, we take a look ahead, suggesting implications and potential future directions for this work.

THE SIX ESSENTIAL ELEMENTS

At the conclusion of Chapter One, we offered six elements that we feel are critical to the success of distance learning: *honesty, responsiveness, relevance, respect, openness,* and *empowerment*. Although these are simple concepts, without any one of them a virtual learning community cannot function. We now discuss each of these in terms of its importance in the creation of a learning community and the contribution each makes to a successful outcome in an online learning experience.

Honesty

In order for participants to connect with each other, there must be a sense of safety and trust. Participants must feel comfortable that the others in the group are who they say they are and that they will post messages that provide open, honest feedback. In addition, participants must feel that their posts will be received in an atmosphere of caring, connection, and trust. If all of this is to occur, members of the online group must be honest with each other, and with the instructor or facilitator as well. If members of the group sense that the instructor is not being honest with them, they will have difficulty being honest with each other. Although honest feedback is sometimes difficult to hear, when delivered respectfully, it is critical to the development of an online learning community and to the transformative nature of this type of learning.

Responsiveness

An online learning community simply cannot exist unless members respond to each other. The instructor must respond quickly to the participants and be involved in the exchange. Unlike the face-to-face educational environment, learning in the online classroom only occurs when the participants interact with each other and with the instructor. Through interactions with each other, the members of the group create an understanding of the material they are struggling with together. They are mutually responsible for the acquisition of knowledge.

In addition, the importance of collaboration in achieving learning outcomes hinges on the group's ability to work with and respond to each other. Dialogue between a given student and the instructor simply is not enough. Faculty members who have never taught an online course have asked us, "Isn't this just like a correspondence course?" The interaction between and collaboration with other members of the group significantly distinguishes online distance learning from a correspondence course, even though online distance learning derives its roots there.

The responsiveness of the instructor to the needs and concerns of the participants is also a crucial element. If participants are struggling with the technology or with each other, the instructor should be prepared to quickly intervene. While an online course is in process, an instructor is on duty several days out of each week, not just while class is in session. This is not a responsibility to be taken lightly, either by faculty or by their institutions.

Relevance

The beauty of online distance learning is its ability to bring life in the outside world into the classroom. In order for students to get their "hands around" the topic they are studying, it must have some relevance for them. Relating the subject matter to their life experiences and being encouraged to seek out and share real-life examples to illustrate it only enhances the learning outcome. This practice also begins to promote a sense of being an expert when it comes to the learning process. Every participant has something relevant to share with the group, whether it is a story from their workplace or family life or a pertinent case example. Encouraging students to bring their experiences into the online classroom helps the entire group in the meaning-making process.

Respect

In order to coalesce as a learning community, members need to feel as though they are being respected as people. This begins with an initial welcome to the group and continues through the respectful receipt of their posts and the receipt of constructive and expansive feedback on the material they present. Students need to feel as though they are equal participants in the learning process. The instructor holds no more power in the learning process than they do. Even the assessment, evaluation, and grading processes can be shared with the group. The creation and maintenance of an online learning community works best when the instructor relinquishes power to the group and, as we like to state it, gets into the sandbox and plays as an equal. This demonstrates that the instructor understands that students are learners who will, given the opportunity, pursue knowledge and meaning with only gentle guidance. If we demonstrate this type of respect for our students, they will respond in kind.

Another indicator of respect is the willingness of the members of the group to preserve its sanctity. In other words, members of the group keep confidential any information of a personal nature that a member may choose to share online. Every effort is made to keep "lurkers" from entering the group without the members' consent. Postings made by one member will not be shared in another forum without consent. Members agree to maintain a code of ethics, including an agreement not to harass or stalk another member. Issues of basic respect for other human beings are magnified in this environment and must not be assumed. Guidelines negotiated by the group need to include the requirement that everyone show respect for the other participants.

Openness

Although related to the topic of honesty, openness relates more to the environment created within the group and is a product of the ability to be honest with and have respect for each other. In an atmosphere of openness, students can feel free to share their thoughts and feelings without fear of retribution. In an open, online classroom, students should not be afraid that their grade will be affected by the nature of their opinions. Again, this represents the ability of all participants to give and receive feedback with respect and the confidence that it will be received in the spirit with which it was offered. If an atmosphere of safety and trust has been successfully created, members can feel confident that, if they are open with one another, only positive outcomes will result.

Empowerment

A sense of empowerment is both a crucial element and a desired outcome of participation in an online learning community. In a learner-centered environment, the learner is truly the expert when it comes to his or her own learning. Consequently, participants take on new roles and responsibilities in the learning process and should be encouraged to pursue knowledge wherever that path takes them. We hope that once students experience this form of learning, it will follow them and provide them with a new foundation from which to experience other forms of learning. In the construction of a transformative learning environment, the participants gain a new view of themselves and a new sense of confidence in their ability to interact with knowledge.

One of our participants summed up the importance of all of these elements in the formation of a successful learning community:

> We find honesty, responsibility, trust and mutually respective behavior—traits that are all too rare in our increasingly paranoid and hostile culture. This medium, then, is where we can turn the tide. Through computer communication, we quickly evolved from individuals embedded in their separateness into community. [This course] celebrates the community spirit of wholeness and connection. *Cyd*

Not only are these traits rare in our culture, they are rarely related to our educational experiences. Just as we hope that students will carry these elements with them into other learning experiences, we also hope that faculty will do the same; electronic pedagogy is the use of our best teaching practices regardless of setting.

THE ESSENCE OF ONLINE LEARNING: COMMUNITY

Without the purposeful formation of an online learning community in online learning, we are doing nothing new and different. In giving us feedback on our earliest online course, Don MacIntyre, former president of Fielding Graduate University, commented: "In talking about distance learning, I keep stressing that our focus is on the learning process and not the technology. Many institutions are jumping on the technology bandwagon so as to become a part of the information superhighway. In doing so, their goal is to use the technology to transmit a tired and stale pedagogy over fiber optic cable—as if the fiber optic cable will somehow transform the pedagogy."

The development of a learning community in the distance education process involves developing new approaches to education and new skills in its delivery. When we present this concept to faculty members, they often comment that this is not new information to them—that they are familiar with these practices. Why, then, do we see so many online learning programs and classes that rely on the technology to create a new environment for learning rather than employing the skills of community building in the classroom? We believe the answer lies in the fact that many instructors have not looked closely at the online learning environment and what it demands in order to create a successful learning outcome. Our efforts to incorporate community building into the process cannot be assumed but must be much more purposeful in this medium.

The creation of a learning community supports and encourages knowledge acquisition. It creates a sense of excitement about learning together and renews the passion involved with exploring new realms in education. The collaboration involved in learning together in this way truly creates a sense of synergy, as Stephen Covey (1989) describes it, or a chemistry between people that creates an atmosphere of excitement and passion for learning and working together. The total outcome of knowledge acquired and shared is far greater than what would be generated through independent, individual engagement with the material. The bonus is the newly developing sense of self and sense of empowerment that accompanies the process. The power of community is great. The power of a learning community is even greater, as it supports the intellectual as well as personal growth and development of its members.

However, because this is still a relatively new and developing area of education with almost daily technological changes, as well as rapid growth and expansion, there continue to be many issues that surface in distance education and remain unresolved and unanswered. We often comment that the field of online learning as we know it today is in its infancy—many forget that the World Wide Web did not exist until 1995 and that the use of the Web to deliver education began shortly thereafter. Some of the continuing issues relate to the work required to develop a learning community online; others relate to the infrastructure required to support it. By the time this book is published, some of these issues are sure to be resolved. However, we are certain that as this field continues to develop, others will emerge to take their place. In the next section, we discuss some of the issues as we see them currently. In so doing, we are striving to create points for further discussion rather than offering solutions.

UNRESOLVED ISSUES AND UNANSWERED QUESTIONS

Many institutions have entered the distance learning arena because they think it makes economic sense for them. The hope has been to attract new nontraditional students, as defined by age, marital status, or employment status, to the academic market. The attempt has been to capture a group of students who might not otherwise attend classes in a traditional setting. However, what we are finding through our own classes, and what universities are noting, is that this form of education also attracts students in residence on campuses who may also be attending traditional face-to-face classes. They are younger and may be attracted to these classes for very different reasons. Many residential students enroll in online learning courses for convenience. But others simply prefer to learn online. They may have experienced this form of learning in high school. In addition, they may appreciate the increased level of individual attention from instructors in online courses, and the fact that they can spend more time reflecting on the content and working on assignments in alternative ways.

The phenomenon being described here is one we have discussed. The introverted student who may not feel comfortable speaking out or asking for help in a face-to-face setting may flourish in the online setting, and all students gain the luxury of control over their time while attending classes and the ability to be more thoughtful about their interactions within those classes (Pratt, 1996). This creates a set of dilemmas with which academic institutions must grapple. How will institutions come to terms with the needs of the student who prefers online learning? How will online courses be offered without jeopardizing face-to-face offerings? Will faculty need to make a choice between offering one or the other, or will departments and institutions make it possible for those faculty who prefer the online environment and who are adept at this form of teaching to offer both types of classes? What will the impact of these decisions be on such issues as faculty compensation, faculty recruitment, department and school budgets, and current marketing efforts to attract the nontraditional student, as currently defined, to the online environment? Although we first raised these questions in 1999, institutions are still grappling with the answers to them.

Perhaps institutions will devise means by which to assess which courses and programs will be appropriate for online delivery. And there may be a need to develop student assessments, such as the one offered by De Anza College, to determine which students would do best in online courses as opposed to face-to-face instruction. Clearly, the old distinctions between market segments are blurring. As a result, institutions must rethink their strategies for attracting students to the online environment and develop ways to attract students based on their learning needs rather than their life status.

Because of the necessity to rethink our educational strategies, Carol Twigg (1994a), then of Educom (now known as Educause), an organization devoted to looking at the transformation of education through information technology, talks about rethinking our current system of education for the purpose of developing a new learning infrastructure:

> Our current system was developed to serve a different student population and is based on old assumptions about teaching (e.g., viewing the teacher and the classroom as the only delivery method) and learning (mastery of a body of knowledge as the way to prepare for life). What was once the most effective and efficient way to teach and learn—the research university model of faculty who create knowledge and deliver it to students via lectures—now cracks under the strain of meeting new learning demands. As an old technology, the traditional classroom suffers from severe limitations, in both its on-campus and off-campus versions. We need a better system of learning to enable students to acquire knowledge. We need to create a support system for faculty who want to teach in this new way. [p. 4]

She further states that "our understanding of how people learn is growing, suggesting that increased individualization of the learning process is the way to respond to the diverse learning styles brought by our students as they enter and re-enter the world of higher education" (Twigg, 1994b, p. 1).

Perhaps the answers to the questions and challenges posed here lie in a change of focus. In order to successfully accommodate the needs of a diverse body of learners and to make room for both traditional and nontraditional students, along with online approaches that may encompass both, institutions should concentrate their efforts on what learners need and are demanding, as well as what our society is demanding of our graduates. It is, as one instructor told us, "the Nordstrom approach"—a customer-service orientation to education. When academic institutions truly begin to acknowledge that students are our customers and that their service needs come first, they will be able to focus on allowing several forms of knowledge delivery to exist side by side without a sense that one is competing with the other. It is a broadening of our thinking about education in general that is needed as institutions move into an increasingly technological future.

LESSONS LEARNED AND A LOOK TO THE FUTURE

One of the basic requirements for education in the twenty-first century is to prepare students for participation in a knowledge-based economy; knowledge is the most critical resource for social and economic development. Curricular content and the approaches to twenty-first-century society are being forged through discussion and debate in the public, business, and academic sectors. These discussions are happening with growing urgency as technology advances. It becomes increasingly clear that current educational models, structures, and approaches are inadequate. Students need new and different information resources, skills, roles, and relationships. The traditional educational model, based primarily on the concept of the school and the teacher in a classroom as islands, standing alone and not interconnected with society or other educational institutions, will not generate competence in a knowledge society (Harasim and others 1996).

The educational opportunities that are created should be responsive to the demands of students and the world in which they work and live. As globalization and the rapid exchange of information required become more of a reality, the need for our faculty, institutions, and students to respond to that reality expands. Increasingly, the corporate sector is attempting to shape education by offering incentives to academic institutions to provide educational opportunities that are more responsive to corporate needs, and are developing corporate universities to more closely address those needs. Although online learning is not the sole response to this reality, it certainly offers a means by which students can practice and acquire the skills needed to compete. In addition to knowledge acquisition, students learn about technology through its use. They learn about themselves and their own learning styles, and about how to collaborate with others in geographically distributed teams. They learn what it takes to pace themselves in order to get the job done. As this is occurring, they become increasingly confident in their abilities, feel empowered to work in a manner that best suits them, and seek out the information they need for the task at hand. All of these skills are transferable to the world of work and gained through participation in an online learning community.

As we stated at the beginning of this chapter, the traditional face-to-face classroom is not likely to disappear. It continues to serve the needs of many students and will do so in the future. However, what we have learned from our experience of facilitating online classes is that regardless of the setting, the creation of community greatly enhances the learning experience and the likelihood of successful learning outcomes.

EXTENDING COMMUNITY BEYOND THE CLASSROOM

As the research continues to show that the online learning community is an effective approach to online learning, new applications of the concept have emerged. Academic institutions, wrestling with the issue of persistence in online courses and programs, have realized the need to reach out to students at a distance in ways that may not be necessary on campus. In other words, student services programs are expanding online, and various means by which a sense of community and connection to the university can be achieved are being attempted. The concept of the institution as the larger community with smaller neighborhoods within, which we discussed earlier in the book, applies here; some of the ways in which this concept is being used include the creation of university-wide discussion forums to enable distance students to engage in conversation about issues that affect or are of interest to them. Through such forums, colleges and universities are able to offer what are known as "push and pull" choices or selections; in other words, institutions are "pushing out" reminders, relevant information, and other services as appropriate to students based on "pulled" information gathered from the students who participate in the discussions or who respond to posted surveys. This allows institutions to create interactive information exchanges and create just-in-time services based on expressed need. Consequently, students feel much more engaged with their institution and are much more likely to stay enrolled. In addition, smaller "neighborhoods" can be created under the umbrella of the larger community through the establishment of communities of inquiry or practice. These neighborhood groups might include students who come together online around social activities, clubs, or sports or who share academic interests. Faculty also may become involved in these neighborhood groups.

The extended learning community concept has also been applied in troubled times. In the wake of Hurricane Katrina in fall 2005, several academic institutions in the Gulf States were forced to use online means to connect with their students and to continue the mission of delivering education. For some, such as Delgado Community College in New Orleans, the significant destruction of their physical plant pushed them to reemerge as a predominantly online institution. An extended online learning community approach through the college's main website has been used to reach both students and faculty who have been displaced all over the United States, allowing them to support one another through this difficult time and to continue delivering education.

Finally, the learning community approach is proving to be an effective means by which to provide faculty development and training regarding online teaching. By putting cohorts of faculty into online training courses with the goal of building a faculty learning community, not only can faculty learn the techniques of building community that can be taken into the classroom, but they also develop their own support network and community that is likely to extend beyond the training period. Through this extended approach, we have seen faculty use one another as resources as they develop their online courses and invite their peers to review their work as they develop syllabi and activities for online delivery.

IMPLICATIONS FOR INSTRUCTOR TRAINING

Clearly, this work has implications for the training and development of faculty. As students who intend to teach become more involved in successful online classes in which the development of a learning community is intentionally built into the process, their experiences should translate into their own teaching. It is also important for institutions to include training for their faculty in the process of online learning that is learning-community-oriented as they move into this arena.

Too often, faculty training involves an introduction to the hardware and software being used to deliver classes, with no emphasis on process. Just as the technology used to deliver an online class should become transparent in the learning process, so should it become transparent in faculty training. Once again, the technology should only be used as a vehicle to convey the ability to create a collaborative, transformative process. It is only the means by which instructors and students can connect to form community. By focusing on electronic pedagogy in faculty training rather than on technology, faculty will become excited about the potential and power of online learning.

Online education is not the panacea that will cure the ills of education today. However, if facilitated in a way that incorporates community into the process, it is a way to promote a generation of empowered learners who can successfully navigate the demands of a knowledge society. As Don MacIntyre stated in observation of our first seminar and the work of the Fielding Graduate University involving distance learning:

> We are trying to do what no one else in higher education has done to date: create a true virtual academic community. . . . You have grappled sensitively and openly with many of the key issues of a virtual community. You have brought together "high tech" with "high touch." You have demonstrated caring, concern, love, and support for one another. I doubt if you could find your kind of interchanges taking place in any other graduate program around the country. It was really beautiful to behold.

We find that we are touched and moved by our students in every online course we conduct. This was true when we first wrote this book and is still true today. We feel that we learn as much or more than they do and that they touch our lives in ways that are difficult to communicate. Not only are we helping to shape the creation of empowered, lifelong learners, our participation as equal members of a group of learners supports us in our own quest for lifelong learning. For us, this is the power of online distance learning.

**JOHN F. KENNEDY UNIVERSITY
SCHOOL OF LIBERAL ARTS
Syllabus: Personality and Psychotherapy
PYC 3200,
4 Units**

Instructor. Rena M. Palloff

Phone. (510) 769–1340

E-mail. rpalloff@mindspring.com

Course Meetings. This course is conducted completely online. To enroll in your course, go to http://courses.jfku.edu and use the keyword "personality" to enroll yourself in the course.

Objectives and Description

This online course approaches the study of personality in a slightly different manner. The author of our text, Lawrence Pervin, notes that the typical approach to the study of personality takes the form of the "grand theories" of personality. This approach, however, does not address current approaches to personality, nor does it necessarily assist us in knowing how to apply the theories in a therapeutic context. In addition, being a more traditional approach, it does not account for issues of gender, culture, or politics in the study of personality, all of which play a significant role. Consequently, our approach will be two-pronged. We will read about the ways in which personality is studied, both through our text and also through articles assigned by me and articles you may find in your research. In addition, you will form presentation groups, allowing you to explore and present the "grand theories" to one another. In this way, we will have the best of both approaches and will learn from one another.

1. Become knowledgeable about the major theories and approaches to the study of personality and their relationship to psychotherapy
2. Evaluate the similarities and differences of the various approaches and theories
3. Become familiar with changes and current developments in the field
4. Critically and creatively evaluate the strengths and limitations of the theories and practices
5. Examine assumptions about human nature and therapeutic relationships, with particular attention paid to multicultural approaches
6. Apply the material studied to personal experience and case examples

Required Reading

Pervin, L. (2003). *The Science of Personality.* New York: Oxford University Press.
    Course Reader: *Please make sure to order your reader asap from Central Services!*

Additional articles assigned by me and researched by you.

Course Format

This course consists of readings, written assignments, small group presentations, weekly responses and check-ins on the course website. All assignments are posted on the discussion board as individual topics, with papers and responses posted as replies to the appropriate topic. Discussion topics will be posted on Sundays and the discussion week will go from Monday to Monday. *Regular participation in the online dialogue and timely posting of assignments and responses are required of everyone in order to have a successful experience.* It is important to check-in and to make substantive postings in response to others at least two to three times a week. If you cannot do so, it is critical that you let the group know what they can expect of you. Silence or the lack of participation will be deemed unsupportive of the group and will be reflected in assessment and grading. During the first two weeks, we will explore the basis of personality theories. In Weeks 3 through 9, the presentation groups will present material to the class. In weeks 10 and 11, we will wrap up our learning experience by focusing on multicultural approaches to therapy and by presenting final reflections on our learning experience. *Because of the highly interactive nature of this course, no registrations will be taken beyond the last day of the first week of class.* I do not want to set you up for failure and want to establish our learning community as quickly as possible—you will find that you depend on one another for your learning in this course!

Guidelines for a Successful Online Course

1. This course is not self-paced and is not the "softer, easier way"! This means that you need to check in regularly, respond to the weekly discussion questions and also to one another. Please remember that this is a 4-unit course!

2. Discussions go from Sunday to Sunday and will be deemed *closed* on the Wednesday following each week, giving you a maximum of 10 days per topic. So, please stay current and up-to-date! There is a fair amount of reading, so please do pace yourselves.

3. I expect you to respond to all of your student colleagues at one point or another in the discussions. I realize that some of you see one another on campus and others are at a distance. Because of this, it's not unusual for you to talk only to the people you know, but push yourselves out of your comfort zone and make some new friends at a distance!

4. Have contingency plans for computer problems as well as late arrival of textbooks. Some suggestions include becoming familiar with the local library, Internet services and community college resources. It is even suggested that you seek out friends, family, and even coworkers who have Internet services in the event your computer crashes. That way you will stay current with your weekly assignments.

5. Online learning happens in real-time. Just as a professional counselor must function regardless of life's challenges e.g., birth, death, travel, family emergencies, medical problems, professional crises, military deployment (etc.), so must the online student. Success is contingent upon the ability to master course content while simultaneously mastering all of life's other challenges. If work is not submitted on time, I assume that an unforeseen event has occurred and that you will be back on track as soon as possible, thus eliminating the need

for apology or excuse. Do contact me, however, to let me know what's going on in your life if you need to be away from the course. I am human and I do understand!!

What You Can Expect of Me as Your Instructor

1. I highly value instructor-learner communication. We can communicate via my personal e-mail and telephone if you need to speak to me. To prevent telephone tag, you may want to e-mail me for telephone appointments. Generally, I can be reached by telephone most days. If I am away from the phone, please leave a message and I will return your call as quickly as possible.

2. If at anytime you are dissatisfied, confused, or unclear about how the discussion is being facilitated, please contact me via e-mail. I will respond to your inquiry within 48 hours, and we will work together to resolve the identified issue. We will use the course discussion area as our primary place of communication. In the event a private conversation is required, we will utilize e-mail. I'll get back to you usually within 24 to 48 hours; and if necessary we can arrange a time to talk/chat/exchange ideas.

3. I will share my travel schedule with you all and will post any away times in the Café area, which I call Rena's Roadhouse. I do travel frequently as I consult as well as teach, but I always travel with a laptop. There are rare times where I have been unable to connect for a couple of days (i.e., very slow dial-ups and travel outside of the US). When those occur, at the very least I will post a message in the Roadhouse letting you know.

4. I do my utmost best to respond to assignments with feedback within a week of receipt. Again, sometimes life and other work intervene in that, but if it does, I'll let you know.

5. I will treat all of you with collegial respect! I believe that you have as much to contribute to this learning process as I do and I look forward to our exchange as colleagues.

6. I will provide a warm, fun course environment where we can have fun and learn together!

Presentation Groups

During the first week of class, you will elect to participate in presentation groups, which will begin in Week 3. The following are the presentation topics:

Week 3—Psychoanalysis and Character Psychology (Theories of Freud, Reich et al.)

Week 4—Analytical Psychology and Transpersonal Psychology (Jung, Maslow et al.)

Week 5—Behaviorism (Skinner, Pavlov et al.)

Week 6—Developmental and Cognitive Psychology (Erikson, Bandura et al.)

Week 7—Self-Psychology and Psychology of Consciousness (Kelly, James, Kohut et al.)

Week 8—Women's Ways of Knowing and Feminist Psychology (Gilligan, Belenky et al.)

Week 9—Hindu, Buddhist, and Islamic Approaches and Traditions

The task of the presentation group is to find and present material related to the topic. If the group feels the rest of us should read an article or visit a particular website to support their presentation, that should be assigned the week prior to the topic to allow for preparation. In addition, the group will link the theoretical material to psychotherapeutic approaches. In other words, in Week 3, the group will present the personality theories related to psychoanalysis and character psychology but will also present approaches to therapy based on those viewpoints.

Presentations must be posted by Wednesday of the week it is assigned. From Thursday to the following Monday, the remaining members of the class will post a brief (1 page) response paper to that group noting what was learned from the presentation along with some brief feedback for the group.

Note: After you have completed your presentation, please send me a personal e-mail that provides the following information:

- A self-assessment of your own contribution to the group along with a letter grade (even if you are taking the course for credit)
- An assessment of your teammates' contributions to the group along with a letter grade for each member
- A brief process assessment—how well did you work together and how much did you learn by completing this assignment?

I would like to receive those e-mails within a week after your presentation ends. If you don't send it, I'll remind you!!

Discussions

In addition to the presentations, I will post a discussion question for the entire class to consider on Sundays. *You are expected to post a response to the discussion question as well as to respond to at least two other student colleagues' postings weekly.* The more the better as it promotes dialogue and deepens our learning!! Reading assignments will be kept short so as to allow you more time for online discussion. Feel free to search out additional websites on topics to add to our learning and list of resources.

Final Paper

The paper should be approximately 10 pages, typed, double-spaced, and in APA format.

Choose one of the following options for your final paper:

1. Theory and personal application—Take one theory or approach to personality and present yourself in reference to this theory or approach. Use at least 3 outside references not read for class. You also have the option of taking a personality inventory, such as the MBTI, and using that as the theoretical basis for your analysis. If you do so, make sure to also discuss the theory to which the inventory relates. Your content should be 60% theoretical and 40% personal process.

2. Watch the film, "Don Juan de Marco" and write a paper that applies the theoretical material we have discussed this term as well as the therapeutic approach used with Don Juan. What theories in action do you see in the film? Support your paper with at least 3 outside references not read for class.

Schedule of Discussion Topics and Assignments

Note: Reading assignments are for the week that *follows.*

Week 1 (October 3)—Introductions, Finding Our Way Online, Selection of Presentation Groups

Assignments:

Online discussion

Reading: Pervin, Introduction (Chapter 1);

Sloan article

Week 2 (October 10)—The Study of Personality

Assignments:

Online discussion

Reading: Pervin, Chapter 2;

Shapiro articles

Week 3 (October 17)—Trait Units of Personality

Assignments:

Online discussion

Psychoanalysis group presents—all respond

Reading: Pervin, Chapter 3

Week 4 (October 24)—Cognitive Units of Personality

Assignments:

Online discussion

Analytical group presents— all respond

Reading: Pervin, Chapter 4

Week 5 (October 31)—Motivational Units of Personality

Assignments:

Online discussion

Behavioral group presents—all respond

Reading: Pervin, Part 2 (Chapters 5 and 6)

Week 6 (November 7)—Personality Development

Assignments:

Online discussion

Developmental/Cognitive group presents—all respond

Reading: Pervin, Chapters 7 and 8;

Barone article;

Kanter, Parker, and Kohlenberg article

Week 7 (November 14)—The Unconscious and the Concept of the Self

Assignments:

Online discussion

Self-psychology/Consciousness group presents—all respond

Reading: Pervin, Chapters 9 and 10;

Diener, Oishi, and Lucas article;

Lawrence article

Week 8 (November 21)—Action, Emotion, Adaptation, and Health

Assignments:

Online discussion

Feminist psychology group presents—all respond

Reading: Pervin, Chapters 11 and 12

Week 9 (November 28)—Change Processes and Personality Assessment

Assignments:

Online discussion

Hindu/Buddhist/Islamic approaches group presents—all respond

Reading: Pervin, Chapter 13;

Gjerde article

Week 10 (December 5)—Multicultural Approaches and Critical Psychological Approaches

Assignments:

Online discussion

Week 11 (December 12)—Final Reflections

Assignments:

Online discussion

Final papers due by December 17 at the latest!!

Grading and Evaluation

Your grade will be determined as follows:

Online participation = 40% (Remember that the requirement is 3 posts per week *minimum*)

Group presentation = 20%

Responses to presentation group = 10%

Final paper = 30%

I have created a 3-point grading scale to evaluate your discussions and will be assigning grades based on the following:

3 = Discussion question is answered at an integrative level that shows critical thinking skills, is well written, and references the reading. There is at least one response to another learner that is constructed at the level of the initial posting.

2 = Discussion question is adequately answered at an analysis level. Some critical thinking is present. There may be some writing issues. There is at least one response to another learner that is constructed at the level of the initial posting.

1 = There is a response to the initial discussion question that is brief and at the summary level. There is little evidence of critical thinking. There may be some writing issues. There are no additional responses to other learners.

0 = No responses present.

Although I encourage supportive and social postings that will help us build and sustain our learning community, they will not be evaluated for a grade.

Feedback to you on your progress in the course will be provided in the form of an e-mail from me after you complete your presentation, at midterm, and after I read your final paper. If you have questions about your individual progress in the course, please don't hesitate to contact me and to ask!

Grading Criteria for the Course

To earn an A, students will

- Complete assignments on time
- "Attend" and participate
- Respond fully to assignments
- Express their purpose clearly and persuasively, but using good "netiquette"
- Present papers and discussion responses in a well organized and well-written fashion
- Provide adequate and supportive documentation and references
- Use good APA format and document sources appropriately
- Written work is free of errors in grammar, punctuation, word choice, spelling, and format
- Demonstrate creativity and originality

To earn a B, students will

- Demonstrate all of the above with strong performance, but may show little or no creativity or originality (analysis rather than synthesis)

To earn a C, students will

- Demonstrate all of the above adequately, but written work may contain errors in writing and thinking (summary level work)

To earn a D, students will:
- Be unable to demonstrate the above adequately. Papers may look like a first draft or are hastily conceived.

To earn an F, students will

- Be unable to follow through with assignments

- Be unable to participate adequately online

- Be unable to demonstrate competence in written work

Credit/No Credit Policy. If you are taking the class for Credit/No Credit, you must earn a C or better in order to earn Credit.

Incomplete Policy. An Incomplete (I) grade can only be given to students who demonstrate that they are unable, due to *extraordinary circumstances* to complete the required work by the end of the term. The granting of an Incomplete grade is at the discretion of the instructor. It is the student's responsibility to request an Incomplete *in writing, stating briefly, but specifically the reasons for the request.* If the I is approved, the student must provide the instructor with the Incomplete Grade Form (See the University catalog for a complete statement of the Incomplete Policy). Given that this course is delivered online, the form must be mailed to the instructor to arrive in a timely fashion so that the request can be considered.

"Attendance"

In order to be considered "present" for class each week, each of you *must* respond to the discussion question posted by me, provide feedback to at least 2 of your peers' responses, and either "present" or respond to a presentation.

Rena's Roadhouse

This is an area of our course where we can relax with one another. So, picture a country inn along a beautiful rural road just outside a small town where the entire community gathers from time to time throughout the day. The food is good and the coffee is great and always flowing. There are also weekly specials to tempt you! This is the place we can go to partake of some casual conversation about any number of things—personal news, group problems or frustrations, or even tangents of interest started in the formal course discussion but left behind as the course moved on. This is also the place that we'll use to inform each other of special events, travel, and absences from the course. Hope to see you there and, by the way, the coffee is on me!

Contacting Rena. Remember, please do contact me with any questions or concerns. I can be reached through the class website by putting my name in the subject line (i.e., Debra to Rena regarding. . .), or through the posting of a question in the Questions for Dr. P discussion forum, by e-mail at rpalloff@mindspring.com, or by phone at (510) 769–1340. If we have a conversation by e-mail or phone, I may ask you to post a synopsis of our conversation on the class website as other students may have similar questions or concerns.

Tips for Success in your Online Class

Guidelines for Discussion

- Before posting anything . . . .
    1. Read the assigned material.
    2. Do the exercises or activities assigned.
    3. Read your fellow students' postings.
    4. Think about what you want to add to the ongoing discussion.
- When posting . . .
    1. Respond to direct questions and inquiries.
    2. Make your points clearly and concisely
    3. Bring in any additional knowledge, sources, etc. you can from the Internet, other material, and/or your personal experience.
    4. Include relevant quotes/sections from previous posts.
    5. Do not include irrelevant quotes/sections from previous posts.
    6. Disagree civilly and respectfully.
    7. Do not post *ad hominem* attacks, embarrassing, or derogatory material (this is called "flaming" and is unacceptable behavior online).
    8. Practice good netiquette.
- Throughout the week . . .
    1. Participate in the threaded discussions several times a week.
    2. Engage fellow students, instructor in a dialogue.
    3. Check the threaded discussion for any responses to your comments.
    4. Be prepared to post follow-up messages if necessary.

Most of all, have fun and learn from one another!!!

Syllabus: OM 373
The Search for the Soul and Spirit in the Workplace

Instructor. Rena M. Palloff, Ph.D., LCSW
Phone. (510) 769–1340
FAX. (510) 769–1340

E-mail. rpalloff@fielding.edu

Introduction, Course Overview, and Objectives

Writers in the area of organizational change talk about the constant change that besieges today's organizations as "turbulence" or "permanent whitewater." Rightsizing, re-engineering, and globalization are but a few of the changes having significant effect on the people who work in organizations. Jack Canfield and Jacqueline Miller (1996) in their book, *Heart at Work* state, "The work environment in modern organizations leads to a parching of the human spirit. In reaction against this, people are speaking out for 'heart at work,' for 'spirit in the workplace.' We find a growing insistence that every part of society—especially the workplace where so many spend so large a portion of their lives—be conducive to the fullest development of the human being." (p. xi) Organizational writers have begun to pay attention to this growing demand and have begun to explore not only the importance of soul and spirit in the workplace, but also their implications for leadership and organizational transformation. This course will explore recent writings regarding the search for soul and spirit in the workplace, as well as how it impacts the notions of meaningful work, leadership, and organizational change. We will also explore these concepts as they pertain to your personal search for meaning in the work you do.

Required Reading:

Bolman, Lee, and Deal, Terrence (1995). *Leading with Soul*. San Francisco: Jossey-Bass.

Briskin, Alan (1998). *The Stirring of Soul in the Workplace*. San Francisco: Berrett-Koehler.

Peppers, Cheryl, and Briskin, Alan (2000). *Bringing Your Soul to Work: An Everyday Practice*. San Francisco: Berrett-Koehler.

Articles from *BizSpirit*, an online journal—links to articles provided.

[*Note:* Some of the links may have changed over time as this journal is no longer published. To access BizSpirit articles, you will need to go into the Archives of this journal. Let me know if you're having difficulty locating any of the articles and we'll either make a substitution or look for another means of locating it.]

Highly Recommended Reading

Whyte, David (1994). *The Heart Aroused.* New York: Currency Doubleday.
Whyte, David (2001). *Crossing the Unknown Sea: Work as a Pilgrimage of Identity.*
New York: Riverhead Books.

Schedule of Discussions

[*Note:* Reading is for the week of discussion. I will be checking all URLs to make sure that they are current. If a URL change is necessary, I will post the change in the course. I may also add or substitute articles from the BizSpirit site as new material becomes available. Feel free to seek out additional soul and spirit resources from the Internet or library to support your facilitation of the discussion as well.]

Discussions for this course will primarily focus on readings which are organized into 2-week blocks. You will be asked to facilitate the discussion for one week by posting a thoughtful question for all of us to consider and respond to, based on the readings and your responses to them. As the facilitator for the week, you will also post a summary of the discussion for that week. All of you are encouraged to bring your own experiences into the discussions as we go.

In addition, I will create a "blog spot" in which I'd like you to post your reflections for the week in journal fashion and an idea or two that the reading and discussion triggered for you regarding interventions in the workplace related to soul and spirit. Feel free to comment on each other's blog entries.

The following is a beginning outline of the discussion topics and the reading assignments. This may be modified as we go dependent upon your interests and needs.

Week 1

Post an introduction and begin a discussion regarding the definition of soul and spirit.

Read article by Rutte, "Spirituality in the Workplace," [http://www.soulfulliving.com/spiritualityinworkplace.htm]

Weeks 2 and 3

Defining the search for soul and spirit organizationally: What are the problems being surfaced? What are the organizational issues related to soul and spirit? Confronting the shadow organizationally.

Read Briskin, *The Stirring of Soul in the Workplace* (entire book) and articles by Johnson and Lewin:

- Johnson, "How to Do Well and Do Good in Business," [http://www.bizspirit.com/bsj/archives/cedric1.html]
- Lewin, "The Reality of Complexity," [http://www.bizspirit.com/bsj/archives/lewin1.html]
- Lewin, "The Soul at Work," [http://www.bizspirit.com/bsj/archives/lewin2.html]

Weeks 4 and 5

How do we define meaningful work? What are the roles of values and ethics in determining meaningful work?

Read Peppers and Briskin (entire book) and article by Levoy, "The Power of Work as a Calling," [http://www.bizspirit.com/bsj/archives/levoy2.html]

Week 6:

Discussion of the organizational assessments. Your assessment should be posted by midnight Pacific Time on Monday.

Weeks 7 and 8

Leadership and motivation as they relate to soul and spirit.

Read Bolman and Deal (entire book) and articles by Madigan and Dreaver:

- Madigan, "Consciousness: A Principle-Based Paradigm for Leadership," [http://www.bizspirit.com/bsj/archives/madigan1.html]
- Dreaver, "Fearless Leadership," [http://www.bizspirit.com/bsj/archives/dreaver1.html]

Weeks 9 and 10

Organizational transformation, soul, and spirit

Read articles by Barrett, Renesch, Marcic, and in HR Magazine:

- Barrett, "Organizational Transformation," [http://www.bizspirit.com/bsj/archives/barrett1.html]
- Renesch, "The Conscious Organization," [http://www.bizspirit.com/bsj/archives/renesch1.html]
- Marcic, Table 2 from *Managing with the Wisdom of Love,* [http://www.marcic.com/books/virtues.htm]

Week 11

Discussion of final papers in dyads

Week 12

Report out from dyads

Submit self-evaluation

Assignments and Evaluation

Grading for this course will be based on a possible 100 points which will be allocated over the following assignments:

Posting an introduction along with why you have chosen this course and your goals for participation—10 points

Mid-term assignment: Complete an evaluation of the organization for which you work or one for which you have worked, addressing issues related to soul and spirit in the workplace. How are they manifested in your place of work, or are they absent?—20 points

Final assignment: Reflect on the totality of your weekly journals and post a 3 to 5 page paper that applies what we have been discussing this term to an organization. You might discuss the "ideal" organization in terms of promotion of soul and spirit and how the concepts we have discussed play out in that organization. Or, you may choose the opposite path and present an organization that is far from ideal with your ideas for organizational interventions designed to promote or increase soulfulness in that organization. Feel free to bring additional resources and references into your discussion. I will put you in dyads to discuss your assignments and then ask each dyad to report out to the larger group on what you've learned from each other's papers—20 points

Complete a self-evaluation at the close of the course outlining what you have gained (or not) from participation in this course—10 points

Participation in the online discussion: Please note that you will not be able to receive credit or the benefit of this course without participating in the online discussion. I will expect each of you to read and respond to the online discussion at least twice weekly. Consequently, if you are having technical or other difficulties with your participation, please contact me immediately. If you will be traveling, please post a message in the course letting us know that. You will be asked to facilitate one week of the online discussion. This will be worth 10 points. Overall participation will be worth an additional 30 points for a total of 40 points.

Guidelines for Online Participation in "The Search for Soul and Spirit in the Workplace"

Should you have questions or comments on any of these guidelines, let's discuss them! Also, please add any guidelines that you feel are appropriate.

"Attendance" and presence are required for this class. You are expected to log on at a minimum of twice per week (at any time during the week) and are expected to post a substantive contribution to the discussion at that time. Simply saying "hello" or "I agree" is not considered a substantive contribution. You must support your position or begin a new topic or add somehow to the discussion when logging on.

Assignments will be posted online. You will be asked to comment on and provide feedback to one another on your work.

Although I strongly suggest that all issues, questions, and problems be dealt with online, you can feel free to call or e-mail me regarding these issues at any time.

Use good "netiquette" such as

1. Check the discussion frequently and respond appropriately and on subject.

2. Focus on one subject per message and use pertinent subject titles.

3. Capitalize words only to highlight a point or for titles—Capitalizing otherwise is generally viewed as SHOUTING!

4. Be professional and careful with your online interaction.

5. Cite all quotes, references, and sources.

6. When posting a long message, it is generally considered courteous to warn readers at the beginning of the message that it is a lengthy post.

7. It is considered extremely rude to forward someone else's messages without their permission.

8. It is fine to use humor, but use it carefully. The absence of face-to-face cues can cause humor to be misinterpreted as criticism or flaming (angry, antagonistic criticism). Feel free to use emoticons such as :) or ;) to let others know that you're being humorous.

[*Note:* The above "netiquette" guidelines were adapted from Arlene H. Rinaldi's article, "The Net User Guidelines and Netiquette," Florida Atlantic University, 1994, available from Netcom.]

Most of all, let's have fun together! This is an exciting and relevant topic for us all. I hope that we will be able to share our thoughts and experiences with one another in the form of an active and stimulating discussion!

Course Assignments
Structure of Course Site/Facilitation Assignments.
In an attempt to make things easier to follow in this heavily discussion-based course, I will create topic folders for each 2-week segment as reflected on the syllabus. Once we agree on facilitation assignments, the facilitator will post a reflection followed by a question or two related to the reading for all of us to consider and respond to. The facilitator generally will be responsible for the first week of a two-week segment and I will follow up in the second week, depending on the number of students enrolled in the course and the popularity of some of the topics to be discussed. In those cases, students may each facilitate one week of a two week block. The second week of discussion should take off where the first week began, meaning that the facilitator will provide another view of the reading or perhaps focus on reading for the 2 weeks that has not yet been discussed, and then offer one or two additional questions to consider.

Facilitation preferences will be negotiated online. Is there a particular book that intrigues you and so you would like to lead that discussion? Or is there a topic you are particularly drawn to? These are questions to consider as you request a facilitation assignment. Once we have completed the negotiation of facilitation assignments, I will post a facilitation schedule in the course.

The following is the schedule for discussions for this term to assist you with your planning:

Week 1–January 30 (Intro's and Definitions of Soul/Spirit—Rena facilitates)

Week 2–February 6 (Organizational Search for Soul and Spirit)

Week 3–February 13 (Organizational Search for Soul and Spirit)

Week 4–February 20 (Meaningful Work)

Week 5–February 27 (Meaningful Work)

Week 6–March 6 (Organizational Evaluations—Rena facilitates)

Week 7–March 13 (Leadership and Motivation)

Week 8–March 20 (Leadership and Motivation)

Week 9–March 27 (Organizational Transformation)

Week 10–April 3 (Organizational Transformation)

Week 11–April 10 (Final papers discussed in dyads)

Week 12–April 17 (Report out from dyads and self-assessments due/Wrap Up)

The following are further description of the written assignments for the course:

Week Six: Organizational Evaluations. Post an evaluation of an organization for which you work or have worked, addressing issues of soul and spirit in the workplace. How are these issues manifested in your workplace? Or are they absent? There is no specific format for these evaluations—you might choose to follow a model you've read about in our reading or create one of your own choosing. The main idea here is to give us a good idea of how the organization functions, what is present, and what is absent and how people within the organization feel and behave in relationship to soul and spirit.

Please remember our guideline of confidentiality as we post and discuss these evaluations!

Week Eleven: Final Paper. Reflect on the totality of your weekly journals and post a 3 to 5 page paper that applies what we have been discussing this term to an organization. You might discuss the "ideal" organization in terms of promotion of soul and spirit and how the concepts we have discussed play out in that organization. Or, you may choose the opposite path and present an organization that is far from ideal with your ideas for organizational interventions designed to promote or increase soulfulness in that organization. Feel free to bring additional resources and references into your discussion. Again, there is no specific format for this paper other than to use general APA format guidelines when producing it and to include references either to course readings or any additional references you find.

Self-Evaluations. What have you gained (or not) from your participation in this course? Have you learned anything new about this topic? About yourself? About yourself as a learner? What suggestions do you have for future groups participating in this course and for me as an instructor?

Course Schedule. The facilitator for the week should plan to post their "kick-off" of the discussion on Monday evenings so that we can begin discussion of the topic by Wednesday of each week. Kicking off a discussion means posting some of your reflections and thoughts about the readings and/or posts from the previous week that lead into the current week's topics. If you cite the readings or another post, please include your references and page numbers so that we can all follow your thinking. Your post should be no longer than a page and should include at the end a question or two that the group can then begin to wrestle with. First responses to the ideas, questions, or readings will be due by Wednesday of each week. Please do not respond to your colleague's questions in lockstep fashion. Instead, consider the questions in relationship to the readings and post a one-page narrative representing your views and reflections. After that, you are free to respond to one another as you see fit!

All papers will also be due on Mondays by 12 midnight Pacific time.

JAMESTOWN COMMUNITY COLLEGE

Syllabus: Intermediate Algebra

Instructor. Stephanie Zwyghuizen

Structure of Syllabi in SLN. Courses in SLN have a "Course Information" area along the left-hand side of the main course page. This course information section houses the syllabus for the course and contains not only instructor-generated document but also some general documents created by JCC.

The following are JCC pages:

- "Registration vs. Access" explains to students that they need to register with both JCC *and* SLN

- "Successful Online Students" provides students with a checklist of recommended characteristics for an online student

- "Academic Integrity Statement" is JCC's cheating and plagiarism policy from the *Student Constitution*

The remaining pages are detailed below.

Welcome! Page

Welcome to Intermediate Algebra! Before you begin Module 0, please read all course information documents, create a private folder by editing and saving your profile in the "Meet your classmates" area, and take the SLN student orientation at http://www.sln.suny.edu/sln/student/lnstorhd.nsf/web?openview.

[*Note:* The professor's introduction/bio is also in the "Meet your classmates" area.]

My Expectations Page

My expectations. . . .

   • *I expect you to put in the amount of time it requires for you to succeed.* Advisors say that you need to study an hour outside of class for every hour you spend in class, and for math you can at least double that amount of time. An eight-week summer course in a traditional classroom would meet for nearly 5 hours per week. You have an extra challenge ahead of you, as you will not have that 5 hours a week in class with a lecture. This time will be yours to read the book and the mini lectures and work with the resources at the MyMathLab site. I would expect that "homework" and studying will be, on the average, at least 5 to 10 hours on top of this. This gives us a grand total of at least *15 hours per week* that you should spend on this course. Certainly there might be a small number of students who can succeed while spending less than 15 hours per week, but I would not be surprised if many students needed to spend more than 15 hours per week to do well. If you believe you are spending an inordinate amount of time on this course, *I need to know* so that we can troubleshoot!

- *I expect you to ask questions on the practice exercises and on the homework questions.* Open the question up to everyone, as someone else in the class will probably have the same question. I will also let you try to answer each other's questions, as you learn the best when you can explain something to someone else. If the class cannot figure out a problem I will then jump in and provide some assistance.

- *I expect you to practice good "netiquette" [TVC group—this would be a link to a page with some guidelines for netiquette] and treat your classmates with respect.* There will be some discussion and group work in this course. Please "listen" carefully to the contributions of each other, respect differences of opinion, be constructive with any criticisms, keep up your end of the workload, and do your part to make this a safe environment where people feel comfortable expressing their comments and questions.

- *I expect you to do your own work.* I encourage you to work with classmates either via the computer, phone, or in person if possible. You may discuss your questions with each other, but when you take tests and when you prepare for the final exam, it will be critical that you can work on your own.

- *You are expected to purchase the required textbooks, MyMathLab access code, and calculator.* You may use any kind of calculator you prefer.

- *I expect you to be online (SLN) at least 3 times a week.* You may find that it is to your benefit to be online more often. It is important to log in so that you can read course announcements, read the postings of your classmates, and check your private folder for new messages.

- *I expect you to keep up with the course schedule.* Do not allow yourself to get behind. Dates for the start and end of the modules are posted the moment the course opens on the Web. You need to plan your schedule around these dates. I understand that emergencies happen. If you have an emergency please notify me ASAP.

Course Objective and Overview Page
Objective.

This imputed-credit *[this would be a link to a definition of imputed credit]* course is intended to help you learn some foundational skills that will be needed at the college level of mathematics. These skills include algebraic competence and "mathematical maturity." *[this would be a link to my definition of mathematical maturity]*

Overview. We will cover the following topics this semester.

Module 1: Chapter 5 "Exponents and Polynomials"

5.1. Exponents

5.2. Polynomial Functions and Adding and Subtracting Polynomials

5.3. Multiplying Polynomials

5.4. Special Products

5.5. Negative Exponents and Scientific Notation

Module 2: Chapter 6 "Factoring Polynomials and Quadratic Equations"

6.1. The Greatest Common Factor and Factoring by Grouping

6.2. Factoring Trinomials of the form $x2 + bx + c$

6.3. Factoring Trinomials of the form $ax2 + bx + c$

6.4. Factoring Binomials

6.5. Solving Quadratic Equations by Factoring

6.6. Quadratic Equations and Problem Solving

Chapter 11: Quadratic Equations and Functions

11.2. Solving Quadratic Equations by the Quadratic Formula

11.3. Solving Equations by Using Quadratic Methods

Module 3: Chapter 7 "Rational Expressions"

7.1. Rational Functions and Simplifying Rational Expressions

7.2. Multiplying and Dividing Rational Expressions

Required Textbook and Software Page
Required Materials.

Calculator: Any style of your choosing.

MyMathLab: It is *extremely important* that you purchase the MyMathLab (CourseCompass) access code so that you can submit homework and take tests using the MyMathLab website. You have three ways to purchase this access code:

purchase instant access through the CourseCompass registration site (credit card required) http://info.coursecompass.com/Website/student_register.html

purchase a stand-alone access code card from the JCC bookstore (ISBN 0131486918), *or:*

Purchase a textbook package containing a textbook and an access code card from the JCC bookstore (ISBN 0131622269).

In any case, the course ID you will need for MyMathLab (CourseCompass) is zwyghuizen67291. See the "What is MyMathLab" [this would be a link to the page] page in Module 0 for more information.

Textbook: Because the MyMathLab site provides an electronic version of your textbook, it is *not required* that you purchase a physical textbook for this course. You could open .pdf files from MyMathLab which contain exact copies of the pages from the textbook *Beginning & Intermediate Algebra, 3rd edition,* by K. Elayn Martin-Gay (Prentice Hall, 2005). If you do intend to purchase this book, I recommend that you purchase the textbook bundle (ISBN 0131622269) from the JCC bookstore so that you can have the MyMathLab access code at *a reduced charge.* Purchasing the textbook and the access code separately will likely cost you more.

Word Processing Software. The student/teacher version of Microsoft Office can be purchased at an exceptional discount at the JCC bookstores. Works or WordPerfect may also be used, so long as you submit files to me in *Rich Text Format* (.rtf file extension). I do not have Publisher, so please do not send me Publisher files.

Course Learning Activities Page

This is a general overview of activities. More details will follow where appropriate.

• You will spend a good deal of time reading your textbook, the mini-lectures provided on this website, and the MyMathLab website that is dedicated to your textbook. With my mini-lectures in hand for guidance, scan through each section in your book to get your bearings and work through the examples provided (for you pencil-and-paper lovers) or watch the video lectures at the MyMathLab site and work through step-by-step examples there (for you more hands-on, audio-visual types).

• *Icebreaker Discussions and group work are meant to help you and your classmates get to know each other while learning about algebra at the same time.*
Homework and practice problems are designed for you to learn about the concepts discussed in the book. Again, you have paper-and-pencil resources as well as online resources through MyMathLab. If you cannot finish a problem you are working on, post it to the class in an SLN discussion area. If you can help a classmate then do so by clicking on "respond." The entire class will see the question and can reply, if they wish. I will also answer questions.

• *Tests will be used to help you pull together all of the concepts from the various chapters.* Each test will combine the various topics from the chapters. These tests should also help you prepare for the comprehensive final exam.

How You Will Be Evaluated Page
I. Summary of Evaluation Tools.
Your grade in the class will include the following activities:

• Icebreaker discussions, group work, and quizzes/assessments 25% of your grade

- Online homework assignments at MyMathLab 25% of your grade

- Timed tests at the MyMathLab website (3) 30% of your grade

- Comprehensive departmental final exam (proctored) 20% of your grade

II. Summary of Related Course Policies.

Grade Scale

Percentage Earned	At Least a Grade of:
90–100	A
80–85.99 / 86–89.99	B / B+
70–75.99 / 76–79.99	C / C+
< 70	F*

[*Note: Students who cannot complete MAT0600 with a 70% of better have very little chance of success in their next college math course, hence the absence of a *D* grade. However, a grade of *D* for percentages 67–69% might be given in special circumstances and only if a student has a score of 70%+ entering the final exam. Please contact me before the exam if you believe you fit into the "special circumstances" category.]

Late Work Policy. Late work will be accepted but will be subject to a 25% reduction in points for each calendar day it is late. (Example: Due by 11:59pm Eastern Time on Saturday but received at 12:01am Sunday = 1 day late.)

Plagiarism Policy. I do not know that plagiarism will be an issue in a course such as this, but do be aware that copying *any* part of an assignment from another person or textbook and turning it in under your name is *plagiarism* and will result in a 0 on the assignment. In addition, instances of academic dishonesty will be reported to the Dean of Academic Affairs.

Missed Test Policy. Because test dates are available the moment this course opens and because you will have several days during which your tests will be available, *no make-up tests will be given*. If you know you will be unavailable during the test days because of an exceptional circumstance (hospital stay, for example), please let me know ahead of time so that we can make special arrangements for you.

III. Description of Evaluation Tools.

Please see the *Course Schedule* [this would be a link to the page] for specific due dates.

Icebreaker Discussions. Most modules will have an Icebreaker Discussion for you to participate in. You are encouraged to respond to your classmates' postings. The discussions will be scored on the following: accuracy of the use of any mathematical terminology or computations, completeness of your answer (i.e., did you speak to all aspects of the discussion topic), thoroughness (giving details, not using vague pronouns or vague descriptions), and correct spelling/grammar.

The objective of the icebreakers is two-fold. First and foremost, I want to get you "talking" to each other. It is extremely important that you realize you *are not alone* in this course and that you have a support structure of other struggling students and a professor who wants to help! Secondly, I hope that you are able to learn something about mathematics in a real-life context through the discussions.

Group Work. Where applicable, you will work on problems in small groups. Being able to collaborate with a group helps you learn from your peers (who can probably give you a more down-to-earth explanation than a professor can!), gives those of you who catch on quickly a chance to "teach" and thus deepen your understanding of the material, and provides you with an opportunity to see problems solved in new ways.

Quizzes/Assessments. Where applicable, you will take short-answer or multiple-choice quizzes / assessments on our SLN course website. These might cover things like the SLN student orientation, a course information scavenger hunt, mini-lectures, and so forth.

Homework. Practice problems will be available in your textbook and at the MyMathLab website. Answers for odd-numbered problems will appear in the back of your book and in your student solutions manual. MyMathLab offers tutorials and practice problems for which you can obtain immediate feedback from the computer.

After practicing on your own, you will complete graded homework problems at MyMathLab. Because MyMathLab can offer you immediate feedback on the correctness of your answers and can offer you an opportunity to re-do an incorrect homework problem (the program will generate a new, similar problem for you to try), you have the option to keep making corrections to your homework until you are ready to turn it in. With your perseverance, every assignment you turn in could have a score of 100%!

Tests. An online test at MyMathLab will be given over the following topics:

Test 1: Sections 5.1–6.5

Test 2: Sections 6.6, 11.2–11.3, and 7.1–7.4

Test 3: Sections 7.5–7.7, 10.1–10.4

For the sake of convenience, these tests will not be proctored, but they will be timed. Although you are *strongly* encouraged to work without using any outside resources (in preparation for the final exam), I cannot stop you from using your books, notes, and technology. You will be on your honor to work alone.

Comprehensive Departmental Final Exam. JCC requires that all students enrolled in MAT0600 take the same comprehensive departmental final exam and that this exam be administered over a two-hour period and supervised by a college-approved official. A calculator will be allowed but no notes or books may be used.

The exam will be proctored as described below.

Jamestown students will take the exam at Main Street tutoring center (2nd floor HULT) or with me on the Jamestown campus.

Olean students will take the exam at the Cattaraugus campus Learning Assistance Center (CTTC building). You will need to contact Deb Simpson to schedule an appointment.

(Directions, contact information, and hours of operation for these tutoring centers can be found at http://www.sunyjcc.edu/college-wide/tutoring.html.)

If you are a student at the Dunkirk or Warren sites of JCC, I might have colleagues on these campuses who could proctor during the summer. I will provide you with their contact information if possible.

For students who are not within a reasonable driving distance from any of our four campuses: If there is a tutoring/testing center on your campus that is willing to proctor your exam, please provide me with a contact person (with e-mail address) there. If you are unable to take the exam at your tutoring/testing center, you may have a supervisor, mentor, librarian, or other teacher proctor your exam. This person cannot be a peer/friend/relative. Please provide me with the proctor's name, title, and e-mail address—I will be sending the exam through e-mail as a Word document attachment.

Course Schedule Page

You may want to print this document.

Course Calendar and Assignment Schedule. All assignments are due by 11:59 p.m. Eastern Time on the due date.

Contact Information Page
Contact Information.

Instructor. Assistant Professor Stephanie Zwyghuizen

Course Number. MAT0600, CRN 3578

Semester. Summer 2006

JCC Office. Arts and Sciences (ARSC) 102. I will seldom be in my office over the summer, but I can arrange to meet you there if necessary.

Mailing Address. Stephanie Zwyghuizen,
Jamestown Community College,
525 Falconer Street,
Jamestown, NY 14702.

E-mail Address. Stephanie.Zwyghuizen@sln.suny.edu. (Please do not e-mail me unless there is some urgent reason to do so. Instead, use your private folder in the Online Office Hours area for all personal communications.)

Phone. 716–665–5220 Ext. 2390. I will seldom be at my office, so please send me electronic communications instead. If necessary, I can make an appointment to have you call me at this number.

Fax. 716–338–1473. (It is very unlikely that you will need this number as I do not accept coursework via fax.)

Log-on Schedule. I will log on frequently throughout the week, often daily. However, I will probably be less active on Fridays, and I generally take Saturdays off.

Exhibit A.1.
Course Schedule Page.

Topics/Activities	Start	End	Assignments Due
	5/29/06	7/27/06	**See Below**
Week 1: Welcome to Intermediate Algebra! (Module 0) Chapter 5 (sections 5.1 – 5.4) **Because a summer math course is very fast-paced and you do not want to get behind, please participate as much as possible even if you are still waiting for your textbook package.**	**"Preview Week" begins 5/29** **Class officially begins 6/5**	6/11	**Please have the following completed by 11:59pm ET 6/7 (Wednesday)** • Read through all Course Information and Module 0 documents. Experiment with Equation Editor (instructions found in Module 0). Nothing needs to be turned in from Equation Editor, but you will need to know how to use this tool before starting the course material. • Create Private Folder (for 5 homework points) • Course Information Tests at the bottom of Module 0 (for a homework grade) • Module 0 Icebreaker Discussion **Due by 11:59pm ET 6/10 (Saturday)** • Group Post #1 – I recommend you start wrapping up discussion on Friday so that your team leader can post on Saturday **Due by 11:59pm ET 6/11 (Sunday)** • MyMathLab Assignment #1
Week 2: Chapter 5 (section 5.5) Chapter 6 (section 6.1 – 6.5)	6/12	6/18	**Due by 11:59pm ET 6/17 (Saturday)** • Module 2 (Chapter 6) Icebreaker Discussion • Group Post #2 – I recommend you start wrapping up discussion on Friday so that your team leader can post on Saturday **Due by 11:59pm ET 6/18 (Sunday)** • MyMathLab Assignment #2

Topics/Activities	Start	End	Assignments Due
	5/29/06	7/27/06	See Below
Week 3: Test 1 (1st 1/2 of week) Chapter 6 (section 6.6)	6/19	6/25	**Due by 11:59pm ET 6/22 (Thursday)** • Test 1 (in MyMathLab) **Due by 11:59pm ET 6/25 (Sunday)** • MyMathLab Assignment #3
Week 4: Chapter 11 (sections 11.2–11.3) Chapter 7 (sections 7.1 – 7.4)	6/26	7/2	**Due by 11:59pm ET 7/1 (Saturday)** • Module 3 (Chapter 7) Icebreaker Discussion • Group Post #3 – I recommend you start wrapping up discussion on Friday so that your team leader can post on Saturday **Due by 11:59pm ET 7/2 (Sunday)** • MyMathLab Assignment #4
Week 5: Test 2 (1st 1/2 of week) Chapter 7 (sections 7.5 – 7.6)	7/3	7/9	**Due by 11:59pm ET 7/6 (Thursday)** • Test 2 (in MyMathLab) **Due by 11:59pm ET 7/2 (Sunday)** • MyMathLab Assignment #5
Week 6: Chapter 7 (section 7.7) Chapter 10 (sections 10.1–10.4)	7/10	7/16	**Due by 11:59pm ET 7/15 (Saturday)** • Module 4 (Chapter 10) Icebreaker Discussion • Group Post #4 – I recommend you start wrapping up discussion on Friday so that your team leader can post on Saturday
Week 7: Test 3 (1st 1/2 of week) Chapter 10 (sections 10.5–10.6)	7/17 7/24	7/23 7/27	**Due by 11:59pm ET 7/2 (Sunday)** • MyMathLab Assignment #6 **Due by 11:59pm ET 7/20 (Thursday)** • Test 3 (in MyMathLab) **Due by 11:59pm ET 7/23 (Sunday)** • MyMathLab Assignment #7
Week 8: Final Exam			**Due 7/27 (Thursday)** • Culminating Activity Survey • Proctored Final Exam

APPENDIX B:
GLOSSARY OF TERMS USED
IN ONLINE EDUCATION

Asynchronous: A type of communication that can occur at any time and at irregular intervals, meaning that people can communicate online without a pattern of interaction. It is the predominant mode of communication used in e-mail, in usenet groups, and on bulletin boards and websites.

Blog (Web Log): A form of online journaling that often offers reflections and commentary on news or a particular subject. Blogs may be personal in nature and take the form of an online diary. Although primarily text-based, blogs can contain images, audio, video, and links to other websites.

Chat/IRC (Internet Relay Chat): A chat system that was developed by Jarkko Oikarinen in Finland in the late 1980s. IRC allows people connected anywhere on the Internet to join in on a live discussion that is not limited to just two people. In order to participate in an IRC chat, participants need IRC Client software and Internet access. The client software runs on the participant's computer and sends and receives messages from an IRC server. The IRC server, in turn, broadcasts all messages to everyone participating in the discussion.

Client-Server Application: A network architecture in which each computer or process on the network is either a client or a server. Servers are computers or processes dedicated to managing disk drives (file servers), printers (print servers), network traffic (network servers), or other processing services. Clients are PCS or workstations on which users run applications. Clients rely on servers for resources such as files, devices, communications, or processing power. Client-server architectures are sometimes called two-tier architectures.

Computer Conferencing: Conducting a conference between two or more participants at different sites by using computer networks to transmit any combination of text, static pictures, audio, or motion video. Multipoint conferencing allows three or more participants to sit in a virtual conference room and communicate as if they were sitting right next to each other.

Course Authoring or Course Management Software: Software specifically designed to assemble and electronically publish educational and training courses. The courses may be interactive in nature, wherein several students can interact, or may involve only the interaction of the student and computer.

Desktop Video Conferencing: A video conference that occurs between two or more participants located at different sites by using personal computers to transmit and receive audio and video.

Extranet: A secure network that allows for the exchange of information between a group and its customers. An extranet might be set up, for example, as a means by which to register students for courses and provide them with ongoing information.

FTP (File Transfer Protocol): Provides the ability to transfer files to and from remote computer systems on the Internet.

Groupware: Software designed to allow groups of colleagues to organize their activities. The group must be connected electronically, whether it be through the Internet, an intranet, or an extranet. The software usually facilitates such things as scheduling meetings and allocating resources; it also facilitates e-mail, telephone utilities, file distribution, and password protection for shared documents.

Intranet: A private Internet operating within an organization. Both require the same network protocols and both use e-mail and World Wide Web standards for communication.

ISP (Internet Service Provider): A company that provides access to the Internet for a monthly fee.

Netiquette: Contraction meaning Internet etiquette. These are the guidelines for etiquette in the posting and sending of messages to online services and to Internet news groups. Netiquette not only covers rules for maintaining civility in interactions but also guidelines unique to the electronic nature of forum messages. For example, the special formatting of text is discouraged because some people would not be able to see the special formatting.

Network: A group of two or more computers linked together electronically.

Real Time Audio/Video: Audio and video that is broadcast and received with very little time delay.

Podcast: A method of distributing multimedia files such as lectures, programs, or music for playback on mobile devices as well as personal computers.

Server: A computer or device on a network that manages network resources. For example, a file server is a computer and storage device dedicated to storing files. Any user on the network can store files on the server. A print server is a computer that manages one or more printers, and a network server is a computer that manages network traffic. A database server is a computer system that processes database queries. Servers are often dedicated, meaning that they perform no other tasks besides their server tasks. On multiprocessing operating systems, however, a single computer can execute several programs at once. A server in this case could refer to the program that is managing resources rather than the entire computer.

Streaming Media: Content that is read, heard, or viewed while being delivered. Generally, this refers to the technology used to deliver audio and video content online. Software applications such as Real Network, Quicktime, and Windows Media are generally used for the delivery of streaming media content.

Synchronous: A type of communication in which those communicating do so at the same time. An example is a chat room where people are all typing at the same time.

URL (Uniform Resource Locator): The global Internet address of documents and other resources on the World Wide Web. The first part of the address—ftp or http—indicates the protocol to use, and the second part specifies the Internet Protocol (IP) address or the domain name where the resource is located.

Usenet Groups: Groups formed around numerous topics that are located or housed on the Internet. The usenet is a worldwide bulletin board system that can be accessed through the Internet or the online server.

Video Conferencing: Conducting a conference between two or more computers at different locations by the use of networks to transmit and receive audio and video data.

Web-Based Application: Software that is designed specifically to be used with the Internet. Frequently, this term is used to describe software through which courses might be delivered, wherein a student interacts only with the computer and not with other participants.

Webcast (or Webinar): The use of streaming media technology to deliver content synchronously from one source to many recipients, generally through the use of a virtual classroom.

WebQuests: A WebQuest is an inquiry-oriented activity in which most or all of the information used by learners is drawn from the Web. First applied primarily to the K–12 arena, it is now being used extensively with all levels of education. It is a scavenger hunt of sorts, but differs in that WebQuests are designed to use learners' time well by focusing on the use of information rather than the search for it, and to support learners' thinking at the levels of analysis, synthesis and evaluation. Most WebQuests contain a rubric for assessment of the final product produced by the team engaging in the quest.

Whiteboard/Whiteboarding: An area on a display screen that multiple users can write or draw on that other remote users can see simultaneously. Whiteboards are often a principal component of computer conferencing applications because they enable shared visual communication.

Wikis: A wiki is a piece of server software that allows users to freely create and edit Web page content using any Web browser. Wikis support hyperlinks and have simple text links for creating new pages and crosslinks between internal pages. Wikis allow for both the organization of contributions to be edited as well as the content itself by any user.

APPENDIX C:
INTERNET RESOURCES
FOR ONLINE EDUCATION

The following is a collection of websites, Internet journals, and course management software for use in and assistance with online teaching and learning. It is not exhaustive but should give readers a place to start in researching additional resources. Inclusion of course resources on this list is for the information of our readers only and does not constitute endorsement of a particular software application. We invite our readers to visit our website at *http://www.xroadsgroup.com* for additional information about our work.

Websites of Interest
The following websites contain useful information for both instructors and students.

Illinois Online Network http://www.ion.illinois.edu/resources/
California Distance Learning Project   http://www.cdlponline.org/
University of Wisconsin Distance Learning Clearinghouse
http://www.uwex.edu/disted/
Distance Educator.com http://www.distance-educator.com/index.php

Resources for Course Development
MERLOT (Multimedia Educational Resource for Learning and Online Teaching)
http://www.merlot.org/Home.po

World Lecture Hall (Free online course materials)
http://web.austin.utexas.edu/wlh/
WebQuests http://webquest.sdsu.edu/

Online Communities for Instructors

Tapped In (primarily for K–12 instructors, but all are welcome)
http://tappedin.org/tappedin/
Learning Times http://www.learningtimes.org/
LERN (Learning Resources Network) http://www.lern.org/

Education and Training for Online Instructors

Fielding Graduate University—Teaching in the Virtual Classroom Program
http://www.fielding.edu/elc/tvc/index.htm
LERN (Learning Resources Network)
http://www.lern.org/edctr/upcoming_online/upcoming_online.htm

Journals

JOLT *(Journal of Online Learning and Teaching)* http://jolt.merlot.org/
JALN *(Journal of Asynchronous Learning Networks)* http://www.sloan-c.org/
publications/jaln/index.asp
American Journal of Distance Education http://www.ajde.com/
Journal of Interactive Online Learning http://www.ncolr.org/jiol/
Journal of Online Learning http://www.iste.org/Content/Navigation-
Menu/Membership/SIGs/SIGTel_Telelearning_/SIGTel_Bulletin2/Archive/20012/V
olume_12,_Number_1_of_Journal_of_Online_Learning.htm

Course Management Systems

EduTools (provides reviews of course management systems)
http://www.edutools.info/static.jsp?pj=8&page=HOME
Review of Course Management Systems http://www.uiowa.edu/~provost/elearn-
ing/resources/DEC0302.pdf
Blackboard/WebCT http://www.blackboard.com/us/index.aspx
Angel Learning http://angellearning.com/products/
Desire2Learn http://www.desire2learn.com/
eCollege http://www.ecollege.com/indexflash.learn

REFERENCES

Adams, J. M., and Sperling, M. B. "Ubiquitous Distributed Learning and Global Citizenship." *The Presidency* EBSCO Publishing: Winter 2003.

Angelo, T., and Cross, K. P. *Classroom Assessment Techniques.* San Francisco: Jossey-Bass, 1993.

Argyris, C. *On Organizational Learning.* Oxford, UK: Blackwell, 1992.

Barkley, E. F., Cross, K. P., and Major, C. F. *Collaborative Learning Techniques.* San Francisco: Jossey-Bass Publishers, 2005.

Beaudoin, M. "Learning or Lurking? Tracking the 'Invisible' Online Student." Orlando, FL: Paper delivered at the 7th Sloan-C International Conference on Asynchronous Learning Networks, 2001.

Benson, B. *How to Meet Standards, Motivate Students, and 'Still' Enjoy Teaching.* Thousand Oaks, CA: Corwin, 2002.

Bolman, L., and Deal, T. *Leading with Soul.* San Francisco: Jossey-Bass, 2001.

Bolman, L., and Deal, T. *Reframing Organizations.* San Francisco: Jossey-Bass, 2003.

Brook, C., and Oliver, R. "Online Learning Communities: Investigating a Design Framework." *Australian Journal of Educational Technology, 19*(2), 2003, pp. 139–160. [http://www.ascilite.org.au/ajet/ajet19/brook.html].

Brookfield, S. D. *Becoming a Critically Reflective Teacher.* San Francisco: Jossey-Bass, 1995.

Brookfield, S. D. *Understanding and Facilitating Adult Learning: A Comprehensive Analysis of Principles and Effective Practice.* Milton Keynes: Open University Press, 1996.

Brookfield, S., and Preskill, S. *Discussion as a Way of Teaching.* San Francisco: Jossey-Bass, 2005.

Brooks, J., and Brooks, M. *In Search of Understanding: The Case for Constructivist Classrooms.* Alexandria, Va.: Association for Supervision and Curriculum Development, 1993.

Caffarella, R. *Planning Programs for Adult Learners.* San Francisco: Jossey-Bass, 2002.

Carr-Chellman, A., and Duchastel, P. "The Ideal Online Course." *Library Trends,* 2001, *50*(1), 16.

Catalfo, P. "America Online." In S. Walker (ed.), *Changing Community.* St. Paul, Minn.: Greywolf, 1993.

Christiansen, E., and Dirckinck-Holmfeld, L. "Making Distance Learning Cooperative," 1995. [http://www-cscl95.indiana.edu/cscl95/chritia.html].

Collins, M., and Berge, Z. "Facilitating Interaction in Computer Mediated Online Courses," 1996. [http://star.ucc.nau.edu/~mauri/moderate/flcc.html].

Collison, G., Elbaum, B., Haavind, S., and Tinker, R. *Facilitating Online Learning: Effective Strategies for Moderators.* Madison, WI: Atwood, 2000.

Conrad, L. D., and Crowell, P. W. "E-mail Addiction." *Business Officer,* National Association of College and University Business Officers, 1997. [http://www.nacubo.org/website/members/bomag/1097_conrad.html].

Conrad, R. M., and Donaldson A., *Engaging the Online Learner: Activities and Resources for Creative Instruction.* San Francisco: Jossey-Bass, 2004.

Covey, S. *The Seven Habits of Highly Effective People: Powerful Lessons in Personal Change.* New York: Fireside, 1989.

Cranton, P. *Understanding and Promoting Transformative Learning: A Guide for Educators of Adults.* San Francisco: Jossey-Bass, 2006.

Cutler, R. "Distributed Presence and Community in Cyberspace." *Interpersonal Computing and Technology: An Electronic Journal for the 21st Century, 3*(2), January 1995, pp. 12–32. [http://jan.ucc.nau.edu/~ipct-j/1995/n2/cutler.txt].

De Anza College Distance Learning Center. "Are Distance Learning Courses for You?" n.d. [http://dadistance.fhda.edu/DLCQuestionnaire.html].

Davidson, M. "Facilitation." Retrieved October 27, 2006 from Teaching in the Virtual Classroom course forum, Fielding Graduate University.

December, J. "Searching for Meaning Online." *CMC Magazine,* Mar. 1997. [http://www.december.com/cmc/mag/1997/mar/ed.html].

Derrick, M. G. "Creating Environments Conducive for Lifelong Learning." New Directions for Adult and Continuing Education, no. 100. San Francisco: Jossey-Bass, 2003.

Donnelly, K. M., and Berge, Z. "Podcasting: Co-Opting MP3 Players for Education and Training Purposes." *Online Journal of Distance Learning Administration, 9*(3), Fall 2006.

Doran, C. "The Effective Use of Learning Groups in Online Education." *New Horizons in Adult Education, 15*(2), Summer 2001.

Duchastel, P. "A Web-Based Model for University Instruction." *Journal of Educational Technology Systems,* 1997, *25*(3), 221–228. [http://www.nova.edu/~duchaste/unimodel.html].

Felder, R. M., and Brent, R. "Cooperative Learning in Technical Courses: Procedures, Pitfalls, and Payoffs." ERIC Document Reproduction Service Report, 1994. (ED 377038.) [http://www2.ncsu.edu/unity/lockers/.elder/public/Papers/Coopreport.html].

Fink, L. D. *Creating Significant Learning Experiences: An Integrated Approach to Designing College Courses.* San Francisco: Jossey-Bass, 2003.

Finkelstein, J. *Learning in Real Time: Synchronous Teaching and Learning Online.* San Francisco: Jossey-Bass, 2006.

Fleming, J. "How Learning in Residence Fosters Transformative Learning and Connected

Teaching." Conference in Adult, Continuing, and Community Education, Michigan State University, Oct. 15–17, 1997. [http://www.canr.msu.edu/aee/research/fleming.html].

Garrison, D. R. "Online Community of Inquiry Update: Social, Cognitive, and Teaching Presence Issues." University of Calgary: Unpublished, n.d. [http://www.communitiesofinquiry.com/documents/Community%20of%20Inquiry%20Issues.pdf].

Garrison, D. R., Anderson, T., and Archer, W. "Critical Inquiry in a Text-Based Environment: Computer Conferencing in Higher Education." *The Internet and Higher Education, 2*(2–3), (2000), 87–105. [http://communitiesofinquiry.com/documents/CTin TextEnvFinal.pdf].

Garrison, D. R., Anderson, T., and Archer, W. "A Theory of Critical Inquiry in Online Distance Education." In M. G. Moore and W. G. Anderson (eds.), *Handbook of Distance Education* (pp. 113–127). Mahwah, NJ: Erlbaum, 2003.

Gergen, K. *The Saturated Self: Dilemmas of Identity in Contemporary Life.* New York: Basic Books, 2000.

Glogoff, S. "Instructional Blogging: Promoting Interactivity, Student-Centered Learning, and Peer Input." *Innovate Online,* 2005 [http://www.innovateonline.info/index.php?view=article&id=126].

Gunawardena, C., and Zittle, F. "Social Presence as a Predictor of Satisfaction within a Computer-Mediated Conferencing Environment." *American Journal of Distance Education, 11*(3), 1997, 8-26.

Harasim, L. "On-Line Education: A New Domain." *Mindweave,* 1989. [http://www.icdl.open.ac.uk/mindweave/chap4.html].

Harasim, L. "Pedagogy 201 for Distance Learning: Enhancing Interactivity." [Television broadcast], STARLINK Uplink, R. Jan LeCroy Center for Educational Telecommunications, Dallas County Community College District, Dallas, TX, September 29, 2005.

Harasim, L., Hiltz, S. R., Teles, L., and Turoff, M. *Learning Networks.* Cambridge, MA: MIT Press, 1996.

Harris, R. "Preventing and Detecting Plagiarism." *The Plagiarism Handbook: Strategies for Preventing, Detecting, and Dealing with Plagiarism."* Los Angeles, CA: Pyrczak, 2002. [http://www.antiplagiarism.com/generic7.html].

Hargrove, R. *Mastering the Art of Creative Collaboration.* New York: McGraw-Hill, 1998.

Horrigan, R. "Pew Internet Project Data Memo: Broadband Penetration on the Upswing." *Pew Internet and Family Life Project,* 2004. [http://www.pewinternet.org/pdfs/PIP_Broadband04.DataMemo.pdf].

Illinois Online Network. "What Makes a Successful Online Student?" *Online Education Resources, Pedagogy and Learning.* Retrieved on May 12, 2006 from [http://www.ion.illinois.edu/resources/tutorials/pedagogy/StudentProfile.asp].

Janov, J. *The Inventive Organization.* San Francisco: Jossey-Bass, 1994.

Johnson, D., and Johnson, R. *Joining Together: Group Theory and Group Skills (9th ed.).* New York: Allyn and Bacon, 2005.

Johnson, D., Johnson, R., and Smith, K. *Active Learning: Cooperation in the College Classroom.* Edina, MN: Interaction Books, 1998.

Jonassen, D., Davidson, M., Collins, M., Campbell, J., and Haag, B. "Constructivism and Computer-Mediated Communication in Distance Education." *The American Journal of Distance Education,* 1995, *9*(2), 7–26.

Jones, S. *Cybersociety 2.0.* Thousand Oaks, Calif.: Sage, 1998.

Kaiser Family Foundation. "Generation M: Media in the Lives of 8–18 Year Olds," 2005. [http://www.kff.org/entmedia/index.cfm].

Kellogg, A. "Students Plagiarize Less Than Many Think, a New Study Finds." *The Chronicle of Higher Education,* February 2002. [http://chronicle.com/free/2002/02/2002020101t.htm].

Kiernan, V. "An Engineering Professor Uses the Web to Run a 'Virtual Laboratory.'" *Chronicle of Higher Education,* Oct. 10, 1997 [http://chronicle.com/].

Laufgraben, J., Shapiro, N., and Associates, *Sustaining and Improving Learning Communities.*San Francisco: Jossey-Bass, 2004.

Lee, E. "Social Sites Becoming too Much of a Good Thing." *San Francisco Chronicle,* November 2, 2006.

Lenhart, A., Madden, M., and Hitlin, P. "Teens and Technology." *Pew Internet and Family Life Project.* July 27, 2005. [http://www.pewinternet.org/pdfs/PIP_Teens_Tech_July2005web.pdf].

Levin, D., Arafeh, S., Lenhart, A., and Rainie, L. "The Digital Disconnect: The Widening Gap Between Internet-Savvy Students and Their Schools." *Pew Internet and Family Life Project.* August 14, 2002. [http://www.pewinternet.org/pdfs/PIP_Schools_Internet_Report.pdf]

Lombard, M., and Ditton, T. B. "At the Heart of It All: The Concept of Presence." *Journal of Computer-Mediated Communication, 13*(3), 1997. [http://www.ascusc.org/jcmc/vol3/issue2/lombard.html].

London, M., and Beatty, R. W. "360-Degree Feedback as a Competitive Advantage." *Human Resource Management,* Summer/Fall 1993, 353–372.

López de Vallejo, I. "Information Security in the Context of eLearning." *Learning Technology, (4)*1, January 2002. [http://lttf.ieee.org/learn_tech/issues/january2002/index.html#18].

Luecke, R. *Harvard Business Essentials: Managing Change and Transition.* Boston, MA: Harvard Business School Press, 2003.

Macduff, I. "Flames on the Wires: Mediating from an Electronic Cottage." *Negotiation Journal,* Jan. 1994, *10*(1), 5–15.

McDonald, S. "The Laws of Cyberspace: What Colleges Need to Know." *Chronicle of Higher Education,* Oct. 31, 1997.

McGrath, J., and Hollingshead, A. *Groups Interacting with Technology.* Thousand Oaks, CA: Sage, 1994.

Meyer, K. *Cost-Efficiencies in Online Learning: ASHE Higher Education Report.* 32 *(1)*. San Francisco: Jossey-Bass, 2006.

Mezirow, J. "Transformative learning as Discourse." *Journal of Transformative Education, 1,* 2003, 58–63.

Mezirow, J. *Learning as Transformation: Critical Perspectives on a Theory in Progress.* San Francisco: Jossey-Bass, 2000.

Mezirow, J. *Transformative Dimensions of Adult Learning.* San Francisco: Jossey-Bass, 1991.

Mezirow, J. *Fostering Critical Reflection in Adulthood: A Guide to Transformative and Emancipatory Learning.* San Francisco: Jossey-Bass, 1990.

Morgan, G. *Images of Organization.* Thousand Oaks, CA: Sage, 2006.

Morgan, C., and O'Reilly, M. *Assessing Open and Distance Learners.* London, England: Kogan Page, 1999.

National Center for Educational Statistics. "Distance Education at Degree-Granting Post-secondary Institutions: 2000–2001," August 15, 2003. [http://nces.ed.gov/pubsearch/pubsinfo.asp?pubid=2003017].

Nipper, S. "Third Generation Distance Learning and Computer Conferencing." *Mindweave,* 1989. [http://www-icdl.open.ac.uk/mindweave/chap5.html].

Ornstein, R. *The Roots of the Self.* San Francisco: Harper, 1995.

Palloff, R. "Confronting Ghosts: Lessons in Empowerment and Action." Unpublished dissertation, Human and Organizational Systems, Fielding Graduate University, 1996.

Palloff, R., and Pratt, K. *Collaborating Online: Learning Together in Community.* San Francisco: Jossey-Bass, 2005.

Palloff, R., and Pratt, K. *The Virtual Student: A Profile and Guide.* San Francisco: Jossey-Bass, 2003.

Palloff, R., and Pratt, K. *Lessons from the Cyberspace Classroom: The Realities of Online Teaching.* San Francisco: Jossey-Bass, 2001.

Palloff, R., and Pratt, K. *Building Learning Communities in Cyberspace: Effective Strategies for the Online Classroom.* San Francisco: Jossey-Bass, 1999.

Peck, M. S. *The Different Drum: Community Making and Peace.* New York: Simon and Schuster, 1987.

Peck, M. S. "The Fallacy of Rugged Individualism." In C. Whitmyer (ed.), *In the Company of Others.* Los Angeles: Tarcher/Perigree, 1993.

Picciano, A. "Beyond Student Perceptions: Issues of Interaction, Presence, and Performance in an Online Course." *JALN,* 6(1), July 2002, 21–40.

Picciano, A. G. *Distance Learning: Marking Connections Across Virtual Space and Time.* Upper Saddle River, NJ: Prentice-Hall, 2001.

Polhemus, L., Shih, L-F., Richardson, J. C., and Swan, K. *Building an Affective Learning Community: Social Presence and Learning Engagement.* Paper presented at the World Conference on the WWW and the Internet (WebNet); San Antonio, TX, 2000.

Pratt, K. "The Electronic Personality." Unpublished doctoral dissertation, Human and Organizational Systems Program, Fielding Graduate University, 1996.

Preece, J. *Online Communities: Designing Usability, Supporting Sociability.* New York: Wiley, 2000.

Richardson, J. C., and Swan, K. "Examining Social Presence in Online Courses in Relation to Students' Perceived Learning and Satisfaction." *JALN, 7*(1), February 2003, 68–88.

Rovai, A. P. "Building Sense of Community at a Distance." *The International Review of Research in Open and Distance Learning, (3)*1, April 2002. [http://www.irrodl.org/content/v3.1/rovai.html].

Rovai, A. P., and Barnum, K. T. "On-Line Course Effectiveness: An Analysis of Student Interactions and Perceptions of Learning." *Journal of Distance Learning, 18*(1), Spring 2003, 57–73.

Rovai, A. P., and Jordan, H. "Blended Learning and Sense of Community: A Comparative Analysis with Traditional and Fully Online Graduate Courses." *The International Review of Research in Open and Distance Learning, (5)*2, 2004. [http://www.irrodl.org/index.php/irrodl/article/viewArticle/192/274].

Salomon, K. D., and others. "Distance Learning Course Ownership and Compensation Policies." *Education Securities, Inc. Newsletter,* July/Aug. 1997, *1*(2).

Seligman, K., "Young and Wired." *San Francisco Chronicle Magazine,* May 14, 2006.

Shaffer, C., and Anundsen, K. *Creating Community Anywhere.* Los Angeles: Tarcher/Perigee Books, 1993.

Shapira, N. A., et al. "Problematic Internet Use: Proposed Classification and Diagnostic Criteria." *Depression and Anxiety (17)* 2003, 207–217,

Shea, P., Swan, K., and Pickett, A. "Teaching Presence and Establishment of Community in Online Learning Environments." Sloan Consortium Summer Workshops (2004), Retrieved 5/10/06 from [http://www.sloanconsortium.org/summerworkshop2004/draft-papers/shea_090104.doc].

Shell, B. (ed.). "Shaping Cyberspace into Human Space." *CSS Update,* 1995, *6*(3) [http://fas.sfu.ca/css/update/vol6/6.3–harasim.main.html].

Short, J., Williams, E., and Christie, B. *The Social Psychology of Telecommunications.* New York: Wiley, 1976.

Smith, B. L., MacGregor, J., Matthews, R., and Gabelnick, F. *Learning Communities: Reforming Undergraduate Education.* San Francisco: Jossey Bass, 2004.

Smith, J., and Doty, E. "CPsquare's Story: Finding A Business Model." *CPSquare and Worklore,* 2003, Retrieved from [http://www.cpsquare.org/News/archives/CPsquare-Early-History.pdf].

Sproull, L., and Kiesler, S. *Connections.* Cambridge, MA: MIT Press, 1991.

Stein, D., and Wanstreet, C. E. "Role of Social Presence, Choice of Online or Face-to-face Group Format, and Satisfaction with Perceived Knowledge Gained in a Distance Learning Environment." *2003 Midwest Research to Practice Conference in Adult, Continuing, and Community Education.* (2003), Retrieved May 10, 2006 from [http://www.alumni-osu.org/midwest/midwest%20papers/Stein%20&%20Wanstreet—Done.pdf].

Sumner, M. R. "Ethics Online." *Educom Review,* Jul./Aug. 1996, *31*(4). [http://educom.edu/web/pubs/review/reviewArticles/3142.html].

Tu, C., and Corry, M. "Research in Online Learning Community," 2002. [http://www.usq.edu.au/electpub/e-jist/docs/html2002/pdf/chtu.pdf].

Tuckman, B. W. "Developmental Sequence in Small Groups." *Psychological Bulletin,* June 1965, 384–399.

Turkle, S. *Life on the Screen: Identity in the Age of the Internet.* New York: Simon & Schuster, 1995.

Twigg, C. "The Changing Definition of Learning." *Educom Review,* July/Aug. 1994a, *29*(4). [http://educom.edu/web/pubs/reviewArticles/29422.html].

Twigg, C. "The Need for a National Learning Infrastructure." *Educom Review,* Sept./Oct. 1994b, *29*(5). [http://educom.edu/web/pubs/review/reviewArticles/29516.html].

Walker, S. (ed.). *Changing Community.* St. Paul, MN: Greywolf, 1993.

Weimer, M. G. *Learner-Centered Teaching: Five Key Changes to Practice.* San Francisco: Jossey-Bass, 2002.

Wenger, E. *Communities of Practice: Learning, Meaning, and Identity.* Cambridge, England: Cambridge University Press, 1999.

Whitesel, C. "Reframing Our Classrooms, Reframing Ourselves: Perspectives from a Virtual Paladin." *Microsoft in Higher Education,* Apr. 1998. [http://www.microsoft.com/education/hed/vision.htm].

Wiggins, G. *Educative Assessment.* San Francisco: Jossey-Bass, 1998.

Wolcott, L., and Haderlie, S. "Institutional Support for Distance Teaching: A Study of Reward Practices." In F. Saba (ed.), *Defining Concepts in Distance Education.* Madison, WI: Magna, 1997.

Young, K. *Caught in the Net.* New York: Wiley, 1998.

INDEX

Software: changes, 55; course management, 89, 96–97, 276; ease of use of, 97–98; technical support for, 101–102

Spelling and grammar in posts, 60, 214–215

Sperling, M. B., 4

Spiritual issues, 46, 58–59

Sproull, L., 37, 46, 47

Stein, D., 30, 142, 143

Student homepage, 99, 100

Student performance: assessment of assignments, 208–214; dialogue and, 207–208; evaluation of, 22, 206–207; grading criteria for, 248–249, 254–255, 263–264

Students: attendance of, 153, 154, 249; expectations of, 161–163; participation of, 42–43, 150–153; personal information about, 87–88; successful learners, 8–9; in teams, 165–167; Week Zero for introducing, 21, 150

Students, roles of: collaboration, 119, 120–121; knowledge generation, 119–120; process management, 119, 121–124

Successful learners, 8–9

Summative evaluation, 205–206

Sumner, M., 62

Swan, K., 4, 12, 26, 30, 31

Syllabi: creating effective, 133; examples of, 134–136, 137, 239–269; guiding questions for, 153–154

Synchronous communication, 13, 67–71, 273

Synchronous presence, 12. *See also* Social presence

T

Teaching presence, 107–108, 109

Teams, forming, 165–167

Technical difficulties, 101–104

Technical facilitation, 117–118

Technology: access to, 20, 96; advent of new, 89–91; attachment phenomenon and, 91–93; as facilitative tool, 96–101; transformative learning and, 192–198

Teles, L., 41

Terminology used in online education, 271–274

Threaded discussion, 11–12, 13

Time constraints, 79–81

Time management, 76–79

Time offline versus time online, 71–73

Time zones, 68, 69

Tinker, R., 19

Topic-driven courses, 133, 138

Transformative learning: conscious reflection, 200–202; defined, 185; final thoughts on, 202–203; guiding questions to promote, 203–204; as outcome, 17, 21–22; process of, 187–192; reflective process, 199–200; self-reflection, 186, 198–199; use of technology and, 192–198

Triple loop learning, 186

Tu, C., 31

Tuckman, B. W., 36

Turkle, S., 92

Turoff, M., 41

12-Step Program, 75–76

Twigg, C., 5, 234

U

Unresolved issues, 232–234

V

Viruses, 87

Visual appeal of site, 98–101

Vulnerability, ethics, and privacy, 46, 61–64